Radio and the Jews
The Untold Story of How Radio Influenced the Image of the Jews

Radio and the Jews

The Untold Story of How Radio Influenced the Image of Jews

By David S. Siegel and Susan Siegel

Book Hunter Press
Yorktown Heights, New York

Radio and the Jews: The Untold Story of How Radio Influenced the Image of the Jews, 1920s-1950s
by David S. Siegel and Susan Siegel
© Copyright 2007. Book Hunter Press

All rights reserved. No part of this book may be reproduced or transmitted in any form or by any means, electronic or mechanical, including photocopying, recording or by an information and retrieval system, without permission in writing from the publisher, except by a reviewer who may quote brief passages in a review to be printed in a magazine or newspaper or published online.

The authors and publisher have made every effort to assure the accuracy of the information contained in this book but assume no legal responsibility for any errors or omissions, regardless of whether the errors or omissions resulted from negligence, accident or any other cause.

Cover by Alice Pfeifer, www.alicepfeifer.com

Printed and bound in the United States of America

Library of Congress Control Number: 2007905311

ISBN: 978-1-59393-428-6

Book Hunter Press
PO Box 193 • Yorktown Heights, NY 10598
(914) 245-6608 • Fax: (914) 245-2630
www.bookhunterpress.com/radio
bookhunterpress@verizon.net

Dedication

This book is dedicated to the memory of the countless refugees, whose efforts to escape from Nazi persecution and find a safe haven in the land of the free discovered that the words of the Jewish poet, Emma Lazarus, inscribed on the base of Miss Liberty, would not apply to them.

Other Books by David S. and Susan Siegel

Golden Age of Radio Books
A Resource Guide to the Golden Age of Radio: Special Collections, Bibliography and the Internet
Radio Scripts in Print: Books Featuring 1,700 Golden Age of Radio Scripts
Flashgun Casey, Crime Photographer: From the Pulps to Radio and Beyond (co-authored with J. Randoph Cox)
The Witch's Tale: Stories of Gothic Horror From the Golden Age of Radio (edited by David S. Siegel)

Available from bookhunterpress.com/radio

The Used Book Lover's Guide Series
Used Book Lover's Guide to New England
Used Book Lover's Guide to the Mid-Atlantic States
Used Book Lover's Guide to the South Atlantic States
Used Book Lover's Guide to the Midwest
Used Book Lover's Guide to the Central/Western States
Used Book Lover's Guide to the Pacific Coast States
Used Book Lover's Guide to Canada

Available in print and online by subscription from bookhunterpress.com

Acknowledgments

Any serious attempt to shed light on an important aspect of the history of American popular culture must certainly acknowlege the assistance of others. The authors therefore offer our sincerest appreciation to the following friends, authorities, archivists, old time radio fans and good Samaritans:

David Goldin, the man who saved radio, a good friend and a most knowledgeable radio person, who spent countless hours editing our text, saving us much embarrassment.

Jerry Haendiges, a wonderfully generous friend, who in our view is the premier provider of old time radio programs to fans worldwide and who had the patience and professionalism to create the enclosed CD that provides readers with a taste of the "Jewish" sound during radio's Golden Age.

Michael Henry of the Library of American Broadcasting who provided us with scripts and photographs and who patiently responded to our many research inquiries.

And in strictly alphabetical order, our profound gratitude to the following people for their invaluable aid and support:

Jeanette Berard, American Radio Archives, Thousand Oaks Public Library; Howard Blue, author of *Words at War*; Charlotte Bonelli, archivist at the American Jewish Committee; Himan Brown, the radio pioneer whose initial success was achieved when in his teens and who, at age 97, twice humored a co-author by sharing reminisces regarding those early years when he was a true "witness to radio history;" Paul Buhle, author of *From the Lower East Side to Hollywood*; Havva Charm, New York Public Library, Dorot Jewish Division; Robert Clark, archivist at the Franklin D. Roosevelt Presidential Library; Christine Colburn, Special Collections, University of Chicago; Diane Cooter, Bird Library Special Collections, Syracuse University; Bryan Cornell, Library of Congress; Irwin Gonshak, writer for *The Eternal Light;* Martin Grams, Jr., prolific author of old time radio books; Alex Hartov, Technical Director, Dartmouth Jewish Sound Archive, Lilace Hatayama, Charles E. Young Research Library, UCLA, Sherry Hyman, archivist at the Jewish Joint Distribution Committee; Ellen Kastel, Ratner Center, Jewish Theological Seminary; Joan Wise Kaufman, granddaughter of Rabbi Jonah B. Wise; Laura Leff, president of The International Jack Benny Fan Club and author of *39 Forever*; Alex Magoun, Executive Director, David Sarnoff Library; Elizabeth McLeod, radio historian; Anne Mininberg, archivist at Central Synagogue; Halyna Myroniuk, archivist at the Immigration Center, University of Minnesota; Bill Nadel, researcher; Charles Niren, old time radio fan; the Reference Staff of the John C. Hart Memorial Library, Shrub Oak, NY, including Maureen Connelly, Maureen Davis, Patricia R. Hallinan, Sandra Norman and Reva Queler; Alan Schwartz, archivist at the Anti-Defamation League; Eli Segal, author of *The Eternal Light*; Glenn "Pete" Smith, Jr., author of *Something of My Own*; Jack Sobel, old time radio fan; Derek Teague, researcher; Jeremy Wise, grandson of Rabbi Jonah B. Wise; and Rabbi Zev Zahavy, researcher.

Table of Contents

On a Personal Note		1
Introduction		3
1.	In the Beginning	9
2.	"Yoo Hoo, Is Anybody?"	19
3.	"Those People"	41
4.	*Americans All, Immigrants All*	73
5.	Forgotten Series	87
6.	Funny, You Don't Sound Jewish	103
7.	*Abie's Irish Rose*	135
8.	Judaism Aired: Religious Oriented Programs	157
9.	Jews in the Mainstream	189
	Part I: The Gathering Storm, 1930-1938	189
	Part II: The War Years, 1939-1945	202
	Part III: The Postwar Years, 1946-1959	229
	Part IV: Biographies of Prominent Jews	240
Appendix I Availability of Programs		253
Appendix II *Abie's Irish Rose* Controversy		259
Selected Bibliography		265
Index		271

On a Personal Note

This book had its genesis in my almost lifelong obsession with old time radio (my wife and co-author would call it a compulsion).

As the current immigration debate began to unfold, it brought back thoughts of earlier times in American history when both pro and anti-immigration forces used radio to pursue their political agendas. I also recalled a significant, but mostly forgotten, radio program, *Americans All, Immigrants All,* a series of 26 broadcasts that aired during the 1938-1939 season on CBS. Produced in cooperation with the United States Office of Education, the series focused on the important contributions that various immigrant and ethnic groups had made to all aspects of American life and culture.

The proverbial light bulb began to glow above my head, and it seemed to me that a book about how various immigrants groups were portrayed on radio during its Golden Age, the 1920s to the 1950s, might be of interest to readers.

In conducting a mental review of my audio collection, I began to picture separate chapters dealing with different ethnic groups: Italians (*Life With Luigi*), Irish (*Duffy's Tavern* and *The Life of Riley*), Jews (*The Goldbergs* and *The Eternal Light*), African-Americans (*Amos 'n' Andy, Beulah* and *Jubilee*), Orientals (Kato and Charlie Chan) and even Native-Americans (Tonto and Little Beaver). It also occurred to me that such a volume could be a joint effort with several experienced old time radio authors, each contributing specific chapters.

To my delight, I received positive feedback to my idea and nods of willingness from potential writing partners. In each case, I prefaced my offer by announcing that I intended to write the chapter on Jews. Consciously or otherwise, I began making notes on the various Jewish programs or characters that I would include in the chapter.

It didn't take long before it became clear to me that a single chapter about Jews would not be sufficient to do justice to the subject. Thus, despite my initial plan (Robert Burns was right when he wrote about plans going awry) I found myself coming to the conclusion that what started out as a chapter could easily grow into an entire volume.

I'm pleased to say that my colleagues took the news of my change of plans quite well. Perhaps, even with a sigh of relief. Who knows? One of these days we may yet see a volume dealing with all the ethnic groups. If so, I want to purchase the first copy.

And now, as the announcer might be cued to say…"Let's get on with the story."

David S. Siegel
August, 2007

Introduction

When the authors first conceived the idea of a book about Jews on radio from the 1920s to the 1950s, it became clear that the subject could be approached from many directions. After examining the different options, including an analysis of what had already been written about the subject, the authors narrowed and defined their focus to an examination of how Jews were portrayed on network radio to listeners across America. At a time when many Americans had little or no knowledge of the Jewish faith, or had ever come into contact with a Jew, we wondered how mainstream listeners reacted when they heard Jewish characters on the radio and what influence, if any, what they heard may have had on their thinking about Jews or their behavior toward Jews.[1]

When told about this book, well meaning friends asked us if we also planned to provide information about the many Jews who participated in radio broadcasting as actors, writers and directors or in other important capacities. Clearly Jewish talent abounded on the radio. But as celebrating the achievements of Jews in radio was not the purpose or focus of this volume, our answer to them was: we would include Jewish personalities *if* their Jewishness was part of their radio persona. That meant we would include Mr. Kitzel, the Jewish character who appeared on the *The Jack Benny Program*, but we would not discuss Jack Benny who, although Jewish, did not present himself as a Jewish performer.

Other friends asked if we planned to include information about the wonderful Jewish-oriented broadcasts that were aired on regional stations in New York, Boston, Philadelphia and other metropolitan areas with a large enough Jewish population to justify a local station aiming its programming toward that group. Our response was, "mostly not," except for rare historical examples. First, we repeated that our focus was network radio which broadcast to a diverse nationwide audience, rather than local stations that catered to smaller, more homogeneous listening audiences. And second, we explained that most of the regional broadcasts were in

Yiddish, which clearly was not of interest to non-Jews. We also reminded these friends that a very fine study of Yiddish broadcasting in America had already been done, thanks in part to the work of the dedicated archivist, Henry Sapoznik and the Yiddish Radio Project.[2]

The authors also caution the reader that this is not a book about Jewish humor, Jewish assimilation, anti-Semitism or the Jewish identity in American popular culture — although these subjects are discussed in the book — but within the framework of the book's major thrust: how Jews were portrayed on network radio during a clearly defined time period.

This book is believed to be the very first comprehensive volume devoted entirely to an examination of the Jewish image on mainstream radio.[3] For the most part, the books and journal articles that have examined the issue of Jewish identity and/or Jewish themes in mainstream popular culture have focused on literature, film, television, the stage and even comic books. The few publications that do discuss radio have generally limited their treatment to *The Goldbergs,* the "radio priest" Father Charles Coughlin, *The Eternal Light* and some wartime programs aimed at building national unity. Why, the reader may ask, so little about radio?

There are two possible reasons. First, because the people writing about popular culture today are simply too young to have experienced radio as it existed from the late-1920s to the mid-1950s. And second, because locating information about programs that aired 50-70 years ago is difficult, although, as the authors have discovered, not entirely impossible.

It may seem strange for anyone born after World War II and raised in a television environment to believe that during the 1930s and 1940s radio was the major medium of mass communication. By 1938, an estimated 91 percent of all urban households and 70 percent of rural households had radios, some more than one.[4] For many Americans, especially during the Depression, radio was the only affordable means of entertainment. Radio was also the main source of news. In many households, the radio was on at least three hours a day. Housewives listened during the daytime while they did their chores. Children tuned in after school. And in the evenings, families gathered around the radio to listen to comedy programs, dramas, quiz shows, variety and music programs and sports events. On Sundays, the airwaves were filled with religious programs as well as public affairs discussions. President Franklin D. Roosevelt used radio to allay the fears of

Americans and to encourage them to support his New Deal policies. Father Coughlin used radio to stir up anti-Semitism. Radio was also used by a variety of government agencies during World War II to mobilize support for the war. Throughout the 1930s and 1940s, radio, more than any other form of communication, was the medium of choice for reaching all Americans, regardless of age, sex, race, color or religion. Radio influenced what people thought and what they bought. It influenced their values. It provided them with jokes to share with their friends and neighbors and it gave them advice on how to raise their children and cope with the usual array of family problems. It influenced how they voted and what church, synagogue or temple they attended. Like television today, radio was a mix of quality and mediocre fare, low brow as well as high brow entertainment.

Consider, for example, how the popular culture literature treats two popular novels dealing with anti-Semitism: "Gentleman's Agreement" and "Crossfire." Both were made into successful films that are frequently discussed in books and journal articles dealing with the subject. But — none of those publications mention the fact that both films were *also* adapted for radio and heard by millions of listeners in homes across America — most who never read the books and very possibly did not see the movies. Both radio adaptations are discussed in Chapter 9.

Researching the radio career of the demagogue Gerald L. K. Smith is another case in point. Although not as famous as Father Coughlin (both men are discussed in Chapter 3), Smith was well known during the 1930s and 1940s (and a lesser extent into the 1950s) for using radio to disseminate his anti-Semitic messages. But the authors have been frustrated in their attempts to uncover information documenting exactly when he was on the air, for how long and on what stations. The word "radio" does not even appear in the Index of the definitive biography of Smith although the fact that he did have a radio program is mentioned in passing on several pages and the archival collection of his papers includes his radio speeches and correspondence with at least two radio stations.

It is the authors' hope that by providing this comprehensive look at how Jews were portrayed on network radio, as well as identifying where additional primary and secondary source material can be found, other writers will be encouraged to take a closer look at the role radio played in shaping the perception of Jews in American popular culture from the 1920s to the 1950s.

6   Radio and the Jews

As American society, and how American Jews saw themselves in that society, changed over the four decades covered in this book, the manner in which Jews were portrayed on radio also changed. In the 1920s, when radio was coming into its own, America was in the midst of absorbing more than 30 million immigrants, primarily from southern and eastern Europe. Radio's earliest, and certainly most well known, Jewish network program, *The Rise of the Goldbergs* (Chapter 2), was the story of an immigrant family and its assimilation into America society, a theme that resonated with millions of listeners, regardless of where they lived, where they came from or what church or synagogue they attended.

As events unfolded in the mid to late-1930s (the emergence of Father Coughlin and the rise of Nazism in Germany) the story lines of Jewish themed programs changed to keep pace with changing events. By the mid-1930s, the Goldberg family became more middle class and moved to the suburbs. By the late-1930s, there were efforts to celebrate the contributions that Jews had made to American society (Chapter 4) and, at the same time, tone down the use of the Yiddish dialect which was perceived, in some quarters, as being demeaning to Jews (Chapter 6).

During the war years, ethnic-based programming declined in popularity and was replaced with several special series that stressed patriotism, the need for national unity and the concept that all Americans, regardless of their race, religion or ethnic background, shared the same American values. Special broadcasts produced under the auspices of Jewish secular groups called attention to the plight of Jews in Germany (Chapter 9). Efforts were also made to eliminate negative Jewish stereotypes from network programs (Chapter 7).

A further evolution in the nature of Jewish religious programming occurred in 1944 with the debut of *The Eternal Light* and its innovative use of dramatizations to explain Judaism to mainstream America (Chapter 8).

In the postwar years, recurring non-religious Jewish themed programs disappeared from the network schedule, but not the subject of anti-Semitism that became the focus of many individual episodes of several popular mainstream programs (Chapter 9).

In selecting programs and characters for this volume, the authors have used the following criteria: story lines, character development, language and dialect and the use of typical Jewish names such as Levy, Cohen, Abraham (or Abe), Finkelstein, Solomon, and Rebecca (or Becky). Biographical programs about prominent Jews are also included — even though the programs generally did not identify the individuals as being Jewish.[5]

To identify and locate Jewish series as well as specific episodes of mainstream programs that featured Jewish themes, the authors have used a variety of resources: program logs for specific series, references to series and special broadcasts mentioned in other books and journal articles, the authors' personal audio collection of over 100,000 hours of old radio programs and Internet searches. The authors note that identifying Jewish-themed programs is complicated by the fact that the ability to search existing databases of old time radio programs based on the *content* of the program, as distinct from the name of the series or the title of a specific episode, is either limited or non-existent.[6] Therefore, the authors acknowledge that in their research they may have overlooked some programs that could have been included in this volume.

Notes

1. Much has been written about early radio, from its technological beginnings to the evolution of commercial programming from a predominately white, Anglo-Saxon, Protestant focus to its effectiveness in building a national cultural identity and to its use as a communications tool for the dissemination of knowledge as well as propaganda. See Michele Hilmes, *Radio Voices: American Broadcasting, 1922-1952* (Minneapolis, University of Minnesota Press, 1997); Erik Barnouw, *The Golden Web: A History of Broadcasting in the United States 1933-1953* (New York: Oxford University Press, 1968); Fred J. MacDonald, *Don't Touch That Dial! Radio Programming in American Life, 1920 to 1960* (Chicago: Nelson-Hall, 1980); Michele Hilmes and Jason Loviglio, eds.*Radio Reader: Essays in the Cultural History of Radio* (New York: Routledge, 2002); Susan J. Douglas. *Listening In: Radio and the American Imagination from Amos 'n' Andy to Edward R. Murrow to Wolfman Jack and Howard Stern* (New York: Times Books, 1999); and Robert J. Brown. *Manipulating the Ether: The Power of Broadcast Radio in Thirties America* (Jefferson, NC: McFarland, 1998).

2. Readers interested in learning more about Yiddish radio should check the Yiddish Radio Project web site at www.yiddishradioproject.org. The site describes the programs aired on National Public Radio that documented the history of Yiddish radio from the 1930s-1950s. The programs are available on

a set of two CDs.

3. For a three page article on the Jewish image on radio see Henry Sapoznik, "Broadcast Ghetto: The Image of Jews on Mainstream American Radio," *Jewish Folklore and Ethnology*, Vol. 16, #1, 1944, 37-39. See also David Weinstein's chapter, "Why Sarnoff Slept: NBC and the Holocaust," in *NBC: America's Network,* Michele Hilmes, ed. (Berkeley, CA: University of California Press, 2007), 98-116.

4. Christopher Sterling and John M. Kittross. *Stay Tuned: A Concise History of American Broadcasting* (Belmont, CA: Wadsworth, 1978), 183.

5. See Chapter 9, Part IV for a discussion of the controversial issue of whether Jews should be identified by their religious affiliation.

6. One valuable online database of old time radio programs that provides content information about the programs is www.radiogoldindex.com. The site can be searched by both program name and performer name. Once a specific program or performer has been selected, the user can do a keyword search across all the matching listings. However, as with any Internet search, output depends on the input. In doing a keyword search on the site's 740 listings of *Lux Radio Theatre*, for example, a search for the word "Jewish" brings up "Gentleman's Agreement" because the word is included in the description. But the search does not bring up "Counselor at Law" about a Jewish lawyer because the word "Jewish" is not included in the program's description. Both *Lux* programs are discussed in Chapter 9.

1
In the Beginning

An understanding of how Jews were portrayed on network radio from the 1920s to the 1950s requires some knowledge of the birth of radio and of the contributions of two men, both of whom just happen to be Jewish. Beyond their common religious heritage, and the fact that neither of the two ever wrote, produced, directed or performed in any radio program, the only other thing they had in common was that they were responsible for the success of the two most powerful networks to broadcast to the American public during radio's Golden Age.

The two giants of network radio, David Sarnoff of NBC and William S. Paley of CBS, grew up in an age when radio was in its infancy. To understand how these two pioneers achieved their success, one must also understand something about the birth of radio itself.

Radio, as we know it today, owes its origin to a number of people. Scientists, practical folks and dreamers from several different nations and spanning several decades saw their combined efforts change the history of wireless sound from that of very faint code heard over short distances to clear voices and powerful music heard across continents and oceans.

- During the 1860's, a Scottish physicist, James Clerk Maxwell, predicted the existence of radio waves.
- In 1866, an American dentist, Mahlon Loomis, claimed to create "wireless" aerial communication between two kites.
- Heinrich Hertz, a German, actually detected the existence of radio waves (1886) and later (1893) was able to cause a spark to leap across a gap that generated electromagnetic waves, using an oscillator and a "resonator."
- A Russian, an Englishman and a Frenchman (Alexander Popov, Oliver Lodge and Edouard Branly) experimented with a process by which electromagnetic waves could be detected, resulting in the development of the "coherer" in 1894.

- In 1894, Guglielmo Marconi perfected the spark-gap transmitter and antenna and in 1896 formed the Wireless Telegraph and Signal Company (later renamed the Marconi Wireless Telegraph Company) in Britain. Shortly thereafter Marconi opened a factory that was to manufacture radio receivers.

A number of other individuals were engaged in research during the final years of the 19th and early years of the 20th century and their efforts, individually and in concert, effectively changed the primitive nature of wireless broadcasting, resulting in greater public interest in this remarkable new invention. Among these often forgotten pioneers were:

- Professor William Gladstone of the University Of Arkansas, who in 1897 is said to have constructed an experimental wireless transmitter.
- Notre Dame Professor Jerome Green, who in 1898 was able to send wireless messages as far one mile, a significant distance at the time.
- In 1903, the German-born scientist Charles Steinmetz developed a high frequency alternator.
- In 1905, Canadian Reginald Fessenden, invented a continuous-wave voice transmitter. He is recognized as being responsible for the very first wireless transmission of the human voice, first on December 23, 1900 using a spark-gap transmitter and again, quite dramatically, on December 24, 1906 when a record of a woman's voice singing a Christmas carol along with Fessenden, who sang and played a violin, was transmitted from the coast of Maine and heard by wireless operators aboard several ships off the Atlantic coast.

It is not particularly surprising that while the scientific accomplishments of almost every person involved in the early development of radio was based on the findings of others, the temperamental nature of some creative people led to feuds and bitter lawsuits regarding the true ownership of certain rights.

Marconi, cited earlier as being a major player in the development of radio and who, to this day is celebrated as the "father of radio," drew resentment and outrage from the likes of Professor Oliver Lodge, who viewed Marconi as a late-comer, taking credit due to others and using the power of his financial backers to purchase patents issued to rivals and gain the support of government officials, all of which eased his path to success. Sour grapes? Perhaps but consider the challenge by Nicola Tesla.

A Serb by birth, Tesla made several revolutionary contributions in the fields of electricity and magnetism. He also brought suit against Marconi for patent infringement. A 1943 decision of the United States Supreme Court found in his favor and invalidated Marconi's patents on the grounds that they were largely based on Tesla's earlier efforts.

These events and others that were to occur during the first half of the 20th Century involving other giants in the world of radio such as Lee DeForest, Philo Farnsworth and Edwin Howard Armstrong are described in a number of excellent books. Of particular note, the authors recommend: *Empire of the Air: The Men Who Made Radio* by Tom Lewis.[1]

David Sarnoff and NBC

The story of how an immigrant boy rose to become the head of the country's first radio network is in many ways the typical Horatio Alger tale of the success that comes from hard work, perseverance, vision and talent, the good fortune to be in the right place at the right time, plus in the case of Sarnoff, the strength to overcome the many obstacles in the path of immigrants in general, and Jews in particular, during the first half of the 20th century.[2]

Born in 1891 in a shtetl (village) in Russia, Sarnoff came to America in 1900 at the age of nine. From his early days, when not in school, he was earning money to help support his family: selling newspapers on the street, running errands for a butcher, selling soda and candy in Yiddish theaters, and even occasionally singing at Jewish weddings.

By the age of 15, he landed a job as an office boy with the American Marconi Company that used wireless technology to transmit messages around the world. Six years later, at the age of 21, he became manager of the company's Wanamaker station.[3] His rise in the company was not accidental: he made sure that he was always available to run errands and take on extra tasks, including delivering gifts to his boss' lady friends. In addition to learning how to transmit and receive messages in code, he also made it a habit to read the company correspondence before he filed the papers, thereby learning a lot more about company matters than some of his superiors. Along the way, he reached the conclusion that his future (and financial success) lay not in the operations side of wireless communications but in where he could influence the company's sales and growth.

On April 14, 1912, when Sarnoff was 21 years old, the unthinkable occurred. The unsinkable Titanic hit an iceberg on its maiden voyage to the United States and sank, taking some 1,500 souls with it. Popular legend has it that Sarnoff, sitting at his post, heard the first wireless messages about the disaster and alerted the press. The more accurate story, however, is that when Sarnoff most likely heard newspaper vendors on the street crying, "Extra, Extra," he rushed to the Wanamaker station where he monitored reports from the rescue vessel providing the identities of known survivors to family members and the press.[4] The coverage of the Titanic story demonstrated for the first time the vital role wireless communications could play in instantaneously reporting important events happening around the world, a boon to the Marconi Company that had been struggling to show a profit since its inception.

Another popular legend about Sarnoff's early career at the American Marconi Company was the "Radio Music Box" memorandum he was supposed to have written in 1916 (and which, so the story goes, was ignored by his superiors as being too far fetched). The memo is often cited by Sarnoff's biographers to show him as a visionary thinker.[5] At a time when most of the people who had anything to do with either the transmission or reception of radio were either employees of one of the wireless companies or radio hobbyists, Sarnoff is reported to have written:[6]

> I have in mind a plan of development which would make radio a 'household utility' in the same sense as the piano or the phonograph. The idea is to bring music into the home by wireless.
>
> While this had been done in the past by wires, it has been a failure because wires do not lend themselves to this scheme. With radio, however, it would be entirely feasible.
>
> For example, a radiotelephone transmitter having a range of say 25 to 50 miles can be installed at a fixed point where the instrumental or vocal music or both are produced. The receiver can be designed in the form of a simple 'Radio Music Box' and arranged for several different wavelengths, which should be changeable with the throwing of a single switch or pressing of a single button.
>
> The 'Radio Music Box' can be supplied with amplifying tubes and

a loudspeaking telephone, all of which can be neatly mounted in one box. The box can be placed on a table in the parlor or living room, the switch set accordingly and the music received. There should be no difficulty in receiving music perfectly when transmitted within a radius of 25 to 50 miles.

Within such a radius there reside hundreds of thousands of families; and as all can simultaneously receive from a single transmitter there should be no question of receiving sufficiently loud signals to make the performance enjoyable...The use of headphones would be obviated by this method. The development of a small loop antenna to go with each 'Radio Music Box' would likewise solve the antenna problem.

The same principle can be extended to numerous other fields as, for example, receiving lectures at home...Baseball scores can be transmitted in the air by the use of one set installed at the Polo Grounds. The same would be true of other cities. The proposition would be especially interesting to farmers and others in outlying districts removed from cities...They could enjoy concerts, lectures, music, recitals, etc. which may be going on in the nearest city within their radius.

World War I had a dramatic impact on the wireless communications industry in the United States — and Sarnoff's future. The war called attention to the fact that the country's leading wireless communications company was owned by a foreign corporation and so, at the urging of the federal government, the American Marconi Company severed its ties with its parent, the British Marconi Company. In November, 1919 the new company became known as the Radio Corporation of America (RCA) with the General Electric company as its majority shareholder. Sarnoff, then 28 years of age, became the new company's commercial manager and in 1921, shortly after his 30th birthday, its general manager in charge of broadcasting. Considering his penchant for "volunteering" and, consciously or otherwise, bringing attention to himself, each of his promotions was brought about as a result of company officials having taken note of the young "Jew boy" who served the company well.

By 1924, RCA owned nine stations, including WJZ in New York City. In 1926, the company acquired WEAF from AT&T and created NBC, jointly owned by RCA (50 percent), General Electric (30 percent) and Westinghouse (20 percent). A year later, owning two stations in New York

14   Radio and the Jews

David Sarnoff (l) and
Guglielmo Marconi (r)

William S. Paley

City, NBC split into two separate networks, the NBC-Red Network with WEAF as its flagship station, and the NBC-Blue Network with WJZ as the flagship station.

In 1927, Sarnoff was elected to the RCA Board, and on January 1, 1929 he was appointed executive vice president. Just one year later, on January 3, 1930, he became president of the company. While Sarnoff didn't create NBC, he most certainly played a significant role in the establishment of broadcasting's first and arguably most influential network.

William S. Paley and CBS

Like his rival, David Sarnoff, William Paley did not "create" CBS. But, like Sarnoff, he became its president during the network's formative years and can be credited with its growth and evolution.[7]

Ten years younger than Sarnoff, Paley was born in the United States in 1901. Like Sarnoff, his parents had emigrated from Russia. Unlike his NBC counterpart who had to work to support his family, Paley's father was a successful businessman and young Bill grew up in comfortable surroundings devoid of any financial worries. Throughout his early years, Paley worked closely with his father and it was generally assumed that when he finished his college education he would join enter the family cigar business. Although Paley did not share Sarnoff's history of financial hardship, he did experience anti-Semitism, particularly as a student at the University of Pennsylvania's prestigious Wharton School of Finance.

It was not until 1925, when he was 24, that Paley listened to his first radio broadcast through earphones connected to a friend's primitive crystal set. He was both stunned and captivated by the experience and had a receiver built for himself. Three years later, and almost by accident, he became president of CBS, the country's second largest network.

During the time that he was completing his formal education and preparing to enter his father's cigar business, changes were taking place in the wireless telecommunications industry that would influence the future direction of Paley's life. With the birth of KDKA in 1920, radio was beginning to emerge as a new industry and new stations were springing up all over the country. By 1926, AT&T began to provide NBC with special telephone lines that made it possible for stations across the nation to receive programs directly from New York headquarters or to send them to the entire system.

Thus, the network system was born.

In 1927, WCAU, a small struggling station in Philadelphia, signed on with the fledgling United Independent Broadcasters (UIB) network that promised to provide its affiliated stations with both talent and income. When UIB found itself unable to meet its contractual commitments and in need of additional financing, it received an infusion of funds from the Columbia Phonograph Company that was interested in securing air time for some of the artists it had under contract, including Howard Barlow and Donald Voorhees. Before making the investment in UIB, however, Columbia insisted that the network change its name to the Columbia Phonograph Broadcasting System.

When the renamed network lost $100,000 in its first month of operation, Columbia Phonograph bowed out. Not ready to call it quits, but still losing money, the network's owners appealed to the Levy brothers, the owners of WCAU, for funds. Not having sufficient funds of their own to rescue the network, the brothers approached their friend, Sam Paley, the prosperous owner of the La Palina Cigar Company. Paley, in turn, decided that in lieu of investing in the troubled network, he would help it out by spending $6,500 a week to sponsor a weekly program. (An earlier experience advertising on radio had resulted in an increase in sales.) In return, the grateful network owners suggested that Paley's son Bill who was young, energetic, experienced in advertising and well educated, might be an ideal person to supervise the network's general operations. Bill turned down the opportunity but did agree to go to New York one day a week to supervise the production of the program, *The La Palina Smoker*. His "hands on" style resulted in a new format for the program — and a significant spike in the sale of La Palina Cigars.[8]

By the time the network began to experience its first month operating in the black, its owners, exhausted from years of frustration, once again approached Sam Paley suggesting that he buy the network for his son. Sam refused, but Bill, less than three years after listening to radio for the very first time, offered to buy the network himself. According to Paley's biographer, Lewis J. Paper, by this time the younger Paley had come to the realization that he didn't like the cigar business and wanted a job with more excitement. "The one thing he liked was to meet people of prominence and importance, and you couldn't meet many people like that in the cigar business."[9]

On September 26, 1928, two days shy of his 27th birthday, Paley took over as president of the Columbia Phonograph Broadcasting System. Shortly thereafter, the name of the company was changed to the Columbia Broadcasting System. Less than four months later, on January 8, 1929, Paley proudly went on the air and announced that with 49 stations in 42 cities, his new network had the largest number of affiliates. Aware that a successful image was sometimes more important than the exact truth, Paley's arithmetic counted the affiliates for NBC-Blue and NBC-Red as two separate networks; when taken together, NBC was clearly the larger network.

Neither David Sarnoff nor William Paley officially founded the networks that they led. However, one cannot challenge the fact that it was the leadership of these two Jewish businessmen that propelled radio into what would eventually become known as its Golden Age.

Notes

1. Tom Lewis, *Empire of the Air: The Men Who Made Radio* (New York: Harper Collins Publishers, 1991).

2. Readers interested in leaning more about Sarnoff and the early days of NBC have several books from which to choose. Eugene Lyons, *David Sarnoff: A Biography* (New York: Harper & Row, 1966); Kenneth Bilby, *The General: David Sarnoff and the Rise of the Communications Industry* (New York: Harper & Row, 1986); Carl Dreher, *Sarnoff: An American Success* (New York: Quadrangle, 1977); Robert Sobel, *RCA* (New York: Stein and Day, 1986); and Leon Gutterman, editor, *The Wisdom of Sarnoff and the World of RCA* (Wisdom Society, 1968). Sarnoff's papers are located at the David Sarnoff Library located in Princeton, New Jersey.

3. Wanamaker was a department store in New York City. The wireless station was located on the building's roof.

4. Both Erik Barnouw in *A Tower in Babel: A History of Broadcasting in the United States to 1933* (New York: Oxford University Press, 1966), 77 and Lyons, *David Sarnoff: A Biography*, 59, cite the popular version of the "Titanic" legend. However, Dreher, *Sarnoff: An American Success*, 28, debunks that heroic version (à la Parson Weems).

5. The story of the "Radio Music Box" memo has a somewhat checkered history and it is possible that the memo may not have been written until sometime in the early 1920s. For more insight into the history of the memo see Alexander B. Maroun, "Pushing Technology: David Sarnoff and Wireless Communications, 1911-1921," presented at the IEEE 2001 Conference on the History of Telecommunica-

tions, July 26, 2001, 6. The paper is available online at: http://www.ieee.org/portal/cms_docs_iportals/iportals/aboutus/history_center/magoun.pdf.

6. Dreher, *Sarnoff: An American Success*, 39-40.

7. For more insights into the life of William S. Paley and the early years of CBS, see Sally Bedell Smith, *In All His Glory: The Life & Times of William S. Paley and the Birth of Modern Broadcasting* (New York: Touchstone/Simon & Schuster, 1990) and Lewis J. Paper, *Empire: William S. Paley and the Making of CBS* (New York: St. Martin's Press, 1987).

8. As with the myths surrounding the Sarnoff's story, there are also contradictory stories about Bill Paley's initial experience with the *La Palina Smoker* program. See Bedell, 57-61.

9. Paper, *Empire: William S. Paley*, 22.

2
"Yoo Hoo, Is Anybody?"

By the mid-to-late 1920s, due in part to "lessons learned" as well as the formation of the two networks (three if one considers NBC's Red and Blue networks as separate entities), a number of new programs were to debut that would enjoy extended runs, thus marking the very beginning of what would later be called radio's Golden Age. The first and, without doubt, what would become radio's most important program devoted to the trials and tribulations of a Jewish-American immigrant family debuted in November, 1929. It was the idea of Gertrude Berg who just a month earlier had celebrated her 30th birthday.[1]

Origins of the Program

Gertrude Berg was born in New York City on October 3, 1899, the daughter of Jake and Dinah Edelstein. In her most charming and informative autobiography, "Molly and Me," co-written with her son Cherney, she wrote most lovingly about the influence that her paternal grandfather had on her. A native of Lublin, Poland, he, like countless other Jews, came to America to follow a dream and to escape the prevailing anti-Semitism that existed in Eastern Europe. A tinsmith by trade, it wasn't long before he was able to send for his wife and children, a common practice among immigrants of that era.

When her father, who managed a restaurant in New York City, purchased an estate in New York's Catskill Mountains and turned it into a summer hotel for middle class Jewish families, Berg's job was to keep the hotel's books and provide entertainment for the guests by writing sketches that she and guests' children would perform. She continued in that capacity for several years, even after marrying an engineer named Lewis (Lew) Berg in 1918 who had been one of the hotel's guests.

What had begun as a daughter contributing her efforts to a family business, rapidly grew into a passion for writing. Buoyed by the positive responses her sketches received from the hotel's guests, a confident Berg decided that her playlets were suitable for radio and that she was ready to turn professional. With the enthusiastic encouragement of her husband, and the reluctant approval of her father, Berg, with script in hand and courage in heart, began calling on people who might help her "open doors." One such person was Herman Bernie, brother of bandleader Ben Bernie and a friend of Lew's. Bernie, in turn, put Berg in touch with Willie Kamen, a Damon Runyonesque character that she described as, "over six feet tall, bald, fat, smoked a cigar and had a voice like a foghorn" and who addressed her as "Boig."[2]

Without giving her a chance to talk about her script, and doubtless based on the build-up about her skills from Herman Bernie, Kamen told her that he had a number of radio projects in the works. When he asked her to write a script for an upcoming musical review, Berg, in what for her must have been a rare, almost speechless reaction, accepted the assignment. In a few days, she submitted a script for which she was praised, paid and promised some future assignments.

Having already penned the very first *Goldbergs* script, a 500 word epic, Berg was determined to test the waters by having Herman Bernie read it, hoping that, if he liked it, he would pass it along to his influential brother. Ben did indeed like the script and arranged for Berg to meet the program director of WMCA, an independent New York City station. After Berg read her script, the program director complimented her on her good radio voice and offered her a job reading a Christmas cookie commercial over the air in Yiddish. Berg earned $6.00 for her first "on air" performance but still had no luck with her *Goldbergs'* script.

Turning to a new subject, Berg wrote a sketch about two young women who worked in a five-and-ten cent store, the popular term given to Woolworth stores, comparable to today's Wal-Mart chain. The script, *Effie and Laura*, had a serious as well as a romantic theme. This time, Berg visited the offices of CBS without an appointment, hoping to meet with someone who would evaluate her script. As the new network on the block, CBS was possibly more open to meeting with writers who could provide usable broadcast material. After giving Berg a chance to read the script, the executive told her to return with another person to act out the second role. When she did, the two women auditioned, were hired, and *Effie and Laura* went on the air. The next day, two things happened. The good news was that Ben Gross, the radio columnist for the New York *Daily News* had heard the show and liked it. The bad news was that Berg was summoned to CBS headquarters and told that the program was cancelled. Apparently, the script hadn't been read by the appropriate CBS executive and so no one had flagged what at the time were off-limit words and topics such as God and a less than traditional approach towards marriage.[3]

Discouraged but, like that other famous Molly (Brown, not Goldberg), Berg remained unsinkable and within days of "Black Friday," October 25, 1929, she was on the phone trying to contact studio executives willing to look at her script. An executive at NBC agreed to read the script for her proposed series, *The Rise of the Goldbergs,* and after two weeks of anxious waiting, Berg was invited to return to NBC to discuss contract terms.

Although there is no doubt that Berg was the creator of *The Rise of the Goldbergs,* Himan Brown, who later became a major figure in radio as the producer of *Inner Sanctum, Grand Central Station* and many other notable programs, has been quoted on more than one occasion as saying that he was the person who "sold" the idea of *The Goldbergs* to NBC. Berg, however, makes no mention of Brown in her autobiography. The only known documentation of Brown's involvement with "selling" the program that appeared while the program was still on the air is a 1939 article in *Radio Parade*, a fan magazine. In the feature, Lorraine Thomas wrote that it was only after Berg heard Brown read dialect stories on radio that she got the idea to write *The Rise of the Goldbergs.* She then contacted Brown who read her scripts and "he agreed to try to sell them." Thomas' version of events was repeated by Brown in interviews he gave later in life and by Smith in his biography of Berg.[4] There remains little question, however, that no matter how much Brown may have been influential in getting NBC to accept the program, the concept of Molly Goldberg and *The Rise of the Goldbergs* theme was purely a Gertrude Berg invention.

The Rise of the Goldbergs, 1929-1934

The Rise of the Goldbergs (renamed *The Goldbergs* in 1936) debuted on November 20, 1929 on WJZ, one of NBC's two New York flagship stations. The original contract called for five 15-minute scripts over a four week period and for Berg to portray Molly Goldberg. In return, Berg was paid $75.00 per week out of which she was responsible for paying the cast. The contract also called for an increase to $100.00 per week if the contract was renewed for an additional four weeks.

Faced with the immediate need to come up with three additional scripts before the first program aired, Berg took refuge in the main reading room of New York's 42nd Street Library where, away from the distractions of home and family, she handwrote the scripts for episodes two, three and four. It was only after a friend told her that other patrons in the library were concerned about the faces she made while acting out what she was writing that she continued her writing endeavors at home.[5]

For ideas for story lines and characters, Berg drew from her personal life, writing that, "I translated my life with my grandmother, my mother and father, my friends, the people I had heard about, into the *Goldbergs* and began to relive it on the air."[6] In the very first episode, for example, Molly's husband Jake, who was working in the dress business, wanted to open his own factory but lacked the cash needed to rent loft space and sewing machines. Berg, drawing from her childhood recollection of a grandmother putting loose change in a jar for a "rainy day," had Molly come to her husband's rescue with the loose change that she too has been setting aside. The experience of living in a three-story walk-up apartment building also taught her that there were few secrets that neighbors could have from one another that would not be revealed by the common dumbwaiter shaft that served each apartment. Berg also credited her frequent visits to New York City's Lower East Side where many of the Jewish immigrants lived for script ideas.[7]

Berg's plots were based on the well known immigrant themes of respect for education, family values and the generational conflict between immigrant parents and their American-born children, themes that resonated with all immigrant groups, regardless of origin or religion. Underscoring those themes was her desire to present an alternative image of Jews from that which was common on the vaudeville stages at the time. As her biographer Glenn Smith explained, Berg strongly objected to the broken dialect and smutty wise-cracks of Jewish comedians as well as the sugar-coated sentimentalities of many of the individuals she considered "the good-willers." Both stereotypes, she believed, were a far cry from the Jewish people she knew — and wanted to write about.[8]

In an early episode, "Sammy's Report Card," Berg dealt with the issue of parental concern for their children's future. Worried about Sammy's poor grades in school and the company he had been keeping, Molly and Jake try to console each other.

Jake: Vhen I read in de newspapers from gangs and loifers, my blood gets cold. Dat's vhy, Molly, I'm begging you, look out for de company he goes, please.

Molly: Don't vorry. You vatch out far de beezness and I'll take care from de children. Vhat else is my life but only de little hope from my children? If Sammy would only be like I would like, I could feel myself, I'm telling you, bigger dan Christopher Columbus, and bigger even dan Abraham Lincoln. Ulleright, only don't vorry yourself. Ve'll have only pleasure from de children. Who knows a child better dan a modder, ha?"⁹

Strip away the Yiddish dialect and clearly Molly and Jake's words could be echoed by any family anywhere in the United States.

Gertrude Berg in an undated photograph.

Immigrant listeners could also relate to Molly's deference to people of authority, as when she had to ask a policeman for directions: "Mr. Policeman, Officer of the law, Your Honor, could you be so kindly if you would to inform me of the location of where is Fourteenth Street?" Relieved at having gotten the answer and not being arrested for asking a simple question, Molly then thanked the policeman: "You are most kind, dear Mr.

Officer...(and) very pleased to have made your acquaintance."

While the use of the Yiddish dialect by Molly and Jake clearly identified the family as Jewish, most of the scripts dealt with generic family themes. The distinctly "Jewish" scripts, when they were used, usually centered around special family events such as Sammy's Bar Mitzvah (a Jewish "coming of age" ceremony when boys reach the age of 13) or the observance of Jewish holidays such as Passover or Yom Kippur. The scripts for these episodes included an array of Yiddish words without any explanation such as "simcha" (a joyous occasion), "shuhl" (a small synagogue), and "tallith" (a Jewish prayer shawl). Two well known Jewish opera singers, Jan Peerce and Robert Merrill, also appeared occasionally on the program, usually on episodes connected to holiday celebrations during which they chanted Jewish prayers such as "Kol Nidre."[10]

By combining universal family themes with Jewish themes, the program brought an understanding of Jews into the homes of millions of Americans who had, until that time, little or no knowledge of Jews or Judaism. Jews, as exemplified by the Goldbergs, were no different than other striving families.

> During its five years on the air 'The Rise of the Goldbergs' became much more than an entertaining and popular sketch. It developed into the most valuable means of building inter-religious and inter-racial good will. The universality of its appeal and its refined and restrained sympathy won for it a huge Christian audience...Farmers' wives, Quaker women, lumberjacks, art connoisseurs, physicians, teachers, sailors and chauffeurs have written in by the hundreds of thousands to tell Molly of the pleasure her sketch affords them.[11]

In its earliest episodes, and with a limited budget, the program featured only four speaking characters, although other "off air" characters were referred to in the scripts.

Molly, the mother, wife, homemaker, philosopher and matriarch was portrayed by Gertrude Berg. The character, Berg wrote, was an amalgam of her mother and grandmother with some added characteristics belonging to the guests at the family's hotel. In addition to her warmth and wisdom, Molly's most distinctive characteristic or trademark was her speaking style: a fractured combination of formal and colloquial English leavened with a healthy penchant for malapropisms. (The American-born Berg was accent free.)

- How is the progressing of my offspring? she asked Sammy's violin teacher.
- Enter, whoever.
- It's late, Jake, and time to expire.
- Give me a swallow the glass.
- Come will and come may, I must face it in real life.

Jake, Molly's husband, father to their children, bread winner and patient soul mate, was initially portrayed by teenager Himan Brown but was replaced after the first season by the veteran actor James R. Waters,[12] possibly because Berg wanted a more mature voice. Waters remained in the role until his death in 1945 when, rather than find a replacement to take on the role, scripts for quite some time thereafter referred to Jake as being on a business trip or at the factory. The character of Jake was modeled to varying degrees on men much like Berg's own father and grandfather; she had him at times being ambitious, sometimes bombastic, but always a loving and forgiving husband and father.

The family's two children, Sammy and Rosalie, were also modeled in part on Berg's two children, Cherney and Harriet. Sammy, who reached the age of 13 in the early episode that centered on his Bar Mitzvah, was portrayed by child actor Alfred Ryder (a.k.a. Alfred Corn) and later, for a while, by Everett Sloane.[13] Rosalie was portrayed by Roslyn Silber, who like the character she played, was only nine years old at the start of the series.

Over time, Berg added additional recurring characters to her plot lines. After seeing Menasha Skulnik on stage in a Yiddish theater production on New York's Second Avenue, she wrote him into the series as her recently widowed Uncle David. It wasn't long before Uncle David moved in with the Goldbergs and listeners would hear him speak often of his son, Solly, the doctor, who, when appearing on air, was played by Sidney Sloan. Other recurring characters who would appear on air, or who were referred to in discussions, included Mendel, Jake's partner, played by George Herman and Tante (aunt) Elka. Perhaps the program's most memorable "off air" character was Molly's neighbor, Mrs. Bloom, with whom Molly would carry on one-way conversations after calling down the dumbwaiter shaft, "Yoo-hoo Mrs. Bloom." (When *The Goldbergs* debuted on television in 1949, Molly's famous "yoo-hoo," would be shouted from an open window.)

As the show's producer, director, writer and star, Berg had complete control over the program.[14] In *On the Air: The Encyclopedia of Old-Time*

Radio, radio historian John Dunning noted that Berg even had control over the sound effects and made sure that when the script called for breaking eggs into a frying pan, that the eggs were real. On other occasions she had the cast rattle their own china and she even gave Roslyn Silber an on air shampoo when the script called for Rosalie's hair to be washed.[15] Whether these stories were true or based on the public relations stories frequently found in fan magazines of the day, may never be known.

For the first year-and-one-half of its run, *The Rise of the Goldbergs* was an unsponsored, 15-minute weekly program heard only on a single NBC station. As a sustaining program, its time slot was subject to change, often with little notice. This did not appear to be a problem for loyal listeners, however: When Berg came down with a case of laryngitis that resulted in the program going off the air for a week, NBC received some 18,000 letters wanting to know, "What became of Molly?" an extraordinary response for an as yet non-network program.[16]

In May, 1931, the program was sold to the Pepsodent Company, the same sponsor for radio's other enormously popular ethic series, *Amos 'n' Andy*. With sponsorship, the program began airing six times a week and NBC added the program to its network line-up, giving the series its first national exposure. Sponsorship also meant that the program had a regular time slot and additional funds that could be used to add cast members, thus increasing the range of plot development.

If NBC had any qualms in 1929 about airing a Jewish program, those doubts were satisfactorily addressed in a 1932 report, "The Goldbergs," prepared by the network's statistical department.[17] As summarized by media historian Susan Smulyan, the report reassured network executives "that there is a large audience for good programs of a 'Jewish type.'" The report went on to note that mail indicated that the audience was not restricted to any geographic region — and it quoted Pepsodent's advertising manager who observed that "although the program concerns a Jewish family, the vast majority...of appeals to keep it on the air came from Gentiles." The report, notwithstanding, Smulyan took note of the fact that the NBC public relations people were still hesitant about releasing photographs of a largely Jewish cast.

For the 1931-1932 season, the series' first full year as a sponsored program, *The Rise of the Goldbergs* was rated the third most popular program according to C.A.B. (Co-Operative Analysis of Broadcasting), a precursor to Hooper and Nielsen, ranking just below *Amos 'n' Andy* and *Eddie Cantor*, but higher than *The Fleischmann Yeast Hour* (Rudy Vallee), *Paul Whiteman, Lowell Thomas, Jessica Dragonette, Sherlock Holmes, Guy Lombardo* and *Kate Smith*.[18]

Letters from listeners confirmed the program's popularity as well as its nationwide appeal. In June, 1932, one year after it became a network program, Pepsodent reported that in the previous month it had received 3,302 letters about the program; 2,838 letters praised the program and only 11 objected to it.[19] NBC's own statistical department, which analyzed the program's mail by station as compared to "total NBC mail," concluded that, "The popularity of this feature is not limited to any one section or to the audience of several stations."[20]

In his essay on the history of *The Goldbergs*, Donald Weber cited a 1931 fan letter in which a listener wrote, "We certainly admire the ideals this family stand [sic] for, and the way they reach the inner and higher feelings of us all. In our estimation they are doing more good than all the World Peace Conferences put together. The Goldbergs are to the mind what Pepsodent is to the mouth — they both leave a clean, wholesome feeling not to [sic] soon be forgotten."[21]

Berg also took note of the fact that, contrary to everyone's belief, the majority of the fan letters she received did not come from Jewish listeners but instead cut across religious divisions. The audience, she wrote,

> ...refused to be typed and from the mail I learned a great lesson: there is no way for anyone to predict what the American public is going to like, going to do, or going to say. I've gotten letters from priests, ministers, and rabbis, and from millionaires and paupers. Letters have been signed by every possible sort of name from Arajiban to Zelinowsky, and I'm proud of it. I didn't set out to make a contribution to interracial understanding. I only tried to depict the life of a family in a background I knew best. The reaction of the people who listened only showed that we all respond to human situations and human emotions — and that dividing people into rigid racial, economic, social or religious groups is a lot of nonsense."[22]

Readers familiar with the very first successful ethnic-based radio classic, *Amos 'n' Andy*, will no doubt see several common patterns between that program and *The Rise of the Goldbergs*. Both programs proved that a well written script featuring sympathetic characters, regardless of ethnicity, could attract wide audience support; both were written by their star performers; both began with a title that eventually was dropped in favor of its more popular title; both went national over NBC; both had the same initial sponsor; both employed heavy dialect; and, as discussed later in this chapter, both featured a move by their main characters to a different community. Finally, both programs emerged from long radio runs to re-emerge as successful television series.

The early popularity of *The Rise of the Goldbergs* can, in part, be attributed to the fact that the family's struggles weren't limited to a single ethnic group but rather touched the lives of a diverse listening public, a theme that radio historian Michele Hilmes pointed out was prevalent in radio's early days. "Radio drama and explorations of national identity and assimilation went hand in hand…(and) Gertrude Berg's early perception of this phenomenon has been echoed many times; one of the most commonly agreed-upon characteristics of the new medium, as seen by contemporaries and later historians alike, was its ability to promote cultural homogeneity."[23]

In his assessment of the series, Erik Barnouw, another radio historian, credited *The Goldbergs'* success to the fact that implicit in the programs "was a sense of escape from old bondage. Its older characters remembered another world, and were held by its beliefs and phobias. There had been a long journey and a Lower East Side sojourn, then emergence into a middle class society." They could all understand, he wrote, the concept of exodus, journey and settlement in a promised land.[24]

Weber came to much the same conclusion when he wrote that another reason for the program's early popularity was that during the uncertain days of the Depression, *The Goldbergs* became, at a certain level, a source of cohesion for its worried listeners, perhaps offering some redemptive hope in the figure of Molly Goldberg, the stabilizing matriarch guiding her own family through turbulent times. "…if Molly's homespun rhetoric of dreaming had an impact, its effect on her audience may be connected to her own identity as a newly arrived American visionary: Molly Goldberg was a *greenhorn* (a newly arrived immigrant) sage recapitulating, indeed reincarnating, the country's innermost ideal of historical optimism and resilient, self-reliant striving…(*The*) *Goldbergs* contained a sediment of national ideals, a rich deposit of folk wisdom unearthed by attentive listeners in the 1930s. Molly, in this respect, looms as an immigrant keeper of the national dream."[25]

While highlighting *The Goldbergs'* universal outlook, Weber also drew attention to the program's special appeal to what was clearly its much smaller Jewish audience. "Berg's representations of Jewish faith and observance, however abridged or attenuated on the radio, inspired a certain pride in her Jewish listeners. In the process Berg herself became an emblem of nostalgia, a figure associated with the incarnation of ethnic memory."[26] After hearing the October, 1935 "Yom Kippur" program, a listener from the Midwest wrote to thank Berg on behalf of the two Jewish families in town: "It touched our hearts as it was so real and reminded me of years gone by." Responding to the same broadcast, a young women from Los Angles admitted to being "a modern Jew of the younger generation, but (the Yom Kippur show) certainly gave a tug at my heart strings."[27] Years later, after listening to the 1943 Yom Kippur program, a Jewish educator from Cleveland thanked Berg because "this series from your facile pen has done more to *set us Jews* [emphasis in the original] right with the 'goyim' than all the sermons ever preached by Rabbis." And in a 1942 letter inviting her to speak before a Jewish group, the assistant superintendent of the Guild for the Jewish Blind wrote, "You symbolize for them the lives that they have lived."

In 1934, when Berg's contract with Pepsodent was up for renewal, negotiations between the parties stalled. There are two versions of what happened. In her autobiography, Berg wrote that given the fact that the program was heard by millions of listeners and received a large volume of positive mail, it came as a shock to her when Pepsodent told her it was not renewing her contract. "It wasn't the show, they assured me. It was just a matter of shortages of material that went into the making of the glass mouthwash bottles. It sounded impossible and I thought they were trying to let me down easy. But it was the truth. I waited to see what show Pepsodent was going to put on the air after me but there wasn't any, and that meant more to me than the money. At least my pride was salvaged."[28] Smith's biography of Berg, however, offered a very different explanation. After reviewing newspaper clippings from the period, he concluded that negotiations between the sponsor and the writer broke down because of Berg's demand for more money as well as greater creative and executive control.[29]

When Berg's contract with Pepsodent ended on July 6, 1934, the writer/producer took *The Rise of the Goldbergs* off the air rather than return to a sustaining basis. Over the next two years, Berg kept busy with a variety of projects. In addition to taking the cast on a nationwide tour, she worked in Hollywood, writing both the story and screen play for the RKO film *Make A Wish* featuring Bobby Breen and Basil Rathbone[30] and started writing a syndicated advice column, "Mama Talks," in the Jewish press that was written in perfect English. She also began working on scripts for a new series, this time based on the summers she spent working at her father's hotel. Thus was born *The House of Glass* (see Chapter 5).

While an audio version of only one *The Rise of the Goldbergs* is known to exist, scripts of 16 early programs were published in 1931 by Barse & Co.[31] Although the text does not follow the usual script format of speaker, followed by dialogue, it does contain what appears to be the original dialogue, complete with the heavy use of the Yiddish dialect.

The Return of *The Goldbergs*: 1936-1945

In January, 1936, the Goldberg family returned to the airwaves on the CBS network as a five-day-a-week, 15-minute daytime program renamed *The Goldbergs*. With the exception of Everett Sloane who took over the role of Sammy for part of the run, the cast featured the same actors who had appeared in the earlier series. (In the post-1940 episodes, Berg added a new recurring character, Seymour Fingerhood, played brilliantly by Arnold Stang, well known for his almost falsetto semi-cracked voice.) The program remained on the air until March 30, 1945, switching between CBS, NBC and Mutual, sometimes being heard on more than one network at a time.[32]

The most significant change in the focus of *The Goldbergs* occurred in 1939 when Berg relocated the family from its humble beginnings on Tremont Avenue in the Bronx where Jake labored as a tailor and a dressmaker, to the fictional Connecticut suburban town of Lastonbury where Jake managed a local mill. Looking back on the 1936-1945 run today, more than 70 years later, one can't help but wonder if the events in Europe during the late 1930s and the stirrings of anti-Semitism at home played a role in the decision to move the family to an "all American" community.

Reflecting back on this period Berg wrote that, "everything about *The Goldbergs* changed except the theme song, Toselli's "Serenade." The stories were still soap opera-like with everything going along smoothly until a Friday cliffhanger. Sammy went to war, Rosalie kept on playing one boy against another and Uncle David continued to argue that his cousin's son, a dentist, really wasn't a doctor. Over the nine year period of its second and longest run, Berg recalled that the series slowly evolved into a situation comedy and tragedies that the family had dealt earlier were treated with a different eye. Although the family remained essentially the same, it changed with the times — but still looked at the world in its own way. Jake continued to make dresses, changing the hemlines as fashion changed, Molly took her friends where she found them and Uncle David took a job as a salesman so that he wouldn't become a burden to the family.[33]

As the plots during this second run became more middle class, they also became less Jewish and Molly's Yiddish accent was replaced by her almost backward way of putting things, in some ways rivaling the "Mrs. Malaprop" habits of Jane Ace of *Easy Aces* fame. The family's Jewishness was, however, still in evidence, especially when it came to celebrating the Jewish holidays or when scripts dealt with the family's concern over the fate of friends and family trying to escape from Eastern Europe ahead of the Holocaust. On an April 3, 1939 broadcast, for example, when the family was celebrating Passover — and singing in Hebrew — from the Haggadah (the book that contains the service for the Passover seder), a rock was thrown through the window of their house, a clear allusion to Kristallnacht, an event that had occurred five months earlier in Germany.[34]

Other programmatic changes involved the country's entry into World War II when, like other soap operas of that time, many of the scripts reflected the patriotic fervor shared by most Americans. When Alfred Ryder, the actor who played Sammy went to war in 1942, the program also sent Sammy off to war and the script that had him leaving home was actually broadcast from New York's Pennsylvania train station before Ryder's troop train left.[35] When asked on the World War II era quiz show, *Double or Nothing,* about Ryder's leaving for war and whether or not she intended to replace him, Berg responded, "Replace Sammy? When you have a son going to the Army, can you replace him?"[36]

In the "station" episode, Molly consoles another woman who is clearly grieving her son's departure to join the war effort.

> Don't cry Madame. Your son. My son. This is no time for crying. Today we have to stand like rocks — and we all have to face the same way...till our bodies become a wall that will lock the Fascists in their...Our sons go to the front, our husbands and our daughters make guns and tanks and bullets. And we dry our eyes and stand like mountains. And when they're tired and weary, we must be their strength. And when they're hurt, we must be their help. And when the dark days come — the dark days will come — we must be their light. And in the end, in the end, when victory...we'll have time to cry...we mothers should make a promise. We should swear to each

other not to cry. Not to cry for the...because unless we win there won't be enough tears in the whole world to sweeten the bitterness...time for tears. There's no time for tears. There's no time for tears now.[37]

Following Molly's inspirational comments, announcer Clayton Collyer continues, "We will be united in victory also. The Goldbergs go back home. Life goes on. And the living must settle the problems that living people create."

As an ensemble, *The Goldbergs'* cast also participated in special patriotic radio programs such as the 15-minute March 1, 1943 episode, "The Rumor," on the government-sponsored program, *Treasury Star Parade*. The plot was about the danger to the country's war efforts when unfounded rumors were spread.

In June, 1944, *The Goldbergs* also made their debut as a comic strip appearing in the *New York Post*.[38] Copies of the strips can be found in Berg's papers.

Roslyn Silber, Gertrude Berg and James R. Waters. Berg was said to have control over the program's sound effects and often had the actors produce the sounds themselves such as rattling the china.

Molly's optimistic outlook on life — from its beginnings in the Bronx to its relocation in suburban Lastonbury — remained a constant throughout the many years of the program, as demonstrated in this 1944 exchange with Uncle David.

Molly:	To understand the whys and wherefores of human behavior. David. Like only God can make a tree. That's only how he can understand. Eh. How much good and how much evil there is in people, David. It's too bad life is so short David.
David:	Why?
Molly:	Because…Because there's too much to learn in one life.
David:	The desire to live leaves you with each page of knowledge, Molly. Believe me.
Molly:	I don't think so David. Knowledge is light.
David:	That's what I mean.
Molly:	Well, to see is to learn. To learn is to change what needs changing
David:	Then we all want to be a fixer, Molly. Eh, Molly, Molly. What I'd like, one day on earth after the alterations were finished.
Molly:	Me too.
David:	What do you think you would find, Molly? Angels on earth Molly?
Molly:	Maybe not angels with wings, David.
David:	Then don't be a dreamer Molly. Dreams can be heavy and a burden that can bend your back too, Molly.
Molly:	I don't think so David. I have one belief David.
David:	Yeh.
Molly:	I think if a man can be bad, he can also be good. I mean if some can be bad and some good, then it's possible for all to be good.

In his pioneering work in the field of radio research in the 1940s, Paul F. Lazarsfeld surveyed women who listened to the daytime serials and asked them: "Do these (daytime serials) help you to deal better with the problems in your own everyday life?" An overwhelming 41 percent of the respondents answered, "Yes."[39] Based on the survey results, Lazarsfeld concluded that one reason for the popularity of the serials, including *The Goldbergs*, was that listeners identified with the sufferings of their radio family, giving them an opportunity to magnify their own woes. The programs, he wrote, gave listeners a chance to express their "superiority over those who have not had these profound emotional experiences." Other listeners, he observed, enjoyed the serials because they gave them the opportunity to "drown out" their troubles or to "fill gaps in their own life." Women, worried that their husbands stayed away from home too much or upset that their daughters had run away from home to marry, could escape reality by listening to stories about a happy family life and a successful wife and mother.[40]

But, Lazarsfeld cautioned, even though listeners said that one reason for listening to the serials was for advice, "Frequently the advice seems confined to good intentions without any substantial influence on basic attitudes." As an example, he cited the apparent contradictory responses of one woman who stated, "They teach you how to be good. I have gone through a lot of suffering but I still can learn from them." And then, when asked whether she disliked any program answered, "I don't listen to *The Goldbergs*. Why waste electricity on the Jews?" Obviously, Lazarsfeld concluded, "the 'goodness' she was 'learning' had not reached the point of materially affecting her attitude towards a minority group."[41]

Other survey respondents said that they looked to the daytime serials for advice on how to handle their husbands or boyfriends or how to bring up children.

> I think Papa David (*Life Can Be Beautiful*) helped me to be more cheerful when Fred, my husband, comes home. I feel tired and instead of being grumpy, I keep on the cheerful side. *The Goldbergs* are another story like that. Mr. Goldberg comes home scolding and he never means it. I sort of understand Fred better because of it. When he starts to shout, I call him Mr. Goldberg. He comes back and calls me Molly. Husbands do not really understand what a wife goes through. These stories have helped me to understand that husbands are like that. If women are tender, they are better off."[42]

Berg herself weighed in on the subject of why she thought her program was as popular as it was. In a magazine article written towards the end of the second run of *The Goldbergs*, she reflected:

> A good radio serial is one which strikes an affinity with its audience by presenting problems with which listeners, as ordinary people, are familiar...When *The Goldbergs* went on the air for the first time, there was a feeling that it might not go across, because it was too down-to-earth, and that what people wanted was escapist material...Through showing how other people live, a radio serial utilizes its medium, the networks, as a powerful channel for the dissemination of progressive ideas, tolerance and understanding.[43]

In October, 1944, Phillip Carlin, a vice president at NBC wrote to Berg, "You have the distinction of putting over the only really successful Jewish program...Others have come and gone but yours goes on forever. See that you keep it that way."[44] A few months later, the show was cancelled.

While no definitive information is available that explains why the program left the airwaves in March, 1945, one reason may have been declining ratings. According to the Hooper ratings for daytime shows, while the program ranked in the top seven programs between 1937-1940, its popularity began to slip after that. Between 1940-1942, the program was not listed in the top 20 daytime programs, although for the 1944-1945 season it was ranked #19.[45]

The Final Years, 1946-1966

After the 1936-1945 run of *The Goldbergs* ended, Berg took her fictional family to Broadway in the play "Me and Molly." The show opened at the Belasco Theater in New York on February 26, 1948 and closed 156 performances later on July 10, 1948. In the play, which was set in the Bronx in 1919, Berg revisited many of the family's earlier concerns such as the fate of Jake's dress manufacturing business and the family's improving economic status that included buying a piano and moving to a larger apartment. Philip Loeb played Jake opposite Berg's Molly. The play was staged by Ezra Stone (of *The Aldrich Family* fame).

It was during the run of "Me and Molly" that Berg realized that television would soon be replacing radio and she began exploring how she could bring *The Goldbergs* to the new medium. After executives at both CBS and NBC turned down her initial request for an audition on the grounds that the program was not suited for television, Berg requested a personal meeting with CBS's William Paley. In a two-minute presentation she told him that "the show might be a flop on TV — or it might be great. I had been on radio for twenty years, fourteen of them on CBS, and I said I thought I deserved an audition."[46] Paley agreed to her request, which eventually led to the program's debut on television on January 10, 1949. CBS also agreed to revive the radio version of *The Goldbergs,* which aired for its third and last time from September 2, 1949 to June 24, 1950. During the initial period when the program was on both radio and television, the scripts and casts for both were almost identical. Berg played Molly, Philip Loeb, her co-star from the play "Me and Molly," was Jake, Larry Robinson was Sammy, Arlene McQuade played Rosalie and Eli Mintz was Uncle David. The plots returned the family to its humble beginnings in the Bronx and Sammy and Rosalie were once again children.

When the radio series came to an end well before its television counterpart, one reason for the cancellation was that for the audience still listening to the radio, the program was, "old hat." And for those who owned television sets, it was, "why listen when you can watch it on the tube." The television version, minus Loeb, who was forced to leave the program when he was accused of communist involvement and blacklisted, struggled along for a few years, moving from CBS to NBC and finally to Dumont where it breathed its final breath in 1954.[47]

In May, 1950, after the conclusion of the program's second television season, the cast went to Hollywood where they filmed the movie *Molly* that was released the following year.

During the final two decades of her life, Berg was involved in a series of other writing and acting projects. In 1955, *The Goldbergs* enjoyed a brief revival on television, although this time, the program was called *Molly* and the family lived in suburban Haverville. In 1961, donning a new persona as a widow going to college, Berg returned to television in *Mrs. G. Goes to College*. Midway through the program's one season run, it was renamed *The Gertrude Berg Show*. Also in 1961, the character of Molly Goldberg was revived when Berg appeared in a series of commercials for SOS scouring pads, intoning, "Yoo-hoo, Mrs. Bloom. Have you tried the new SOS? With soap, it's loaded."

When she died in 1966 at the age of 66, Berg left an indelible crater (certainly not a dent) on the image that Americans of all walks of life had of their Jewish neighbors. In the more than 20 years that *The Goldbergs* was heard on radio, seen on the stage, in film and on the screen, and read about in books and in comic strips, Berg did more in her creative writing and sympathetic portrayal of a loving and caring wife and mother to bring about a decent respect for the lifestyle of ethnic minorities than any amount of purposeful propaganda could achieve.

In November, 1973, seven years after her death, *The Goldbergs* was adapted as a Broadway musical, "Molly," starring Kaye Ballard in the title role. The musical ran for only 68 performances.

Notes

1. Given its position in radio history, *The Rise of the Goldbergs*, renamed *The Goldbergs* in 1936, has been written about extensively, and in far more detail, than the space allowed in a single chapter. Readers wishing to learn more about the program and its creator, Gertrude Berg, are advised to check the following additional sources: Gertrude Berg and Cherney Berg. *Molly and Me* (New York: McGraw-Hill, 1961); Glenn D. Smith, Jr., *Something on My Own: Gertrude Berg and American Broadcasting, 1929–1956* (Syracuse, NY: Syracuse University Press, 2007); David Weber, "Goldberg Variations: The Achievements of Gertrude Berg," in J. Hoberman and Jeffrey Shandler, *Entertaining America: Jews, Movies, and Broadcasting* (Princeton, NJ: Princeton University Press, 1994); Morris Freedman, "The Real Molly Goldberg," *Commentary*, Vol. 21, #4, April, 1956; Gilbert Seldes, "The Great Gertrude," *Saturday Review*, June 2, 1956; and William Birnie, "Molly Goes Marching On," *American Magazine*, November, 1941.

2. Berg, *Molly and Me*, 158.

3. In her autobiography, Berg recalled that when she read the script to the CBS executive the first time, "he didn't seem to be listening." Ibid., 161. Smith, *Something on My Own,* 29, writes that one of the offending lines was when the more outspoken Laura tells Effie that, "marriages are never made in heaven."

4. Thomas' article, in the authors' personal collection, is undated, but does say that it is written 10 years after the program debuted. See also Smith, *Something of My Own,* 31. One of the authors also discussed the Berg/Brown connection with Smith in a 2007 telephone interview and also with Himan Brown in a 2007 phone conversation.

5. Ibid., 169.

6. Ibid., 166-167.

7. During the program's first year, Berg also relied on a Sophia Civoru to develop ideas for the program. The arrangement ended when Civoru sued Berg in 1930. For more details, see Smith, ibid., 38-39.

8. Ibid., 31.

9. Berg, *The Rise of the Goldbergs*, 81. As the text is not written in typical radio format where the name of the speaker is identified, it is not always clear which lines are delivered by Molly and which by Jake.

10. Although several Internet references state that the singers appeared on the program more than once, the authors have not been able to identify any specific dates.

11. Bernard Postal, "The Story of Gertrude Berg, Author and Actor," *Jewish Toronto Canada*, October 5, 1934, 22, cited in Smith, *Something of My Own*, 58.

12. Waters had earlier appeared in the stage productions of *Potash and*

Perlmutter and *Abie's Irish Rose*, both of which were later adapted into radio programs.

13. Berg fired Ryder at one point when his mother asked for a raise. Sloane took over the part for a while but Berg later rehired Ryder. Smith, *Something on My Own*, 50. While the dates for these changes are uncertain, photographs of Sloane as Sammy appear in an October 23, 1938 issue of *Radio Guide*. In a photograph accompanying a 1939 article that appeared in *Radio Parade* (the exact date of the article is not known), Ryder is shown as Sammy.

14. Although Berg is always credited with writing the scripts, she was not the sole writer. The authors have been able to identify at least two writers who contributed to the scripts. Abraham Polonsky, who went on to become an Oscar-nominated screenwriter and director, is known to have written scripts in 1937. He came to Berg's attention while working at a law firm and was assigned to provide some legal background information to one of the firm's clients, Gertrude Berg. Polonsky went on to write for the *The Columbia Workshop* and *The Mercury Theatre of the Air*. The second writer was Abram Ginnes who later wrote extensively for television.

15. John Dunning, *On the Air: The Encyclopedia of Old-Time Radio* (New York: Oxford University Press, 1998), 286.

16. Berg, *Molly and Me*, 170.

17. Susan Smulyan, *Selling Radio: The Commercialization of American Broadcasting 1920-1934* (Washington, DC: Smithsonian Institution Press, 1994), 115-116.

18. http://www.dg125.com/Gazette/BestOfTheBest/1930's/mainmenu.htm.

19. Weber, "Goldberg Variations," 113-114. It is not clear why the number of positive and negative letters do not add up to the total number of letters received.

20. Smuylan, *Selling Radio*, 116.

21. Weber, "Goldberg Variations," 113.

22. Berg, *Molly and Me*, 190-191.

23. Michele Hilmes, *Radio Voices: American Broadcasting, 1922-1952* (Minneapolis, University of Minnesota Press, 1997), 4. See also Hilmes' discussion on early radio's influence on cultural diversity and assimilation, 1-33.

24. Erik Barnouw, *A Tower in Babel: A History of Broadcasting in the United States to 1933* (New York; Oxford University Press, 1966) 274-275.

25. Weber, *"Goldberg Variations,"* 116-117.

26. Ibid., 119.

27. Ibid., 118-119. Weber associated the letters with an October, 1935 "Yom Kippur" episode. However, as the series was off the air in October, 1935 and did not return until 1938, the reference must be either a typographical error or the result of having transposed a number when copying the date from Berg's papers.

28. Berg, *Molly and Me*, 187.

29. Smith, *Something of My Own*, 44, 57-60.

30. In later years, from October 7, 1940 to April 3, 1942, in addition to writing for and staring in *The Goldbergs*, Berg also co-wrote the scripts for another CBS soap opera, *Kate Hopkins, Angel of Mercy*.

31. Gertrude Berg, *The Rise of the Goldbergs* (New York: Barse & Co., 1931). Copies of the book may still be found by contacting a used book dealer.

32. According to Smith, *Something of My Own*, 73-74, CBS and NBC entered into a "bidding war" for *The Goldbergs*. The result was that between 1936-1945, the program changed networks five different times and at various times was off the air. Berg's 1937 contract with Procter & Gamble allowed the sponsor to offer the program to more than network simultaneously.

33. Berg, *Molly and Me*, 189-190.

34. Smith, *Something of My Own*, 77-81, discusses how Berg wove some of her personal political beliefs into her scripts, including her strong support for President Roosevelt. He also notes that "With a nation listening, Molly and her family often disregarded their usual dinner conversation to focus on the struggles of their European cousins."

35. Berg, *Molly and Me*, 172.

36. In a 2007 email message, Smith advised the authors that the remark may have been PR hype, but, he added, "It was classic Berg." See also *Something of My Own*, 95.

37. The surviving recordings of *The Goldbergs* covering the 1940-1942 period are numbered but not dated. The "Sammy Going to War" episode is listed in the authors' collection as Episode #1297. Another example of the program's support for the war can be found in the August 31, 1942 episode excerpted in Smith, ibid., 95. Molly says: "Is what the German people are doing good or bad. And our answer is…it's evil…it's absolutely cruel and bad and evil…and that means we're going to keep killing them until they stop doing what they're doing…and every man or woman who makes a bomb or digs a ditch or helps in any way to keep Hitler's armies from killing our Allies… You've got to believe what are doing is right. It is right. Completely right…until the last Nazi throws down his gun or his shovel and says I'm not fighting you."

38. The strip was written by Stanley Kaufman and drawn by Irwin Hasen. It was carried on a daily basis by the New York Post Syndicate from June 8, 1944 through December 21, 1945. *Stripper's Guide Index to US Comic Strips and Panels*, 392.

39. Paul F. Lazarsfeld and Frank N. Stanton. *Radio Research 1942-1943*. (New York: Essential Books, 1944), 25.

40. Ibid., 24-25.

41. Ibid., 29.

42. Ibid., 27.

43. Gertrude Berg, "Why I Hate the Term 'Soap Opera,'" *Everywoman's Magazine*, February, 1945, 28, as cited in Weber, "Goldberg Variations," 114-115.

44. Smith, *Something of My Own*, 97.

45. http://www.dg125.com/Gazette/BestOfTheBest/1930's/mainmenu.htm. According to Smith, ibid., 85-91, the Berg family suspected that the show was cancelled because of Gertrude's strong — and outspoken support for President Roosevelt in the 1944 presidential election. However, CBS and Procter & Gamble cited the show's slipping ratings as well as Berg's desire to travel overseas to entertain the troops as the reason for the show's cancellation.

46. Berg, *Molly and Me*, 207. See also Smith, *Something of My Own*, 112-116 for a discussion of the concerns at CBS and other networks about the acceptance of "Jewish" programs on television.

47. For more insights into how Berg dealt with the Loeb controversy see Smith, ibid., 129-161.

3
"Those People"

The history of the world is replete with examples of individuals, some organized, some not, who for various perceived reasons, have developed deep seated hatreds of entire groups of people. From biblical times through the centuries, and in almost every part of the globe, historians have recorded various acts of oppression committed against peoples based on their belonging to a tribe, nationality, language group, religion, sect, family or sexual group. A classic source of information about how such behavior had an impact on the lives of people living in the United States is the *History of Bigotry in the United States* by Gustavus Myers.[1] Other important studies updating Myers' work have since been published.

How did network radio portray "those people?" Shush, you know: the Jews; Kikes; Hebes; Christ killers; money lenders and war profiteers; funny looking people with big noses and long beards; communists, anarchists and union leaders; the people who controlled Hollywood, radio, Tin Pan Alley and the press; the men who wanted to seduce good Christian girls; the women who wanted to tempt decent Christian men; and the people who kidnapped innocent Christian babies and sacrificed them to make Passover wine and matzah. These and other derogatory terms were commonly used to describe Jews in the United States during the first half of the 20th century.

Long before America entered World War II, the seeds of fear and hatred towards Jews had been planted and nurtured by various individuals and organizations. Using the print media, mass rallies and radio, rather than alert their audiences to the evils of Fascism and Nazism, these diverse groups instead aimed their invective against the international bankers, war profiteers and, more pointedly, shush, you know, "those people."

America was ripe for such demagogues. The stock market crash of 1929 brought about the Great Depression, which in turn created havoc throughout every level of society. People from almost all walks of life lost their jobs as well as their life savings as factories closed and businesses and banks failed. Many individuals, some wealthy, others not, who had invested in the stock market lost, their shirts. The apocryphal image of sad looking men booking hotel rooms on the upper floors so that they could end their misery by leaping from a window became all too common.

An examination of how radio may have influenced anti-Jewish attitudes in the years preceding America's entry into World War II, begins with a brief look at how the purveyors of hate used the print media to disseminate some of the more severe and outrageous portrayals of Jews. Because the airwaves were subject both to government regulation and censorship by sponsors and network executives who didn't wish to alienate listeners who were potential customers,[2] when anti-Semitic messages were broadcast, they were generally toned down with euphemisms and other verbal techniques.

Henry Ford

Much has been written about Henry Ford, the genius who is frequently credited with developing the concept of the assembly line as a means of reducing manufacturing costs. He was also the businessman who offered his employees a better wage ($5 a day) so that they could afford to buy the product they were producing. However, Ford also became one of the leading figures responsible for fomenting anti-Jewish feelings during the 1920s.[3] While Ford always maintained that he had no dislike of Jews, and indeed employed a number of them in his plant, he felt it his duty to educate the public about the dangerous conspiracy he learned about from reading *The Protocols of the Elders of Zion,* a publication repeatedly proven to be a forgery and a hoax. The discredited book, which had its origin in Russia in 1903 where anti-Semitism was endorsed by the Czar, described a Jewish conspiracy for world domination.

Ford's "educational" campaign began when he purchased the *Dearborn Independent*, a newspaper he used to spread his views on "The Jewish Question." Beginning with the May 22, 1920 issue, and continuing over the next 91 issues, the weekly publication featured articles based on the fabricated *Protocols*. Not long after the entire series of articles appeared, many were reprinted in book form in a four volume paper-bound series collectively called *The International Jew: The World's Foremost Problem.* The book was subsequently translated into German, Spanish and several other languages. Copies continue to be sold to this very day, not only in the United States but also in the Middle East.

As a result of a series of damaging lawsuits, some negative impact on the bottom line of Ford's business, and the strong opposition of Henry's son Edsel and grandson Henry Ford II, the *Dearborn Independent* eventually stopped printing its anti-Semitic articles. In 1927, Ford issued a public apology for any remarks of his that had been, in his words, misconstrued as being anti-Semitic.[4] That, however, did not stop the perception by many that privately Ford continued to harbor anti-Semitic views. In July, 1938, on the occasion of his 75th birthday, Ford was one of four non-Germans (and the only American) to be awarded the German Order of the Eagle, created by Hitler as the highest honor a foreigner could receive from the Nazi government.[5] At the time, outspoken Jewish-American radio comedian Eddie Cantor was quoted as saying, "Mr. Ford, in my opinion, is a damned fool for permitting the world's greatest gangster to give him this citation," further pointing out that the German press would play this as American support for their cause.[6] On Hitler's birthday in 1939, the Ford Company of Germany sent the Fuehrer a gift of 50,000 marks as a token of its loyalty.

Unlike Charles Lindbergh, Father Charles Coughlin and Gerald L. K. Smith, whose anti-Semitic views were heard on the airwaves, Ford was not known to have made personal appearances on radio. He did, however, underwrite a prestigious weekly radio program, *The Ford Sunday Evening Hour,* that provided him an opportunity to have his views heard on the air as part of the broadcast's mid-program intermission feature. The program, heard from 1934-1942 and again from 1945-1946, featured members of the Detroit Symphony Orchestra, well known opera stars, prominent instrumentalists and Fred Waring's Orchestra. Its host and intermission speaker was William J. Cameron, the former *Detroit News* reporter hired by Ford to work for the *Dearborn Independent.* Called by some a "walking dictionary" and described as a short stout round-faced man, a bit like W. C. Fields minus the humor, Cameron is said to have begun his service for the *Independent* as a moderate thinker who more and more would reflect his employer's views regarding "those people." It was Cameron, in fact, who actually wrote the infamous articles that were to become known as *The International Jew.* In addition to being broadcast to a national audience, Cameron's talks were also printed and distributed to Ford dealers and interested listeners. At six-month intervals, the talks were collected, bound and made available to the public.

While many of Cameron's intermission talks were patriotic, inspirational and uplifting in nature and incorporated much of Ford's anti-New Deal philosophy, they did not include any mention of "The Jewish Question." That changed, however, when during a February 15, 1942 broadcast, Cameron was heard condemning anti-Semitism as "the negation of humanity, intelligence and Christianity. It is not the Jew we pity most, he is not the real victim of anti-Semitism; the real victim is the anti-Semite himself whose soul is eaten by the deadly acid. *Any* (Cameron's emphasis) antagonism toward *any* people *as people* because of color, race or religion, is a vestige of tribal barbarism." Could it be that this amazing reversal from the lips of Ford's spokesperson came about because the country was in the third month of a World War — or were there other reasons?

Charles Lindbergh

While there is little doubt regarding Henry Ford's views regarding Jews, to this day there are those who question the degree to which America's greatly admired aviation hero, Charles Lindbergh, may have shared those opinions. The evidence suggests that he did, but that until at least 1941, he failed to give public voice to those views.

Lindbergh's early life, including his history-making solo flight across the Atlantic and the tragic kidnapping and murder of his son, all of which contributed to his heroic image, is well known. In the mid-1930s, Lindbergh made frequent trips to Germany, culminating in his personally receiving the Service Cross of the German Eagle from Reichmarshal Hermann Goering, commander of the Luftwaffe.[7] Also during the 1930s, Lindbergh began a close association with Dr. Alexis Carrel, a Frenchman and recipient of the Nobel Prize for medicine. In addition to being a world famous surgeon, Carrel was also an enthusiastic proponent of eugenics, the belief that people with undesirable characteristics should not be permitted to reproduce, and that by encouraging breeding between people possessing highly desirable characteristics, the human race would improve. Although impressed by the concept, Lindbergh did not necessarily support the extreme measures later adopted by the Nazis who used eugenics as the scientific justification for cleansing the Third Reich of all of its undesirables, i.e., Jews, gypsies, homosexuals, communists, the disabled, etc.

By 1939, Lindbergh's frequent references to the need to protect the civilized "white" population from the threat of other racial groups, and his continuing public sympathy for Germany was enough to cause New Jersey

Attorney General David P. Wilentz, the prosecutor at the Hauptmann trial[8] to say, "The people of England are about finished with him. Americans are beginning to feel the same way, and the halo of hero worship around Lindbergh's head is getting pretty well tarnished."[9]

In 1939, Lindbergh joined forces with an anti-war movement known as the America First Movement. At least four United States Senators, all progressive Republicans (Burton K. Wheeler of Montana, Gerald Nye of North Dakota, Hiram Johnson of California and Robert La Follette of Wisconsin), were actively involved in the movement, as was Robert E. Wood of Sears Roebuck who headed the organization. Although the Committee's membership never exceeded more than 850,000, Lindbergh's popularity, waning as it may have been among some people, gave the group greater public exposure, especially as his speeches were broadcast by the networks.[10]

Lindbergh gave at least eight major talks on behalf of the America First Movement that were aired on radio. All have been archived and are available for anyone wishing either to hear them or read his words. The speeches, beginning with September 15, 1939 ("America and European Wars") set a pattern in which his emphasis on saving the white race and his sympathy for Germany's position would become more clear. Other radio addresses followed:

- October 13, 1939 ("Neutrality and War")
- May 19, 1940 ("Air Defense of America")
- June 15, 1940 ("Our Drift Toward War")
- August 4, 1940 ("Our Relationship With Europe")
- April 23, 1941 ("We Should Not Enter a War We Can't Win")
- May 23, 1941 ("Challenge Canada's Right to Draw Us Into War")
- September 11, 1941 ("Three Groups Who Want Us to Intervene")

It was the September 11, 1941 speech, delivered to an America First audience in Des Moines, Iowa, that was to turn a larger segment of public opinion against Lindbergh and, by association, the organization that sponsored him. One wonders if it was merely coincidence that less than a month prior to the September 11th speech, Senator Wheeler announced that he would investigate "interventionists" in the motion picture industry where many of the studio heads were Jews. He questioned why so many foreign-born people were allowed to shape American opinion, causing President Roosevelt to observe that the Bible, too, had been written "by mostly foreign-born and Jewish people."[11] Senator Nye echoed his colleague's sentiments when he accused Hollywood (translation: the Jewish movie executives) of attempting to "drug the reason of the American people" and "rouse war fever."

Significant segments of the Lindbergh's Des Moines speech are excerpted below.[12] While Lindbergh attempted to demonstrate his sympathetic understanding of the Jewish position, he nonetheless condemned them as self-serving and un-American. He said:

> The three most important groups who have been pressing this country toward war are the British, the Jewish and the Roosevelt administration. Let us consider these groups, one at a time...
>
> The second major group I mentioned is the Jewish. It is not difficult to understand why Jewish people desire the overthrow of Nazi Germany. The persecution they suffered in Germany would be sufficient to make bitter enemies of any race. No person with a sense of the dignity of mankind can condone the persecution of the Jewish race in Germany. But no person of honesty and vision can look on their pro-war policy here today without seeing the dangers involved in such policy both for us and for them. Instead of agitating for war, the Jewish groups in this country should be opposing it in every possible way for they will be among the first to feel its consequences.
>
> Tolerance is a virtue that depends upon peace and strength. History shows that it cannot survive war and devastation. A few far-sighted Jewish people realize this and stand opposed to intervention. But the majority still do not. Their (the Jews) greatest danger to this country lies in their large ownership and influence in our motion pictures, our press, our radio and our government.
>
> I am not attacking either the Jewish or the British people. Both races, I admire. But I am saying that the leaders of both the British and the Jewish race, for reasons which are not understandable from their viewpoint as they are inadvisable from ours, for reasons which are not American, wish to involve us in the war. We cannot blame them for looking out for what they believe to be in their own interests, but we also must look out for ours. We cannot allow the natural passions and the prejudices of other peoples to lead our country to destruction.
>
> In selecting these three groups as the major agitators for war, I have

included only those whose support is essential to the war party. If any one of these groups — the British, the Jewish, or the administration — stops agitating for war, I believe there will be little danger of our involvement. I do not believe that any two of them are powerful enough to carry this country to war without the support of the third. And to these three, as I have said, all other war groups are of secondary importance...

Our theaters soon became filled with plays portraying the glory of war. Newsreels lost all semblance of objectivity. Newspapers and magazines began to lose advertising if they carried anti-war articles. A smear campaign was instituted against individuals who opposed intervention. The terms 'fifth columnist,' 'traitor,' 'Nazi,' 'anti-Semitic were thrown ceaselessly at any one who dared to suggest that it was not to the best interest of the United States to enter the war. Men lost their jobs if they were frankly anti-war. Many others dared no longer speak.

It did not take long for radio's power and effectiveness as a means of communicating with millions of Americans to produce results. However, it was not quite the results that Lindbergh had anticipated. Reaction to the speech was immediate.

The *Des Moines Register* observed, "...it may have been courageous for Colonel Lindbergh to say what was in his mind, but it was so lacking in appreciation of consequences — putting the best interpretation on it — that it disqualifies him for any pretensions of leadership of this republic in policy-making...(The speech was) so intemperate, so unfair, so dangerous in its implications that it cannot but turn many spadefuls [sic] in the digging of the grave of his influence in this crisis." The *Kansas City Journal* commented: "Lindbergh's interest in Hitlerism is now thinly concealed."

Time magazine reported in the September 22, 1941 issue published the following week that, "Last week — freedom-loving U.S. citizens — heirs of Patrick Henry, Thomas Jefferson, Abraham Lincoln and a great host of heroes — had genuinely good reason to fear that Freedom might perish from their land. For last week Charles Augustus Lindbergh and Gerald Prentice Nye cast aside all but the last veil of pretense and, in the pattern established by Adolph Hitler years ago, sought to make the Jews a public national issue in the U.S." Citing Lindbergh's remarks that the Jews would be the first to feel the consequences should the United States go to war, the article continued, "The plain implication was that the Jews will be blamed for war if it comes and will be persecuted because of it when opportunity arises. If this is not a threat it was the next thing to it."

Other newspapers, including those owned by isolationist William Randolph Hearst, were equally critical. Even the *Chicago Tribune*, no friend of the British, condemned the speech. Wendell Willkie, the Republican nominee for president in 1940, referred to the speech as, "...the most un-American talk made in my time by any person of national reputation." Thomas Dewey, who was to be the Republican nominee for president against Franklin Roosevelt in 1944, called the Lindbergh speech, "...an inexcusable abuse of the right of freedom of speech." Even conservative Republican Robert Taft observed that Lindbergh's reference to the Jews as if they were a "foreign race" and not Americans at all was a grossly unjust attitude.

Lindbergh had been scheduled to give one more speech, on December 11, 1941 in Boston, on the subject of "What Do We Mean By Democracy and Freedom?" The action taken by a joint session of Congress on December 8th in response to the attack on Pearl Harbor resulted in that speech to be cancelled and led to the dissolution of the America First Committee. It also marked the end of Lindbergh's influence on public opinion.

Father Charles E. Coughlin

A third, and certainly the most influential advocate who shared the anti-Roosevelt, anti-war and blame "those people" views with both Ford and Lindbergh was Father Charles Edward Coughlin. While not the very first clergyman to take to the airwaves, he is certainly the best remembered of his generation. As this book focuses only on Coughlin's use of radio to disseminate his anti-Semitic messages, readers interested in learning about other aspects of the priest's early personal history, his involvement with the National Union For Social Justice and the Union Party, and his other economic, social and political causes are directed to several books that document his multi-faceted life.[13]

The power of Father Coughlin to influence a nation's perception of the Jews via the airwaves is best described by Donald Warren in his book, *Radio Priest, Charles Coughlin, The Father of Hate Radio*.

> Time and again over the next decade the radio priest would give his audience suspense and excitement, using the behind-the-scenes exposé format of the gossip columnist. He had brought scoop journalism to the radio, a technique employed later by (Walter) Winchell.

With a mixture of biting political attack, soothing organ music, and spiritual discourse, Coughlin 'tried each season to give his audience something new, something that would 'hold' them, yet enlighten them.' Anticipation, week after week, was the secret of his success.[14]

Warren also cited Wallace Stegner's description of Coughlin's baritone voice as:

> ...of such mellow richness, such manly, heartwarming, confidential intimacy, such emotional and ingratiating charm, that anyone tuning past it on the radio dial almost automatically returned to hear it again. It was without doubt one of the great speaking voices of the twentieth century. It was a voice made for promises...his range was spectacular. He always began in a low rich pitch, speaking slowly, gradually increasing in tempo and vehemence, then soaring into high and passionate tones...His diction was musical, the effect authoritative...[15]

Coughlin's radio career began on Sunday October 17, 1926 over Detroit station WJR,[16] some six years after the very first scheduled radio broadcast had been aired and one week prior to his 35th birthday. The program, *The Golden Hour of the Little Flower*, was carried as a remote hook-up from the altar of his own church, the Shrine of the Little Flower in Royal Oak, Michigan. From the very beginning, his broadcasts were popular with listeners and resulted in an ever increasing number of letters, several of which contained contributions, most in small denominations, but a few containing as much as $50 or $100. Seeking a way to increase the flow of donations, Coughlin created The Radio League Of The Little Flower: For a donation of $1.00, members of the League and other enrollees (deceased members could also be enrolled) would be included in the "remembrance in the daily Mass offered at Calvary Hill, Jerusalem." By the fall of 1929, after two additional stations picked up his program, WMAQ (at the time, a CBS affiliate) in Chicago and WLW in Cincinnati, the priest was getting some 3,000 letters a week.

Initially, the program featured organ music, a male choir and a Coughlin sermon that was generally of a religious nature. However, on the January 12, 1930 broadcast, Coughlin changed the format and the entire program was devoted to attacking Communism and Socialism. As the country moved deeper into the Great Depression, his sermons continued to focus increasingly on populist issues, including attacks on people of wealth and power, but he also began talking about the "red menace." It was at this time that he also started using the "naming names" technique that would be used twenty years later in another anti-communist crusade led by another Midwesterner, this time a United States Senator from Wisconsin. In 1930, Coughlin attacked Norman Thomas, the leader of the Socialist Party. The criticism backfired, however, when Thomas enlisted the help of a senator-friend who also happened to be on the Federal Radio Commission. The end result was that WJR was instructed to tell Coughlin that he could no longer make any direct mention of the Socialist Party on his broadcasts. The rebuke was the first time that Coughlin's veracity and the accuracy of his statements would be challenged—but not the last time. (See the discussion below of Coughlin's November 20, 1938 broadcast.)

Whether due to Coughlin's speaking style, his understanding of mass psychology, the nature of his messages or simply the uniqueness of hearing matters heretofore ignored on other radio broadcasts, word spread about the program. As additional stations throughout the state picked up his broadcasts, the priest was given ever wider exposure and the size of his listening audience increased. Money kept pouring in until it reached the point that the post office had to build a new facility in Royal Oak just to serve the daily flow of incoming donations. It was not unusual for Coughlin himself to make trips to the bank each day with deposits in small denominations totaling several thousand dollars each. Coughlin's church, which initially had far greater seating capacity than parishioners, found itself filled beyond capacity on Sundays with fans of the priest, many of who moved to Royal Oak to become regular members of his congregation.

In an article analyzing Coughlin's rhetorical style, Diane Cypkin raised the intriguing question of how a priest could acquire the power to influence the secular thinking of so vast a listening audience.[17] His method, she concluded, was "simple and exceptionally effective," adding that because Coughlin's initial audience was overwhelmingly Catholic, it shared with him a basic set of values. All Coughlin had to do was:

> ...draw the secular into the realm of the sacred — his realm. In so doing, he, as a priest whose priestly words were vested with 'extra-human origins,' with 'extra-human authority,' became empowered. He became empowered to interpret the current situation (exigence) to his flock. He became empowered to identify the good and bad characters in this Depression drama: the Christian and anti-Christian. He could save his flock from the anti-Christs — to be identified by the Father. And if all else failed, he could always talk to his

audience as American patriot to American patriot, calling up another shared 'rhetorical vision.'

Cypkin also observed that part of Coughlin's persona was creating an "image of erudition and credibility" and that this led him to lace his sermons with "facts" which he offered to make available in print to his listeners. Most listeners, of course, were not in a position to question the accuracy, relevance or source of his "facts," and even when others discredited the priest's "facts," the damage had already been done.

Coughlin's attacks on Jews began as early as February, 1930 when, in a less-than-subtle remark, he linked Jews to the social and economic problems that his listeners were facing. In the talk, the priest traced Socialism (which he had already defined as an evil) back to an 18th century atheist and also associated it with the Old Testament. Later in the year, he drew an analogy between Shakespeare's Shylock and modern day Shylocks who "have grown fat and wealthy, praised and deified, because they have perpetuated the ancient crime of usury under a modern racket of statesmanship."[18] The following week, he returned to his February theme, and after warning about the evils of Communism, reminded his listeners that Lenin, Trotsky and Béla Kun were all followers of "the German Hebrew, Karl Marx."[19]

In the fall of 1930, CBS head William Paley began negotiations with George Richards, the owner of WJR, in an effort to get the station to switch its affiliation from NBC to CBS. Richards agreed, with the proviso that Paley agree to carry Coughlin's broadcast as a network program for 26 weeks. The deal also called for Coughlin to pay CBS for the airtime, which had the added bonus of providing CBS with additional revenue.[20] In what Sally Bedell Smith, Paley's biographer, referred to as a "blunder," Paley was willing to overlook Coughlin's earlier anti-Semitic statements for what he viewed to be a pragmatic business decision. When NBC's Sarnoff complained to Paley that the deal with WJR violated network etiquette, Paley responded, "Mr. Sarnoff, radio broadcasting is a highly competitive business."[21]

Coughlin's first CBS broadcast aired on October 5, 1930. The program was carried on 16 stations in 23 states that reached from coast to coast and included most large cities. The size of the potential audience was estimated at 40 million listeners.[22] During the first three months, the priest concentrated on non-controversial economic and social justice issues. His tone changed, however, in 1931 when the talks became increasingly inflammatory. One may wonder if it was the larger audience that emboldened

Coughlin to express his views about "The Jewish Question" more openly. For his January 4, 1931 broadcast, Coughlin planned to deliver a sermon entitled, "Prosperity," that attacked the Treaty of Versailles and the League of Nations, but also raised what was to become one of the priest's recurring themes: that the international bankers (read Jews) had caused the 1929 stock market crash and that the crash was linked to the ideas of Karl Marx, a Jew. When CBS executives requested that certain inflammatory passages in the talk be dropped (the contract called for Coughlin's text to be submitted in advance), the priest refused and decided not the broadcast the sermon. Instead, he devoted the January 4th broadcast to denouncing CBS' censorship — a move that resulted in a deluge of pro-Coughlin, anti-CBS mail. The original talk was then broadcast — in its original form — the following week.[23]

Despite the program's popularity, in April, 1931 CBS decided not to renew Coughlin's contract. When Coughlin sought airtime on another network, he discovered that NBC wasn't interested in carrying him. But that didn't stop the priest. With the help of WJR's Richards, and armed with a successful track record as someone who could attract a substantial listening audience, Coughlin proceeded to build his own network by purchasing time on a number of independent radio stations serving major population centers.[24]

In an article about Coughlin that appeared in the October 29, 1933 Sunday magazine section of *The New York Times*, it was reported that probably more people heard Coughlin over the radio than the most seductive jazz band or the most plaintive torch singer. The article also noted that in 1932, 2.5 million copies of the priest's radio talks had been mailed to listeners. Asked by the reporter what were the secrets of his success, Coughlin answered that he took pains to express himself in the language of the people and that he kept away from religious controversy. Explaining how he went about writing his sermons, he said:

> I write the discourse first in my own language, the language of a cleric. Then I rewrite it, using metaphors the public can grasp, toning the phrases down to the language of the man-in-the-street. Sometimes I coin a word to crystallize attention. Radio broadcasting I have found, must not be high hat. It must be human, intensely human. It must be simple, but it must be done up in metaphors. It must deal with something vital to the life of the people, and it must be positive.[25]

The article focused entirely on Coughlin's social and economic views, his opinion of President Roosevelt and his religious beliefs — but it never mentioned the words Jews or Communists or the phrase "international bankers" that were becoming increasingly frequent in the priest's talks.

Estimates of the total size of Coughlin's radio audience as well as the number of stations that carried his program varied widely between 1932 when he formed his own network and 1940 when he ceased broadcasting his program on a regular basis. Not only were the number of stations that broadcast him in a state of flux, but there also were discrepancies as to what "listeners" were being counted: regular listeners, those who listened occasionally or at least once, or the size of the station's overall potential listening audience. Interpreting changes in the number of stations that carried the program is complicated further by the fact that frequently the numbers were not associated with specific years. An early 1938 Gallup Poll reported that 10 percent of all families owning radios listened to Coughlin on a regular basis, 25 percent heard him occasionally and that 83 percent of those who listened each week approved of what the priest said.[26]

The above notwithstanding, the two figures most frequently cited when describing the size of Coughlin's audience are either 30 million or 45 million listeners, although it should be noted that both estimates came from sources either friendly to Coughlin or from Coughlin himself.[27] The number of stations that carried his program ranged from 16 in 1930 to at least 63 when he resumed broadcasting in January, 1938, having been off the air during the 1937-1938 season.[28] At his peak, Coughlin was heard from Maine to California.

Another measure of Coughlin's growing popularity was the volume of mail he received: at one time his office reported receiving up to 80,000 letters per week from listeners.[29] Also, many of Coughlin's loyal radio audience subscribed to or purchased copies of his weekly publication, *Social Justice*, which served the priest in much the same way as the *Dearborn Independent* had earlier served Henry Ford. The newspaper also gave the priest the opportunity to expand his message well beyond his weekly radio talks. While Coughlin "claimed" in 1936 that the paper had a circulation of one million, the only two years for which actual figures are available showed a circulation of 228,678 in 1940 and 194,929 in 1941.[30]

Free from any network censorship, Coughlin picked up the anti-Jewish theme in February, 1933. In his sermon, "Gold: Private or Public," he spoke about the role of Jews in European history (how the Rothschilds had financed the Napoleonic Wars) and how that history related to the nation's current economic ills. Again he spoke about how the international bankers, the Morgans, Kuhn-Loebs and Rothschilds (the last two were Jewish) were growing fat at the expense of the millions of oppressed people. A week later, he attacked the Rothschilds again, this time charging that, "Under the flag of their leadership, there assembled the international bankers of the world...the horrible, hated word spelled W-A-R was the secret of their success."[31]

As Nazism took hold in Germany in 1933, concern over Coughlin's comments about Jews began to grow. The priest, however, repeatedly denied that he was anti-Semitic and said that he wanted "good religious Jews" to join him in attacking Communism. He considered the attempt to label him an anti-Semite to be a smear campaign. Coughlin also cultivated the support of some members of the Detroit Jewish community, many of whom shared his concern for social justice.[32]

Father Charles Coughlin

Until 1938, the argument could be made that the articles in *Social Justice* and Coughlin's remarks on his weekly broadcasts about "international bankers," while perhaps misguided, were not clear evidence of out-and-out anti-Semitism.[33] When, however, in the summer of 1938, *Social Justice* began reprinting the infamous and long discredited *Protocols of the Elders of Zion*, there could be little doubt about the priest's views concerning what he would frequently refer to as, "The Jewish Question." Alarmed at the article, members of the Detroit Jewish community met with Coughlin to express their concern. The priest's reaction was to tell his visitors, "there are Jews who are not Jews but who belong to the synagogue of Satan."[34]

Coughlin's true feelings towards Jews became even clearer in the aftermath of Kristallnacht, the night of the broken glass, that followed the assassination of a minor German official in Paris by a young Polish-German Jew. On November 10, 1938, in a single evening, some 267 synagogues in Germany were partly or totally destroyed, Jewish-owned businesses were attacked, some 39 Jews lost their lives, and, in a series of mass arrests, upwards of 20,000 Jews were sent to concentration camps. The Germans also levied a collective fine of $400 million on the entire Jewish community. While the events of Kristallnacht, widely reported in the international press and on radio, shocked and angered even the most hardened reader or listener, Coughlin's response on November 20th, just over a week later, painted a somewhat different picture of the events.

The November 20th program began with a hymn and selection by the choir that set the tone for a religious program. The announcer then informed listeners that, "Father Coughlin will discuss one of the most vital and burning questions of our day — the question of the Jew and of the Christian, and of persecution."[35] Coughlin began his talk by recapping the events that had led to Kristallnacht. He then expressed his "sincere sympathy to the millions of humble, religious Jews, both in America and elsewhere, who have been persecuted by a thoughtless world." He explained that he wanted to trace the origins of the "serpent of hate" and he encouraged "intelligent" Christians to unite with "intelligent" Jews to annihilate the evil of persecution forever.

Following what appeared to be his genuine expression of sympathy for the Jews, Coughlin then deftly changed the subject by asking the rhetorical question: "Why is there persecution in Germany today?" What he did, Cypkin observed was, "what many a lawyer defending a client accused of murder, rape, or some other violent crimes does. He shifted the focus away from the actions of the perpetrator to the culpability of the victim, in this case, the aggressive Jews."[36] In Coughlin's role reversal, the actions of the Nazis against the Jews were no more than a legitimate defense mechanism designed to protect the country from the communists — most of whose leaders Coughlin identified as being Jewish and/or were financed by the

Jewish bankers such as the Kuhn-Loebs — who wanted to take over Germany and other countries as prophesied in the *Protocols*. "Thus Nazism was conceived as a political defense mechanism against Communism and was ushered into existence as a result of Communism. And, Communism itself was regarded by the rising generation of Germans as a product not of Russia, but of a group of Jews who dominated the destinies of Russia."

In an effort to minimize the significance of both Kristallnacht and other anti-Jewish measures that had been taken by the Nazi government, Coughlin reminded his listeners:

> German citizen Jews were not molested officially in the conduct their business. The property of German citizen Jews was not confiscated by the government, although a few synagogues and stores were destroyed by mob violence. The children of German citizen Jews were permitted to attend public schools with other children. The German citizen Jewish bankers pursued their business as usual. The German citizen rabbis were permitted the practice of their rites. Until this hour no German citizen Jew has been martyred for his religion by government order although restrictions were placed upon Jewish professional men.
>
> While it is true that foreign citizen Jews resident in Germany were disparaged and expelled, it is likewise true that many social impediments were placed in the pathway of Catholics and Protestants by the Nazi government — impediments which are revolting to our American concepts of liberty. But despite all this, official Germany has not yet resorted to the guillotine, to the machine gun, to the kerosene-drenched pit as instruments of reprisal against Jew or gentile.

While repeating his opposition to all persecution, in an ironic twist, Coughlin suggested that the Jews might have been responsible for their own persecution because of their successes in so many fields of endeavor. "Despite having no nation of their own, no flag, they (the Jews) are closely woven in their racial tendencies...(they are) a powerful minority in their influence; a minority endowed with an aggressiveness and an initiative which, despite all obstacles, has carried their sons to the pinnacles of success in journalism, in radio, in finance, in all sciences and arts." He also repeatedly tied the Jews to the Communist Party and described Nazism as a defense against the evils of Communism.

Coughlin also belittled the $400 million fine levied against the Jews as a result of Kristallnacht. "Jewish persecution," he told his listeners, "only followed after Christians first were persecuted." He blamed the communists (read Jews) for the murder of over 20 million Christians. He compared the $400 million to the $40 billion of Christian property that had been appropriated "by the Lenins and Trotskys...by the atheistic Jews and gentiles." And while he said he was in accord with President Roosevelt's decision to recall the country's ambassador to Germany in response to Kristallnacht, he reminded his listeners that when at least 25,000 Christians had been killed by communists in Russia, Spain and Mexico, the United States government had not issued any formal protests.

More than once in the talk, Coughlin denied that he harbored negative feelings about Jews. Instead, he advised the "good" Jews that, "Nazism, the effect of Communism, cannot be liquidated in its persecution complex until the religious Jews in high places — in synagogue, finance, in radio and in the press — attack the cause, attack forthright the errors and the spread of Communism."

After setting forth his thesis that the "real" problem was the communists, Coughlin, describing himself as a "student of history," then presented a series of "facts" clearly designed to make the words "communists" and "Jews" virtually synonymous in the minds of his listeners. He even invited his listeners to send in requests for print copies of the documents referred to in his talk.[37] As was his style dating back to his 1930 misrepresentation of Norman Thomas, Coughlin conveniently omitted and/or ignored other well documented facts that contradicted his position. Among them was the fact that Jewish children had been prohibited from attending German schools and that the restrictions on Jewish professionals were more severe than he had implied.

Today's readers can judge, as no doubt listeners at the time did, the sincerity of Coughlin's concern for the welfare of Germany's Jews when, in his closing remarks, he said, "By all means let us have the courage to compound our sympathy, not only from the tears of Jews, but also from the blood of Christians — 600,000 Jews whom no government official in Germany has yet sentenced to death."

The broadcast ended with Coughlin leading his radio audience in a prayer that asked for "deliverance from evil...from hate and lust...from pride and self...from false prophets, false leaders and false philosophy."

Reaction to Coughlin's Kristallnacht broadcast was immediate — and especially strong in New York City. The exact sequence of events at

WMCA, the New York City station that carried Coughlin's broadcast, and its immediate rebuttal is unclear as there are at least two somewhat contradictory versions of what occurred in the days leading up to the broadcast. According to *The New York Times* article the following day,[38] the station had been "tipped off" to the content of Coughlin's remarks by Professor Johan Smertenko, the director of the Nonsectarian Anti-Nazi League who had obtained an advance copy of the talk from an independent source. WMCA therefore had a rebuttal program ready to air immediately following Coughlin's broadcast. The rebuttal began with the announcement, "Unfortunately Father Coughlin has uttered certain mistakes of fact"[39] and went on to present several speakers who showed, point-by-point, how Coughlin had made mistakes and misrepresented documents.

Warren, however, described a slightly different version of events based on his interview with Donald Flamm who owned WMCA at the time.[40] According to the Warren/Flamm version, when Coughlin signed on with the station, it was with the clear understanding that the priest would not engage in any anti-Semitic statements. With that assurance, the station waived any requirement that it receive advance copies of the priest's talks. However, prior to the November 20th broadcast, Coughlin voluntarily sent the station a copy of the script. Flamm, feeling betrayed, likened the script to Marc Antony's oration at the funeral of Julius Caesar and asked that modifications be made. Although the station was still dissatisfied with the slightly revised version it received, it allowed the talk to be aired[41] — but opened the broadcast with the statement, "At this time, WMCA wishes to reiterate its position that the views expressed by Father Coughlin on these broadcasts are his own, and do not necessarily reflect the views of the station."

The following Sunday, November 27th, Coughlin broadcast a recording of the previous week's talk — along with a defense of its content — but the program was not heard on three stations that normally carried his program: WIND in Gary, Indiana, WJJD in Chicago — and WMCA in New York. At 4pm that Sunday, the program's regular broadcast time, a WMCA announcer went on the air and explained that the station did not believe that words that might bring "religious or racial strife and dissension to America" were in the public interest. Coughlin's words were heard in New York City, however, over WHBI broadcasting from nearby Newark, New Jersey.[42]

It didn't talk long for Coughlin's supporters to react to his being cancelled by WMCA. On December 18th, 2,000 supporters picketed the building that housed the station's offices and many of the marchers carried anti-Semitic signs as well as signs protesting WMCA's decision.[43] The demonstrations continued for several weeks, albeit on a smaller scale. On January 8, 1939, the pickets added the CBS studios to their target list.[44] *Variety* reported that for the 15-day period beginning January 16, 1939, the Federal Communications Commission received 21,118 pieces of mail (the largest number of letters received to that date over a 15-day period) relating to Coughlin.[45] While some letters denounced the priest, others denounced the people who were not allowing Coughlin to talk. Mob attacks against people who "looked" Jewish and storefronts with Jewish sounding names occurred more frequently in the final month of 1938 and the early months of 1939. At the other extreme, on April 8, 1939, a crowd of several thousand people mobbed ten Coughlin supporters who were distributing copies of *Social Justice* in Times Square. Police were able to disperse the crowd in a few minutes but not before several hundred copies of the paper had been torn up and two of the protesters arrested.[46]

If there was a turning point in Coughlin's ability to influence American public opinion regarding the Jewish people, it was, without doubt, his November 20th talk, viewed by many as an excuse for the events of Kristallnacht. Any doubts that Jewish leaders may have had about the sincerity of the priest's denial of anti-Semitic sentiments were removed. As was the case of Charles Lindbergh when large segments of the public turned against him following his September 11, 1941 Des Moines speech, additional local stations that had carried Coughlin's weekly broadcasts either cancelled them or refused to renew contracts.[47]

While the Catholic Church was officially silent, some churchmen saw the necessity to limit the damage done by the talk. One such church leader was George Cardinal Mundelein of Chicago who said in a statement that was aired on NBC: "As an American citizen, Father Coughlin has the right to express his personal views on current events, but he is not authorized to speak for the Catholic Church, nor does he represent the doctrine or sentiments of the church."[48]

Even Coughlin's superior, Archbishop Mooney, felt it necessary to weigh in on the priest's talk. In a statement published in the *Michigan Catholic*, he said, "Totally out of harmony with the Holy Father's leadership are Catholics who indulge in speeches or writing which in fact tend to arouse feelings against Jews as a race."[49] Mooney also worked with other

Catholic organizations and prominent laymen to try to stop the deterioration of Jewish-Catholic relations that had been caused by Coughlin's broadcasts.

Coughlin did, however, garner the support of some members of the Catholic hierarchy. An editorial in *The Brooklyn Tablet,* the newspaper of the diocese of Brooklyn, New York, stated that there should be no concern over Coughlin and the correctness of his facts.

> The feeling is abroad that in the present crisis in Germany, the Jews in America have overreached themselves...They have corralled everyone from the President down to plead their case. Yet they have shown no similar willingness to create public sympathy for the persecuted in other lands. WMCA itself has not had a broadcaster ready to check 'mistakes of facts' when speakers over its facilities pleaded for help for 'Loyalist' Spain and other like causes. This was the whole point of Father Coughlin's address. That it went home and that it carried a weighty truth is proven better by the action of WMCA than by any word of Father Coughlin.[50]

The December 8, 1938 issue of the *Michigan Christian Advocate* reminded its readers that the documents Coughlin used to justify his statements had been branded as fakes and that "the total effect of the broadcast was to stir latent hatreds against Jews in an hour when a kindling of hatred might rush our own land into a devastating fire beyond all control. The Father seems to forget that the same class that can be stirred to hate the Jews is the very same class that can be stirred to hate the Catholics and the Negroes."[51]

Rather than toning down his subsequent weekly talks, the contents and spirit of Coughlin's later broadcasts became more and more pro-German, with more and more blame for Europe's troubles being laid upon "those people." At the same time, he continued to maintain that he and his supporters were not anti-Semitic and he continued to talk about the "good" Jews and the "bad" Jews.

> Were my advice of any value, I should counsel the Jews to refrain from joining with others in adopting a program — even through constitutional — which breeds resentment to their race...Intolerance towards men is always reprehensible. But often times intolerance is provoked by injudicious and erroneous policies...I am giving voice to a sentiment which is expressed in millions of homes and in thousands of gatherings. Thus, for his collective safety, the American Jew must repudiate the atheistic Jew...Communism must be

stamped out, else an illogical world will build up a defense mechanism against it in these United States paralleling, if not surpassing, the same illogical defense mechanism which operates under Nazism. We are concerned, then, with extinguishing this fire before it consumes our inheritance and before its flames of hatred enfold themselves around the millions of innocent Jews and gentiles in a holocaust of persecution."[52]

In July, 1939, the National Association of Broadcasters (NAB)[53] proposed new guidelines that placed rigid limits on the sale of radio time to speakers who dealt with controversial issues.[54] As the code permitted the discussion of controversial public issues during free airtime that the radio stations controlled, it was clear that Coughlin was the chief target of the prohibition. Although WJR, Coughlin's flagship station, protested the proposed change in the NAB standards, the change went into effect on October 1, 1939. The result was that more stations dropped Coughlin's program. The priest's followers, in turn, protested the suppression of Coughlin's views to the Federal Communication Commission. For the 1939-1940 broadcast season, Coughlin was, however, able sign contracts with 48 stations, including 15 along the East Coast.[55]

Unlike Charles Lindbergh who decided to support the war effort after Pearl Harbor, Coughlin continued to expound a pro-Nazi position even after the United States was at war with Germany, and eventually the government began to investigate his pro-Axis activities. In May, 1942, with Coughlin facing possible indictment by a federal grand jury,[56] Archbishop Mooney directed Coughlin to remain silent on political matters and to restrict his activities to that of a parish priest or else be defrocked. From that day forward, except for rare interviews given later in life, Father Coughlin was only heard by parishioners at the Shrine of the Little Flower. Having accumulated monies of his own over the years, he retired in 1966, lived comfortably, and continued to write pamphlets denouncing Communism until he passed away on October 27, 1979.

Looking back, it is clear that Coughlin's radio talks, coupled with his articles in *Social Justice*, while not the only source fueling a rise of anti-Semitism in the United States, most certainly played a major role in feeding it, and at the same time, distracting the efforts of many American Jews from focusing their attention on the plight of Jews in Europe.[57]

In summarizing Coughlin's impact on the 1930s listening audience,

Cypkin wrote:

> Father Coughlin — before Roosevelt, before Hitler, before Goebbels — realized the power of broadcasting. He realized that the radio had the potential of making him a national figure with the nation his 'flock' — a tantalizing idea for a man with ambitions beyond his parish. He realized the capabilities and the demands of the medium. It could 'convey the original sound of the human voice' and touch the emotions of listeners as no 'cold print' media could. It demanded, for particular success, a skilled voice, a dramatic voice, a voice that appeared as if it was speaking to each listener individually. He knew there was an audience out there hungry for direction and 'clinging to the radio as to a last link to humanity,' even as the Depression and resultant destitution 'forced them to give up an icebox or furniture or bedding.' He knew all of this and, knowing, used this knowledge to gain fame — and infamy.[58]

Gerald L. K. Smith

A contemporary of Father Coughlin, Gerald L. K. Smith spent his early years as a Protestant minister, but gave up the pulpit in 1933 to enter the world of politics, becoming an organizer for the populist Louisiana Governor-turned-Senator Huey Long. After Long's assassination in 1935, Smith joined Father Coughlin and Francis E. Townsend in forming the Union Party whose goal it was to defeat Franklin D. Roosevelt's re-election, thus ending the New Deal. The journalist H. L. Mencken called Smith, "the gustiest and goriest, the loudest and the lustiest, the deadliest and damndest [sic] orator ever heard on this or any other earth."[59] Another unnamed journalist wrote, "he (Smith) makes Father Coughlin seem somewhat less articulate than a waxworks."[60] Coughlin, possibly jealous of Smith's oratorical skills, later broke with his political ally and called Smith a "viper...a leech...who was anti-Christian, anti-Semitic and anti-God."[61]

When the Union Party was resoundingly defeated, Smith organized the Committ ee of One Million with the goals of preserving the sanctity of private property, wiping out Communism, Fascism and Nazism and repelling all threats to a Christian civilization. In 1937, with the backing of some wealthy supporters, he turned to radio to voice his extremist views, broadcasting first from Cleveland before moving his headquarters to Detroit where he was heard on WJR, the same station that broadcast Father Coughlin.[62] Following the practice of the day, Smith offered listeners copies of his talks — and the requests for them, along with contributions, poured in. Smith used the money to purchase additional airtime, which in turn enabled him to build lists for direct mail campaigns, which in turn brought in additional funds, which in turn helped finance the publication of the monthly newspaper he started in 1942, *The Cross and the Flag*.[63]

By 1939, operating with a staff of 38, Smith was broadcasting twice a week, staging mass rallies and sending out a steady stream of direct mail. Between 1939-1942, his broadcasts could be heard by a potential audience of between 30-40 million listeners, primarily in the Midwest. At the same time, Smith claimed to have three million members in his Committee of One Million and boasted of adding between 3,000-6,000 new members each week.[64]

Smith's voluminous papers, housed at the Bentley Historical Library of the University of Michigan in Ann Arbor, include print copies of radio speeches he made in 1932 and from 1938 to 1977. However, with the exception of a brief period between 1941-1942, little is known regarding the specific details of his radio appearances (dates, times, stations, size of listening audience, etc.). Based on published accounts of Smith's life, in all likelihood, most of the radio speeches from the mid-1940s on were broadcast on an ad hoc basis.[65]

In his detailed biography of the rabble-rouser, author Glen Jeansonne traced the seeds of Smith's anti-Semitism to his strict childhood upbringing that was grounded in evangelical Protestantism and his early relationship with William Dudley Pelley, founder of the pro-Nazi Silver Shirts movement. Smith, however, credited Henry Ford with having revealed to him the connection between Communism and the Jews, writing that, "The day came when I embraced the research of Mr. Ford and his associates and became courageous enough and honest enough and informed enough to use the words, 'Communism is Jewish.'"[66] At one point, Ford gave Smith $2,000 to finance three radio broadcasts.[67] The industrialist also loaned Smith the services of several investigators who helped him compile lists of alleged communists.[68]

Between 1937 and the early 1940s, Smith used his radio program to spread his extremist Christian-only philosophy as well as to further his own career. As his radio texts were subject to advance approval, and the National Association of Broadcasters had issued guidelines on the content of broadcasts in reaction to Father Coughlin, Smith's anti-Semitic message was masked by his rhetoric calling for an all-Christian society as the only way to save America from its decadent ways.[69] Indeed, according to Jeansonne, one reason Smith started *The Cross and the Flag* was because his broadcasts were censored and he could be more aggressive in the newspaper. At one point, Smith is reported to have said, "I will praise Heaven on Sunday night and cuss Hell in the magazine."[70]

The underlying anti-Semitism in Smith's radio addresses was evident in a January 25, 1942 talk broadcast during his unsuccessful campaign for the Republican nomination for senator from Michigan. On the program, Smith warned his listeners about the evils of paganism, atheism and the forces of anti-Christ that were widespread in the United States:

> The germ of the anti-Christ, the virus of the Christ-killer is as treacherous as malaria, as malignant as cancer, more vicious than the tuberculosis bacilli. It rides on the winds of hell. It spews out from the mouth of Satan. It thrives in the battlefield. It offers cynicism as a substitute for faith. It replaces love with hate. It makes of a nation at war a cesspool of revolution as a substitute for the atoning statesmanship as exemplified by the Washington's and Lincoln's as they patterned their liberty-loving statesmanship after the liberty-giving Saviorhood of Christ.[71]

In an analysis of 63 of Smith's radio talks broadcast during the 1942 campaign, Morris Janowitz concluded that of the 14 most frequent themes, the one heard most (52 out of 63 speeches) was "That Gerald L. K. Smith is an able Christian leader." The second most popular theme, that he stood for social improvements, appeared in 50 speeches, while returning to the ways of Christ as a necessary way to save America was heard in 43 talks.[72]

Smith continued his call for an all-Christian nation, founding the Christian Nationalist Crusade with the goal of returning the United States to its roots as a Christian nation.[73] He also championed the anti-communist cause and campaigned against the civil rights movement and the United Nations which he called a "Jew-infested" organization. He likened the United Nations flag to the Israeli ("Jew") flag and noted that it also resembled the hammer and sickle of the Soviet Union.

Although no sound recordings of Smith's radio broadcasts have as yet been uncovered, the Smith collection at the Bentley Library does contain a 37-minute recording entitled, "The Plot to Undermine the Republic." Made sometime in the early 1950s, copies of the recording were possibly sent to Smith's supporters: It is unlikely that any radio station would have broadcast the strong, no-holds-barred anti-Semitic message that the Jews had organized a worldwide conspiracy and plotted to destroy the constitutional republic of the United States as well as all Christian civilizations.

After examining Smith's life and work as well as its impact on the American public, Jeansonne concluded that:

> He orated and threatened and traveled and sent out tons of junk mail, but he never won respectable adherents. In another time and place, under different conditions, Smith might have caused great harm. Had the depression continued, or had a weak leader been president in the 1930s and 1940s, his agitation might have gotten results. Demagogues like Smith surface sporadically in America; perhaps they are always present but gain power in times of privation and turmoil. We can never rest assured that, should troubled times persist 'it can't happen here.' Smith's decline was a matter of luck as well as deliberate policy.[74]

Although Smith's career as a demagogue lasted longer than Coughlin's, from the late-1930s into the 1970s, he is less well remembered today for several reasons. His efforts after World War II were restricted to that of a small right wing fringe movement; his messages tended to be heard by those who were already adherents to his cause; and Jewish organizations discovered a new, more effective approach for dealing with Smith — silence. After realizing that Smith's rallies were less well attended when they were unopposed and unpublicized, they approached publishers and radio stations and urged them not to cover Smith's activities. On some occasions, they went as far as threatening boycotts of the media and advertisers if there was no compliance with their wishes. The result was that, over time, Smith got less and less publicity and became more and more irrelevant.

Notes

1. Gustavus Myers, *History of Bigotry in the United States* (New York: Random House, 1943).

2. In 1935, when Alexander Woollcott, on his program, *The Town Crier,* spoke about the dangers of Hitler's anti-Semitic and jingoistic policies, his sponsor, the National Biscuit Company, makers of Cream of Wheat, received a "torrent" of mail criticizing the broadcaster. When the sponsor asked Woollcott to "use better judgment in the future," the writer refused and the company

cancelled its sponsorship. See Lewis J. Paper, *Empire: William S. Paley and the Making of CBS* (New York: St. Martin's Press, 1987), 63. See also Chapter 8.

3. For more information about Ford's anti-Semitism, see Albert Lee, *Henry Ford and the Jews* (New York: Stein and Day, 1980); Neil Baldwin, *Henry Ford and the Jews: The Mass Production of Hate* (New York: Public Affairs, 2001); and Jonathan R. Logsdon, "Power, Ignorance, and Anti-Semitism: Henry Ford and His War on Jews" in *The Hanover Historical Review*, Vol. 7, Spring, 1999. Also available online at http://history.hanover.edu/hhr/99/hhr99_2.html.

4. In an Introduction to a new edition of *The International Jew* that he published, Gerald L. K. Smith wrote that Ford told him in a 1940 interview that he had never signed the apology and that he had no regrets for having published the articles in the first place. See also Logsdon, "Power, Ignorance, and Anti-Semitism" for additional insights into the Ford apology.

5. To stem the damage from the picture of Ford receiving a German award, Ford and his advisors developed a plan to enlist the support of a Detroit rabbi, Leo M. Franklin, to show that he was truly interested in helping German Jewish refugees. With the assistance of one of his aides, Harry Bennett, Ford issued a public statement expressing his sympathy for the Jewish refugees – but at the same time – had the statement disavowed on Father Coughlin's radio broadcast. In effect, Ford manipulated the statement so that it could appeal to Jews as well as anti-Semites. See Sheldon Marcus, *Father Coughlin: The Tumultuous Life of the Priest of the Little Flower* (Boston, Little, Brown and Company, 1973), 166-168 and *The New York Times*, December 5, 1938, 4.

6. Herbert G. Goldman, *Banjo Eyes: Eddie Cantor and the Birth of Modern Stardom* (New York: Oxford University Press, 1997), 200.

7. There are two schools of thought regarding Lindbergh's visits to Germany. Were they undertaken as a result of requests by the American government to measure the strength of the German military machine OR were the visits motivated by his admiration for the German people and for the Nazis whose policies were seen as providing the leadership that brought that nation out of a state of morass? In any event, his visits received considerable publicity from his hosts, who were proud that such a prominent American hero was interested in their affairs. Some historians have speculated that the Germans knew of Lindbergh's reports back to the United States and purposely exaggerated their strength in order to discourage any thought of America taking part in any future conflict.

8. Bruno Hauptmann was convicted and executed for the kidnapping and killing Lindbergh's infant son in 1932.

9. The Wilentz quote appears on several Internet sites, none of which show the source of the quote.

10. For the most part, Lindbergh and other America First spokesmen

opposed President Roosevelt's policy of ignoring the Neutrality Act by passing legislation such as the Cash and Carry and Lend Lease bills that were designed to assist Britain. In his arguments, Lindbergh reminded Americans of the heavy price they had paid in lives and resources after having been drawn into the first World War. The aviator stressed the need for America to build up its own military machine, particularly its air power, rather than waste resources by giving them to nations like France and Great Britain, both of which would surely be defeated by a well-oiled German military. The idea that Germany would defeat the Soviet Union, thus ending the threat of international Communism, was particularly appealing to those who viewed Fascism as less threatening to America than the "Red Menace."

11. David Gordon, "America First: The Anti-War Movement, Charles Lindbergh and the Second World War, 1940-1941." Paper delivered to a joint meeting of the Historical Society and the New York Military Affairs Symposium, September 26, 2003. Available online at http://libraryautomation.com/nymas/americafirst.html

12. The speech is available at http://www.charleslindbergh.com in both audio and print formats.

13. For more information about the life of Father Coughlin see: Marcus, *Father Coughlin;* L. B. Ward, *Father Charles E. Coughlin* (Detroit, Tower Publications, 1933 (a friendly, authorized biography); Alan Brinkley, *Voices of Protest: Huey Long, Father Coughlin, and the Great Depression* (New York: Knopf, 1982); Charles J. Tull, *Father Coughlin & the New Deal*, (Syracuse, NY: Syracuse University Press, 1965); Donald Warren, *Radio Priest, Charles Coughlin the Father of Hate Radio* (New York, The Free Press, 1996); and Wallace Stegner, "The Radio Priest and His Flock," in *The Aspirin Age: 1919-1941*, Isabel Leighton, ed. (New York: Simon and Schuster, 1949).

14. Warren, *Radio Priest,* 29, 312 (n25).

15. Ibid., 25.

16. Leo Fitzpatrick, the station manager of WJR (who was a Catholic), brought Coughlin to the attention of George "Dick" Richards, the station's owner. Known as the "Goodwill Station," WJR was one of a group of stations owned by Richards who had been accused of being overtly anti-Semitic. In the late 1930s and 1940s, the station also provided airtime to Gerald L. K. Smith who also espoused anti-Semitic sentiments. Radio historian Erik Barnouw noted, "He (Richards) was obsessed with a personal crusade to get 'the Jews' out of government. He repeatedly told his news staff that Jews were communists and communists were Jews and that the patriotic mission of the Richards stations, expressed in innumerable memoranda as well as staff meetings, was to drive them out of positions of influence. He sometimes used 'Arab' as a euphemism for Jew. "The Arabs were taking over Washington." Erik Barnouw, *The Golden Web: A History of Broadcasting in the United States 1933-1953* (New York:

Oxford University Press, 1968), 221-224.

17. Diane Cypkin, "A Rhetorical Critical Analysis of Father Coughlin's November 20, 1938 Radio Broadcast," *Journal of Radio Studies*, Vol. 4, #1, 1997, 134-150.

18. Warren, *Radio Priest*, 133. Although the text refers to this broadcast as having occurred in 1930, the footnote indicating its source lists the broadcast as having been aired on February 19, 1933. However, as the comments about the broadcast "the following week" are taken from a 1930 broadcast, it would appear that the February 19, 1933 citation is incorrect.

19. Kun, a Hungarian communist was not raised in the Jewish faith; his mother was a Protestant, his father a non-practicing Jew. Nonetheless, opponents would commonly refer to him as a Jew, as though Communism and Judaism were equal evils. When referring to Marx as being a Jew, Coughlin would neglect to mention that Marx was not only a non-practicing Jew, but that he also attacked religion as "the opium of the people."

20. An August 24, 1931 article in *Time* magazine reported that when CBS decided to drop Coughlin's program in 1931, the station would lose an estimated $10,000 a week in revenue.

21. Sally Bedell Smith, *In All His Glory: The Life &Times of William S. Paley and the Birth of Modern Broadcasting* (New York: Touchstone/Simon & Schuster, 1990), 90.

22. The program was also heard overseas through the short-wave facilities of Philadelphia's WCAU.

23. Marcus, *Father Coughlin*, 35-37 and Warren, *Radio Priest*, 34-37. Estimates of the number of letters ranged from 350,000 to 400,000.

24. In 1932, the network grew from 11 to 27 stations, reaching from Bangor, Maine to Kansas City. By the mid-1930s, with contributions continuing to pour in, Coughlin was able to spend $14,000 a year to finance broadcasts that reached coast to coast.

25. *The New York Times*, Sunday Magazine section, October 29, 1933, 8-9.

26. Brinkley, *Voices of Protest*, 266. See also "Analysis of Who Listens to Coughlin," AJC, Box 235, Folder 1937-1939 for a February, 1939 demographic analysis of Coughlin's listeners.

27. The 30 million figure was used by Charles Tull, Coughlin's official biographer. The 45 million figure came from Coughlin himself. Marcus, *Father Coughlin*. 235, (n2). The October, 1933 *New York Times* article cited in footnote 25 stated that his program was carried by 27 stations with an estimated audience of 30 million listeners.

28. Marcus, *Father Coughlin*, 154. Coughlin cancelled his 1937-1938 season rather than submit to the demands of this new Archbishop, Edward Mooney, who wanted the ability to censor his broadcasts. This coincides with other information that Gerald L. K. Smith purchased the contracts for Coughlin's

network in October, 1937. When Coughlin resumed broadcasting on January 9, 1938, he lost the WOR outlet in New York City when the station adopted a new policy of not accepting religious broadcasts on a commercial basis. According to Marcus, the WOR experience convinced Coughlin "that Jews controlled the nation's communication system and that they were responsible for his difficulties in securing broadcasting outlets." When another New York City station, WMCA, picked up the program, the station was assured by Coughlin and his representatives that the program would not include any anti-Semitic comments.

29. Most likely, the figure was from 1934.

30. Marcus, *Father Coughlin*, 182. Based on the paper's financial records, Marcus concluded that the one million circulation figure had to be an exaggeration.

31. Warren, *Radio Priest*, 134. Excerpts of February 26, 1933 broadcast.

32. In 1934, when he created the National Union For Social Justice with the goal of promoting the common welfare of all Americans, Coughlin invited Catholics, Protestants, Jews and blacks to join the organization. Also, Coughlin's newspaper, *Social Justice*, was printed for a portion of 1938 by Morris and Myron Steinberg. The latter Steinberg told Warren in a 1989 interview that "Jews in Detroit were divided about whether he (Father Coughlin) was an anti-Semite. "How could he be anti-Semitic if he had the Ten Commandments carved in Hebrew on the tower of the Shrine of the Little Flower?" Ibid., 135, 328, (n20).

33. Brinkley, in an Appendix to his book, *Voices of Protest*, 269-273, appears to downplay evidence of Coughlin's anti-Semitism prior to 1938. Although he states that Coughlin could hardly be termed a "warm friend" of the Jew, "At best, his message in the early and mid-1930s was neutral on the subject. At worse, his rhetoric — with its excoriation of 'international bankers' and its references to 'money changers' and the 'sin of usury' — may have worked in a diffuse way to evoke images and produce stereotypes that could be translated easily into hostility toward Jews. But Coughlin himself did little before 1938 to encourage such a translation." Brinkley also ignores Coughlin's repeated references to "Karl Marx, the Jew" when railing against Communism.

34. Warren, *Radio Priest*, 152. At the meeting, Coughlin invited Philip Slomovitz, editor of the *Detroit Jewish News*, to submit a rebuttal article. When Slomovitz's article appeared two months later, a second article by a "Ben Marcin," identified as a Jew, attacked the Jewish position. In 1970, Coughlin told his biographer, Sheldon Marcus, that "Ben Marcin" never existed and that in fact the articles that carried the Marcin byline had been written by others at the newspaper. Marcus, *Father Coughlin*, 252-256. See also Mary Christine Athans "A New Perspective on Father Charles E. Coughlin," *Church History*, Vol. 56, #2, June, 1987, 224-235. In the article, Sister Athans examines Coughlin's increasing attacks on Jews in 1938 and links them to his relationship with the

Irish priest, Father Denis Fahey. According to Athans, Fahey had published numerous anti-Semitic books and his writings provided Coughlin with the theological foundation for his own anti-Semitism.

35. Excerpts of the November 20, 1938 broadcast are in Warren, *Radio Priest*, 155-156. Audio copies of the program are available on the Internet.

36. Cypkin, "A Rhetorical Critical Analysis," 141.

37. The print version of Coughlin's November 20, 1938 talk included several pages from Fahey's *The Mystical Body of Christ in the Modern World*. On the November 27th rebroadcast, Coughlin cited "Professor Denis Fahey as one of the most outstanding scholars in Ireland." Athans, "A New Perspective," 230. For a rebuttal to the "facts" presented by Coughlin, see Marcus, *Father Coughlin*, 255-256.

38. *The New York Times*, November 21, 1938, 7.

39. Cypkin, "A Rhetorical Analysis," 144.

40. Warren, "*Radio Priest*," 157-159. Both Cypkin's article and Warren's book carry a 1997 publication date. As Cypkin did not list Warren as a reference, it is possible that the book came out after she wrote her article.

41. Flamm recalled that immediately after Kristallnacht, he urged Coughlin, through a representative, to say something about the event. Coughlin agreed and said that he would submit a copy of his comments in advance, even though his contract did not require advance approval of his text. When the station received the talk prior to the broadcast, Flamm said he felt "cruel disappointment." He then called Coughlin's staff and told them that the talk could not be broadcast as originally submitted. The staff, in turn, assured Flamm that the facts were correct. Although he was dissatisfied with a subsequent revised text, Flamm decided to air the broadcast with the proviso that the comments were those of Coughlin and did not reflect the views of the station.

42. *The New York Times*, November 28, 1939, 1. The article includes the full statement by WMCA.

43. *The New York Times*, December 19, 1938, 24.

44. *The New York Times*, January 9, 1939, 2.

45. *Variety*, January 24, 1940.

46. *The New York Times*, April 9, 1939, 15.

47. Using Gallup survey data (but not actual audience counts), Warren calculated that Coughlin lost 1.5 million listeners after the November 20th Kristallnacht broadcast, dropping to 6.7 million listeners in December, 1938 from 8.3 million April, 1938. Warren, *Radio Priest*, 303.

48. Marcus, *Father Coughlin*, 162-163 and 244, (n52).

49. *Michigan Catholic*, December 12, 1938, as cited in Warren, *Radio Priest*, 217. See Warren for a more detailed discussion of the ongoing conflict between Mooney and Coughlin over the priest's radio talks.

50. *The New York Times*, November 26, 1938, 5.

51. Marcus, *Father Coughlin*, 162.

52. Broadcast of December 18, 1938 as excerpted in Warren, *Radio Priest,* 164-165.

53. The National Association of Broadcasters was a voluntary trade association. Stations did not have to join the organization, nor were members required to abide by the organization's guidelines.

54. The controversy over how to handle the "Coughlin" issue was raised in December, 1938 when Neville Miller, president of the NAB denounced as "an evil not to be tolerated" radio talks "plainly calculated or likely to rouse religious or racial hatred and stir up strife." According to *The New York Times*, Miller said it was the right and duty of radio stations to reject such speeches. The journalist Dorothy Thompson who spoke out against the horrors of Kristallnacht as early as November 14, 1938 (see Chapter 9), sent an open letter to the FCC chairman, Frank R. McNinch, asking the agency to begin an investigation into Coughlin's broadcasts. The Commission, the *Times* reported, moved "warily" on questions that might involve censorship. See *The New York Times*, December 23, 1938, 4.

55. Warren, *Radio Priest*, 222-223, 338 (n80). Warren explains that because of a loophole in the NAB code, existing contracts for the 1939-1940 broadcast season had to be honored. Marcus, *Father Coughlin*, 177, notes that despite the loophole, many stations in larger cities such as Indianapolis, Scranton and Milwaukee cancelled existing contracts saying that they were abiding by the NAB guidelines. By 1940, with access to only a few smaller stations, Coughlin concluded that the smaller audience could not justify the time and money it took to put on the program. Therefore, on the September 23, 1940 broadcast, he announced that he was "temporarily" retiring from the air due to circumstances beyond his reach.

56. The Justice Department had been accumulating evidence of Coughlin's anti-war efforts, including his ties to a German spy, for possible prosecution for seditious activities.

57. See Warren, *Radio Priest*, 333 (n28). Warren cites several historians who have written about Coughlin's role in fomenting a climate of anti-Semitism of the United States. He also quotes from the autobiography of Arnold Forster, retired general counsel of the Anti-Defamation League, about how fighting domestic anti-Semitism was a distraction for American Jews, 333 (n29).

58. Cypkin, "A Rhetorical Critical Analysis," 149.

59. H. L. Mencken, "Why Not Gerald?"*Baltimore Evening Sun*, September 7, 1936, quoted in Marcus, *Father Coughlin*, 103-105.

60. Glen Jeansonne, "Gerald L. K. Smith: From Wisconsin Roots to National Notoriety," *Wisconsin Magazine of History*, Winter 2002-2003, 2. The source of the quote is not identified.

61. Marcus, *Father Coughlin,* 105. Despite considerable evidence to the

contrary, Coughlin later denied having any connection with Smith.

62. In 1937, Smith contracted to take over the 48-station network that had carried Father Coughlin's program. *The New York Times,* October 30, 1937. This is likely to have been the brief period when Coughlin cancelled his broadcasts rather than submit to his Archbishop's censorship. When Coughlin resumed broadcasting in January, 1938, it is not clear if Smith's broadcasts were aired on stations other than WJR.

63. Smith continued publishing *The Cross and the Flag* until 1977.

64. Glen Jeansonne, *Gerald L. K. Smith: Minister of Hate,* (New Haven, CT: Yale University Press, 1988), 69.

65. A closer examination of Smith's papers may possibly provide additional insights into these aspects of Smith's radio career. While Jeansonne's biography, *Gerald L. K. Smith: Minister of Hate*, is the most comprehensive examination of Smith's life, the author provides very little detail about Smith's use of radio; the word "radio" is not even listed in the book's Index.

66. Jeansonne, "Gerald L. K. Smith," 26. See also Chapter Six of Jeansonne's *Gerald L. K. Smith: Minister of Hate* for a fuller discussion of Smith's anti-Semitism.

67. Harry Bennett, Ford's right-hand man, denied that the money was for radio broadcasts and said that it was to be used, "to fight Communism and labor racketeering and not for any other purpose." *The New York Times*, October 5, 1944, 10.

68. Jeansonne, *Gerald L. K. Smith: Minister of Hate,* 74.

69. In 1937, WXYZ in Detroit refused to broadcast a Smith speech over his recently acquired network because he had not submitted his manuscript in advance in accordance with station policy. *The New York Times*, November 22, 1937, 21.

70. Jeansonne, *Gerald L. K. Smith: Minister of Hate*, 138.

71. As cited in Morris Janowitz, "The Technique of Propaganda for Reaction: Gerald L. K. Smith's Radio Speeches," *The Public Opinion Quarterly*, Vol. 8, #1, Spring, 1944, 88.

72. Ibid., 87.

73. In 1964 he republished *The International Jew* and serialized the text in his publications.

74. Jeansonne, *Gerald L. K. Smith: Minister of Hate*, 217.

4
Americans All, Immigrants All

From our very foundation as a nation, and with the possible exception of people we today refer to as "native Americans" (although many anthropologists suggest that they may originally have migrated from Siberia), America has been a nation of immigrants.

Of the approximately 1.85 million people living in the American colonies in 1765, the best estimates are that 65 percent to 70 percent were of English origin while another 15 percent to 20 percent came from other parts of Great Britain, including Scotland, Wales and Ireland.[1] Others living in the colonies included some 175,000 Germans, 55,000 Hollanders, 40,000 Frenchmen, 20,000 Swiss, 15,000 Swedes and 1,500 Jews. Among the many ethnic minorities to reach the shores of this continent, African-Americans can hardly be considered immigrants, having been brought to North America as slaves beginning a year prior to the Pilgrims' historic landing at Plymouth.

Considering that it was the history of sectarian conflict in England and throughout the rest of Europe that motivated much of the migration to what promised to be a "New World," it should not be surprising to learn that the seeds of intolerance would take root on this side of the ocean as well. Among the earliest laws enacted by a Federalist dominated Congress were the infamous Alien and Sedition Acts of 1798 that were intended to limit the political power of recent immigrants, the majority of whom supported the Jeffersonian Republicans. In contrast to the Federalists, George Washington and other men of good faith believed in the principle best expressed by Jefferson who wrote, "Shall we refuse to the unhappy fugitives from distress that hospitality which the savages of the wilderness extended to our fathers arriving in this land? Shall oppressed humanity find no asylum on this globe?"[2]

Between 1890-1921, more than 30 million immigrants, most from southern and eastern Europe, made their way to America. By 1930, the number of foreign-born people in the United States had reached 14.2 million, with 56 percent coming from central, eastern and southern Europe.[3] With 21 percent of the country's native-born population of foreign or mixed parentage in 1930, it was not surprising that the question being asked with increasing frequency was, "What does it mean to be an American?"

Jews, who numbered approximately 4.2 million in 1927,[4] were only one of several ethnic groups that did not easily fit into the prevailing definition of what it meant to be an American: white, Protestant and of Anglo Saxon or northern European heritage. Along with African-Americans, more commonly referred to as Negroes, and less politely as "colored folks," Italians, Slavs, Hispanics and Orientals also felt the sting of prejudice and discrimination, although to a lesser extent. One way or another, often depending on where they lived or how long they had been in a community, members of these ethnic groups experienced some degree bigotry. Native Americans living outside their reservations were also treated with suspicion and distrust.

During the 1920s and 1930s, Americans were exposed to two contradictory messages regarding immigrants in general, and more specifically, Jews. At one extreme, there were the efforts of individuals and groups who used the print media and radio to spread their anti-ethnic messages of hate and bigotry: Henry Ford, Charles Lindbergh, Father Charles Coughlin, Gerald L. K. Smith, Fritz Kuhn, the Silver Shirts and the Ku Klux Klan. But, at the other extreme, a cadre of lesser known men and women began to emerge who were deeply concerned about these not-so-subtle trends of anti-immigrant, anti-Semitic, anti-black messages, some of which actually came from houses of worship. Ironically, many of the same people who listened to Father Coughlin also listened to *The Goldbergs*. It was from the efforts of this group of concerned Americans that a unique radio series emerged, *Americans All, Immigrants All*.

Although only one of the 26 programs in the series was devoted exclusively to Jews, that program is significant because, by 1939 when it aired, with the exception of the Jewish characters that appeared from time to time on mainstream programs (see Chapter 7), the only secular network program that featured Jews on a regular basis was *The Goldbergs*. And, as discussed in Chapter 2, by 1939, even that program had begun to downplay its Jewishness.

The inspiration for *Americans All, Immigrants All* came primarily from two people, Rachel Davis Dubois and Avinere Toigo. Independent of one another, each realized the potential radio had for fighting prejudice and bringing immigrants into the mainstream of American society. When each of these activists began searching for support for their ideas, both found a receptive listener when they met with John Studebaker, the U.S. Commissioner of Education, in what was then the Interior Department's Office of Education.

The authors are indebted to Barbara Dianne Savage for the chapter "Americans All, Immigrants All" that appears in her book, *Broadcasting Freedom: Radio War and the Politics of Race, 1938-1948*.[5] Savage's research draws heavily on the personal papers of Rachel Davis Dubois as well as the files of the Office of Education and other sources and provides valuable insights into the creation of the series as well as the individual programs.

Dubois was an early proponent of "multiculturalism," a term that later became known as "intercultural education." A white Quaker high school teacher from New Jersey, she was active in developing educational materials that could be used in the classroom to teach tolerance of various ethnic groups by stressing their history, culture and other contributions. Ironically, it was Father Coughlin's anti-immigrant, anti-Semitic broadcasts that gave Dubois the idea to use radio to disseminate her message of tolerance to a broader audience and which eventually led her to approach Studebaker in the hope of getting his office to underwrite such a series.

At the same time Dubois was pursuing her dream, Toigo, an Italian-American from Illinois who was active in state politics, conceived a plan for encouraging better understanding among the various ethnic groups that made up what was then frequently called "The Melting Pot." Like Dubois, his idea involved a series of radio broadcasts that would highlight the contributions each group had made to American society. However, when Toigo tried to interest NBC in his idea, he was turned down by the network's education consultant, James R. Angell, the retired president of Yale University. Angell warned that such a program would not attract a national audience and carried the risk of, "deeply offending one national group as a consequence of magnifying the achievements of another." Not ready to give up, Toigo took his idea to Studebaker. And, as they say, "the rest is history."

Studebaker's first challenge was to find a network interested in carrying the proposed series. Despite Toigo's earlier failed attempt to interest NBC in the program, the Commissioner's first choice was NBC because the network enjoyed a reputation for supporting and promoting educational causes. With two networks, the Red and the Blue, NBC also had a large listening audience. Studebaker fared no better than Toigo, however, and Angell again advised against the proposed series writing, "I think I should let this dog sleep. Certainly I am not disposed to stir up the menagerie just at the moment."[6] When Sarnoff later asked his staff why NBC had rejected the series, he was assured that it was a low quality program and that the network hadn't lost anything.

Fortunately for Dubois and Toigo, the people at CBS were far more receptive to Studebaker's idea. The network had previously worked with the Office of Education on a series of 26 broadcasts about Latin America that had received positive audience response and which was coming to an end. CBS executives also saw the connection between the proposed series and developments in Europe. They sensed that the subject matter had timely appeal and was likely to attract sizeable audience. Once the decision was made to pick up the series, CBS assigned Gilbert Seldes, one of its new writers who was already a well known and highly respected writer and literary critic, to prepare the scripts using the information that Dubois had already gathered about various ethnic groups.[7]

Not surprisingly, intellectual differences can, and in this instance did, arise among people of good will. Dubois had hoped that each episode would focus on a specific ethnic group and that by highlighting the group's contributions to American society prejudice towards that group would be reduced. Seldes, on the other hand, was more inclined to stress the concept that each ethnic group was important more as a brick in the total structure that unified America. In effect, he saw his approach to fighting prejudice as being more subtle and, in the long run, more effective than Dubois'. Considering the recent debate regarding the issues of immigration and the importance of political correctness, it seems that these two collaborators were well ahead of their time. Eventually, Studebaker suggested the compromise that resulted in 15 episodes focusing on the contributions of specific ethnic groups while 11 highlighted the cumulative contributions of immigrants to American culture, society and the arts.[8]

The series, which was co-sponsored by the Service Bureau for Intercultural Education, a clearinghouse for multicultural educational materials, was broadcast between November, 1938 and May, 1939 on Sundays at 2pm. Each half hour broadcast began with the lead in:

Let us raise a standard to which the wise and honest can repair. Americans All-Immigrants All. This is the story of how you, the people of the United States, made America — you and your neighbors, your parents and theirs. It is the story of the most spectacular movement of humanity in all recorded time — the movement of millions of men, women and children from other lands to the land they made their own. It is the story of what they endured and accomplished — it is also of what this country did for them. Americans All, Immigrants All.

The decision to devote an entire episode of the series to the Jews was controversial from the very beginning of the planning process. As documented by Savage, there was an impressive list of individuals and organizations on both sides of the issue.[9] Dubois, given her strong anti-assimilationist approach, supported highlighting the group's special identity. Toigo, however, recommended against a separate Jewish program, believing that bringing attention to the Jews would actually hurt them more than help them. Jews, individually and as a group, were divided on the question. Many third and fourth generation Jews who were already assimilated opposed the idea. Even the American Jewish Committee (AJC), which was providing some financial support for the series, objected to a separate program about Jews. Indeed, Dubois and the AJC had clashed earlier on the very same issue when the educator was preparing materials for New York City school programs and wanted to treat the Jews as a separate ethnic and cultural group. At that time, the AJC opposed the idea on the grounds that the Jews should be considered a religious, not an ethnic group. "You don't have a separate program on the Baptists, why on the Jews?" an AJC official argued.[10] Mrs. Arthur Hays Sulzberger of *The New York Times* publishing family added her voice to the argument warning, "there is a great mistake being made at the present time in regarding Jews as a race, when they are merely a religious group."[11]

The Service Bureau also expressed reservations about a separate Jewish program. Speaking for the group, its vice chair, Theresa Mayer Durlach, said that while she agreed on the need for a separate program about the Jews, she suggested that the way to resolve the "danger" inherent in a separate episode was "parallelism of treatment": By incorporating the Jews into a program that covered all religions, she argued, the "Jewish problem" would be "merely a part of the general suppression of all liberal and non-conformist elements in the present totalitarian states...the difference being one of degree rather than kind."[12]

Concern was also raised over whether a separate Jewish episode would help or hurt efforts to liberalize America's immigration laws. By 1938, American Jews had become increasingly concerned over the plight of their co-religionists in Europe and there was pressure within the United States to allow more Jewish refugees to enter the country. While some members of the program's Advisory Committee, including the United States Commissioner of Immigration and Naturalization, saw the inclusion of a Jewish episode in the series as helping to win public support for allowing more Jewish refugees into the country, others thought such as episode would increase the already growing hostility towards weakening the country's immigration laws. CBS executives, sensitive to the accusation that the network was controlled by Jews, were especially worried that airing a separate episode about the Jews would exacerbate that issue.

Surprisingly, Seldes, who in general opposed DuBois' separatist approach, agreed with the need for a separate Jewish program on the grounds that the prejudice against the Jews transcended their immigrant status or country of origin. A non-observant Jew, Seldes had nonetheless felt the sting of anti-Semitism early in his career, an experience that may have influenced his decision. The controversy ended when Studebaker accepted Seldes' argument that there was a "Jewish problem" and that the problem should be faced directly.[13]

The Jewish episode was broadcast on February 5, 1939, the thirteenth broadcast in the series. The decision to hold the episode until midway in the series may have been motivated, in part, by an effort to avoid the prevailing belief of some that Jews received favorable treatment in Hollywood and on radio.

Following the same format used for the other episodes, the script combined a series of dramatized sketches and narratives to highlight the positive contributions that members of the Jewish community had made to American life. The Jews were introduced as "many people" who "came to the United States from many countries" and who are "united by the fact that they are Jews." The introduction went on to explain that Jews, like Catholics and Protestants, had come to America to escape religious persecution and oppression and that they were grateful to be living in a land in which they were free to pursue their aspirations. After noting that Jews were among the very earliest settlers of our country, the script went on to stress that since coming to America, Jews had distinguished themselves as loyal patriots, from the Revolutionary War to World War I.

In the opening sketch set in Valley Forge during the Revolutionary War, General George Washington meets Haym Solomon, a Jewish financier and immigrant from Poland who, until the meeting, had been an anonymous donor to the colonists' cause. The scene then shifts to a synagogue where, a year later, Solomon is observing Yom Kippur (the most solemn day in Judaism). When a dispatch arrives from General Washington desperately seeking additional financial aid, Solomon, over the objections of some congregants but with the support of the rabbi, interrupts the service to make a plea for money to help *our* soldiers (the word *our* is used in the script). Solomon raises $160,000 that evening, and the next day adds his own money to the collection and sends a total of $400,000 to General Washington.

The narrator[14] then expands on the patriotic theme by giving several examples of Jews who helped defend America: Uriah P. Levy, who served in the navy during the War of 1812, later reached the rank of Commodore (which at that time was the highest rank) and is credited on his tombstone as the father of the law that did away with corporal punishment in the navy; the 6,000 Jewish privates and 600 Jewish officers (including nine generals) who served in the Union Army during the Civil War; Judah Benjamin, a southerner of West Indian birth, who at different times served the Confederacy in the positions of Attorney General, Secretary of War and Secretary of State; and finally, during World War I, the more than 1,000 Jewish soldiers who received medals of valor for their service.

Other dramatizations highlighted the contributions of Jews in the fields of social service and health, including the work of Lillian Wald, the founder of the Henry Street Settlement (that served all immigrant groups) and businessman Nathan Straus who spent his own money to build plants for the pasteurization of milk because he believed in Louis Pasteur's theory that contaminated milk was one of the major causes of the high death rate among children.

The Wald and Straus dramatizations were followed by a narrative about the contributions of other Jewish Americans in the fields of science, the arts, law and other areas of achievement: Adolph Lewisohn, a philanthropist who financed the building of a stadium in New York City for the free performances of outdoor concerts for everyone; Julius Rosenwald, a businessman who gave millions of dollars for educational programs for Negroes; anthropologist Franz Boas; impresario Oscar Hammerstein who made opera available to the general public; art patron Otto Kahn; physicist Albert Michelson; Supreme Court Justices Louis Brandeis, Benjamin Cardozo and Felix Frankfurter; labor leader Samuel Gompers; publisher Joseph Pulitzer; athlete Hank Greenberg; pathologist Joseph Goldberger; and composer George Gershwin.

Over the subdued strains of *Hatikvah*[15] that built to a crescendo by the time the narrator finished reading the text, the program concluded by celebrating both the Jewish people *and* the United States:

> Yet, the contributions of any group is never merely that of its great men. It is the combined creation of all. More persecuted than most people before they came to the United States, the Jews came to this country with a background of sorrows. In many lands they have been barred from taking part in the national life. They were able to make their contribution to American life because the whole of American life was open to them, as to all others, without discrimination of race or creed. They have helped to build the United States because the United States has welcomed them as Americans all.

The active participation of the Jewish people in all aspects of American society was repeated again in episodes 20-23 that highlighted the contributions of all ethnic groups in the fields of industry, science, arts and crafts and social progress.

Given the controversy surrounding the question of whether there should even have been a separate program about the Jews, it is of interest to note what was, and was not, included in the script. By stating that the Jews were "many people" coming from many countries, the program appeared to play down the idea that the Jews were a single people or a single ethnic group. This controversial issue was simply avoided. And, with the exception of the Haym Solomon/Yom Kippur scene, there was no mention of the fact that Jews, regardless of what their country of origin may have been, or how long they had lived in the United States, shared a common religion and heritage. Absent from the program was any mention of how Jews had been oppressed in the United States or that there was bigotry and intolerance towards them in America. The only time oppression was mentioned, it was in the context of it happening elsewhere. (The generic closing lines of the program did talk about the "sickness" of hate and the need to cure it.)

Comparing the Jewish script to those celebrating the other ethnic groups featured in the series, Savage concluded:

> It is hard to imagine a more politically cautious script than the one on Jewish Americans. Although American Jews were made visible, a listener unaware of anti-Semitism, Hitler, the encroaching European war, or the flood of Jewish refugees would have gleaned nothing of any 'Jewish problem' from the broadcast. Certainly none of the shows in the series openly addressed contemporary concerns, but in many instances they confronted stereotypical beliefs, however clumsily. No attempt was made to do that in this script. (The Office of) Education and CBS network officials probably feared that a direct attack on anti-Semitism would have been perceived in the administration, in Congress, and elsewhere as a political pitch regarding the Jewish refugee issue or perhaps even the question of U.S. intervention in the war.[16]

Savage also observed that in sharp contrast to the Irish, Italian and Slavic immigrants who were portrayed as laborers in the other ethnic episodes, the Jews were presented as being middle class Americans. "With its emphasis on individual actors rather than on a mass of Jews, it made a case for their acceptance and support based simply on their status as long-settled and deserving Americans, delicately balanced between claiming group status and avoiding it."[17]

Responsibility for publicizing and promoting the series was shared among the Office of Education, CBS and the Service Bureau. These efforts included the free distribution of phonograph records of each episode for use in the classroom and by community groups, along with a free 128-page guidebook containing the story of immigration and teaching aids. It was the job of the Service Bureau, however, to publicize the individual programs to specific ethnic groups. This targeted approach to promoting the program proved especially effective for increasing the listenership for the Jewish episode, thanks in part to the cooperation of many Jewish groups that took steps to spread the word about the upcoming program to their members. The national office of Hadassah (a secular Jewish women's organization), for example, sent letters to all its chapters urging them to organize listening parties and encouraging members to bring non-Jews to listen to the program. In an article about the program that appeared in the *Hebrew Union College Monthly*, rabbis were urged to talk about the program in their sermons, sponsor listening parties and write to the Office of Education thanking them for the broadcasts.

Listener reaction to the Jewish episode was greater than that for any previous episode. In less than two weeks following the broadcast, the Office of Education received over 9,000 letters and cards asking for more information.[18] (At the conclusion of the broadcast, listeners were encouraged to send postcards requesting a free copy of the text of the broadcast.) While some listeners criticized the program, expressing the view that it was designed to open the door to more refugees, by and large, public response was favorable. Typical of some of the responses were:

- (The program was) educational, beautiful, and touching, in view of the raw deal we Jews are getting at the hands of various ignorant, bestial tyrants.

- God only knows how much your work is needed at this time.

- (The series) will go a long way in combating the evil influence of Father Coughlin's broadcasts.

Despite the positive response to the program, the Service Bureau, which had originally opposed a separate Jewish episode, continued to express its concern that by putting the spotlight on the Jews, the program may have done more harm than good. That fear was voiced in a letter written by the Bureau's Edward Bayne to Jeanette Sayre, a member of the staff of NBC's *America's Town Meeting of the Air*. Bayne wrote, "some of us have felt that the emphasis on the Jew made by giving him a special program, and constantly referring to him as a national group although he may be a German Jew, Russian Jew or what not, added fuel to the concept that we are pro-Jew and the whole series is designed as pro-refugee propaganda." Sayre's response, however, may not have been what Bayne expected. In her reply, she acknowledged that while there had been some negative feedback to the episode, she wrote that some of the people she had spoken to about the program believed that CBS, which was perceived as being a Jewish network, had aired the program in order to generate sympathy for permitting more Jewish refugees to enter the country.[19]

Several months after the episode aired, Father Coughlin commented on the program – and as he often did, took statements out of context and/or misquoted them. According to the November 27, 1939 issue of *Social Justice*, "It (the program) lauded the Jews in the making of America, declaring that they were responsible even for Columbus' discovery of America."[20]

In point of fact, the only reference in the program to Columbus was that five Jews had accompanied him on his voyage to America.

In retrospect, while the program may not have turned the tide of public opinion on the refugee issue (nor, despite what critics said, was it designed to), it did help to put a different face on the nation's Jews, a face that was far different than that which had been painted on the pages of Ford's *Dearborn Independent*, in Father Coughlin's *Social Justice* and on the priest's radio broadcasts.[21] And, with the overall series winning awards from such diverse groups as the American Legion (the Auxiliary Radio Award, with a special "honorable mention" for the Jewish episode) and the influential Woman's National Radio Committee, the series may have made network executives less skittish in the future about airing programs about Jews and other ethnic groups.

Indeed, after CBS won awards for the series and the *New York Post* radio columnist wrote that the network was "so far ahead in the field of educational radio that the race isn't even close," NBC's David Sarnoff asked his staff why his network had turned the program down. Lamely trying to defend his earlier position, Angell went on the offensive and described the *Post* writer as someone with a "somewhat pinkish complexion" who was only interested in "radical" programming.

In 1941, in an analysis of listener response to the series, Dorothea Seelye looked at the overall impact of the program.[22] Her findings may have surprised the program's supporters. Whereas the series was "designed to help the intolerant become tolerant," what Seelye found was that those actually listening to the program were the individuals least likely to need it: the responses were from individuals belonging to the more recently arrived foreign groups who appreciated the information about their own groups as well as other groups. Seelye concluded:

> As far as I can tell from my material, it did not promote inter-group tolerance in the sense of changing a great many individuals' opinions from very prejudiced to very unprejudiced. The major proportion of the letter-writers were already convinced, relatively unprejudiced listeners.

The overall positive response to the program notwithstanding, Seelye's findings did have implications beyond *Americans All, Immigrants All*. Paraphrasing the work Paul Lazarsfeld, her mentor and a pioneer in the field of radio research, she observed:

...the effect of radio in molding opinion does not operate so long as people in need of change are not intrinsically interested in subject matter which will change their opinions; and the alleged accessibility of radio is not even existent psychologically for people who do not feel the need of that information which will change their opinions...If radio is to influence the stand-patters, the reactionary, the prejudiced, those who are not already interested in social change and improvement, it must promote its serious broadcasts through appropriate institutions...More and more effort must be put into the development of radio listening as part of the cultural activities carried on by institutions.

Readers may want to keep Seelye's conclusions in mind when they read Chapter 9 that deals with radio's efforts counter anti-Semitism during and after World War II.

Notes

Abbreviations

AJC   American Jewish Committee Radio Department Archives at Yivo Institute, New York, NY.

1. J. Joseph Huthmacher, *A Nation of Newcomers* (New York: Delacorte Press, 1967), 7.

2. Ibid., 11. For additional insight about intolerance towards immigrants in the early United States, see Gustavus Myers, *History of Bigotry in the United States*, (New York: Random House, 1943).

3. *The Statistical History of the United States From Colonial Times to the Present* (New York: Basic Books, 1976), 116-117.

4. www.jewishvirtuallibrary.org. By 1937, the Jewish population of the United States was estimated at between 4.6-4.8 million and by 1950 between 4.5-5.0 million.

5. Barbara Dianne Savage, *Broadcasting Freedom: Radio, War and the Politics of Race, 1938-1948* (Chapel Hill, NC: University of North Carolina Press, 1999), Chapter 1, 21-62.

6. Ibid., 25.

7. The political sensitivity surrounding the immigration issue was evident in the extended discussions over the name of the proposed series. After the program's Advisory Committee (composed of representatives of concerned private organizations and federal officials), Studebaker and CBS finally settled on *Immigrants All-Americans All*, network officials realized that the title would

be shortened to *Immigrants All* in the newspaper radio listings. Believing that that would be too "depressing," the title was reversed to *Americans All, Immigrants All* in order to give the program a broader patriotic appeal. See Savage, *Broadcasting Freedom*, 26-27.

    8. The series included the following 26 programs. Some scripts and audio of the programs are available at the Hoover Institution at Stanford University, the National Archives, the Immigration History Research Center at the University of Minnesota and in the special collections at other libraries.

1:	Nov. 13, 1938	"Opening Frontiers" (John Studebaker, Introduction/The Colonies)
2:	Nov. 20, 1938	"Our English Heritage"
3:	Nov. 27, 1938	"Our Hispanic Heritage"
4:	Dec. 4, 1938	"Scots, Irish and Welsh in the United States"
5:	Dec. 11, 1938	"Winning Freedom" (early immigrants defend liberty)
6:	Dec. 18, 1938	"The Negro in the United States"
7:	Dec. 25, 1938	"French Speaking Peoples"
8:	Jan. 1, 1939	"The Upsurge of Democracy"
9:	Jan. 8, 1939	"Irish in the United States"
10:	Jan. 15, 1939	"Germans in the United States"
11:	Jan. 22, 1939	"Scandinavians in the United States"
12:	Jan. 29, 1939	"Closing Frontiers"
13:	Feb. 5, 1939	"Jews in the United States"
14:	Feb. 12, 1939	"Slavs in the United States" (Pt. 1 Russia, Ukraine and Yugoslavia)
15:	Feb. 19, 1939	"Slavs in the United States" (Pt. 2 Poland, Czechoslovakia and Slovakia)
16:	Feb. 26, 1939	"Orientals in the United States
17:	Mar, 5, 1939	"Italians in the United States"
18;	Mar. 12, 1939	"Near Eastern Peoples in the United States"
19:	Mar. 19, 1939	"Immigrants from smaller countries" (Hindus, Roumanians, Lithuanians, etc.)
20:	Mar 26, 1939	"Contributions in Industry" (combines the various ethnic groups)
21:	Apr. 2, 1939	"Contributions in Science"
22:	Apr. 9, 1939	"Contributions in Arts and Crafts"
23:	Apr. 16, 1939	"Contributions in Social Progress"
24:	Apr. 23, 1939	"A New England Town" (Immigrants change a town in Massachusetts)
25:	Apr. 30, 1939	"An Industrial City" (Immigrants change St. Paul, Minnesota)
26:	May 7, 1939	"Grand Finale" (A summing up)

9. Ibid., 45-52.
10. Ibid., 46.
11. Ibid., 47.
12. Ibid., 47-48.
13. Writing about the program in 1964, Seldes recalled that of the 26 episodes, his favorite was the first one that "dealt with America as a whole, not with any one group." Michael Kammen, *Lively Arts: Gilbert Seldes and the Transformation of Cultural Criticism in the United States* (New York: Oxford University Press, 1996), 262.
14. The narrator was Ray Collins, well known for his appearances on the *Mercury Theater*. The names of other cast members are not known.
15. A 19th century poem that was later set to music and which became the official Israeli national anthem.
16. Ibid., 50.
17. Ibid.
18. The total number of letters received for the first eleven programs ranged from a low of 596 letters for the "French" broadcast to 6,562 for the "Germans" episode. "Mail Tabulation for Americans All, Immigrants All," AJC, Box 236, Folder Americans All, Immigrants All. In 1964, Seldes wrote that the people who sponsored the program were especially gratified that 20 percent of the letters received for each episode came from groups other than the group featured in that week's episode. (The authors assume that this "analysis" was based on the last names of the letter writers.) Kammen, *Lively Arts*, 262.
19. Ibid., 51-52.
20. Ibid., 52, 299 (n92).
21. The Jewish episode aired approximately two months after Coughlin's controversial November 20, 1938 broadcast during which he justified what had happened during Kristallnacht as a legitimate defense by the Nazis against Communism.
22. Dorothea Seelye, "Broadcasting Tolerance to the Tolerant, Americans All-Immigrants All: With Special Reference to Audience Response," Master's Thesis, American University, Washington, D.C., 1941. What appears to be a shortened version of the thesis can be found in AJC, Box 236, Folder Americans All, Immigrants All. A note on the cover page of the document indicates that a complete copy of the dissertation is available from Columbia University.

5
Forgotten Series

In the sixty-odd years that have passed since television dramatically changed the nature of radio, archivists and old time radio fans alike have attempted to rescue the remnants of what for too many years has been a forgotten part of America's rich cultural heritage. The audio aspect of this history comes from 16" diameter transcription discs, and in some cases, home recordings or primitive audio tape (plastic, paper or even wire). Some of the programs have survived as complete episodes; others may be simply air-checks (off-the-air recordings that often omitted commercials and/or musical interludes). These recordings have been located in places as diverse as the estates of people associated with broadcasting, junk shops, flea markets, defunct radio stations and even the attics and barns of people who have no idea where they may have come from. Sadly, as respected radio historian Elizabeth McLeod has pointed out, a very small number of the programs that were aired in the late 1920s and early 1930s were ever actually recorded, thus the audio for the vast majority of these programs has been lost forever.[1]

Although some print information regarding these programs has been patiently pieced together based on surviving station records, diaries, scripts, contracts, fan magazines, scrapbooks and other similar sources, cautious researchers recognize that appearing in print is not necessarily a guarantee of accuracy. Over a 70 year period, inconsistencies have sometimes made their way into published material. Unfortunately, with the exception of *The Goldbergs*,[2] very little documentation regarding the more obscure Jewish themed network programs broadcast during the 1930s appears to have survived.

But there are some exceptions. NBC not only maintained written records, it also had the foresight to donate sound recordings to the Library of Congress; the collection has become a treasure-trove for researchers. CBS also maintains its own archive that includes publicity materials regarding some of its early programs. Although less is known about this archive, serious researchers may be able to access its records.

What follows is the result of the authors' efforts to shed some light on a number of Jewish themed series, most of which aired during the 1930s. As even the most ardent of old time radio buffs are not likely to be familiar with these programs, the authors have dubbed them, "the forgotten series." Who knows? Perhaps some master detective will be inspired by these pages and will be able to uncover more information about them — and possibly other, as yet, unknown series.

Meyer the Buyer

One of the earliest of these "forgotten series" is *Meyer the Buyer,* a program that had a relatively short run on CBS during 1932. The authors owe a debt of gratitude to Charles Niren, an old time radio fan from Louisville, Kentucky, who brought this program to their attention. Niren recalled having listened to the program as a child. Much of what is known about the program is a result of his unrelenting research efforts.

The program was based on the comic strip *Abie the Agent* created in 1914 by the multi-talented comic strip artist and humorist Harry Hershfield (1885-1974), best known to radio buffs for his appearances on *Can You Top This?* (see Chapter 6) and *One Man's Opinion.*

Hershfield created his first comic strip, *Homeless Hector,* which appeared in the *Chicago Daily News,* in 1899 when he was only 14 years old. Other strips followed, including *Rubber, the Canine Cop; Dauntless Durham of the U.S.A.; Desperate Desmond;* and *According to Hoyle.* His most famous creation, *Abie the Agent,* was distributed nationally through Hearst's King Features Syndicate. Possibly the first strip based on a Jewish character, *Abie* was a stereotypical Jewish salesman always out to make a buck and, at least until the 1930s, spoke with the heavy Yiddish dialect that was common among the Jewish comedians who appeared in vaudeville in those days.

In 1931, when Hershfield had a dispute with Hearst and found himself embroiled in a "rights" controversy with the publisher over his comic character, he did what Freeman Gosden and Charles Correll did a few years earlier. Just as they changed the names of their characters from *Sam 'n' Henry* to *Amos 'n' Andy* when they left WGN, Hershfield's *Abie the Agent* became *Meyer the Buyer,* the renamed strip was picked up by another newspaper syndicate and the cartoonist brought his popular character to radio.[3]

As no audio of *Meyer the Buyer* has as yet been uncovered, what is known about the program comes from local newspaper clippings that were based on CBS press releases. The network carried the program on several of its major outlets, including WABC, WCCO, WTAQ, WISN, WJAS, WHAS, KMOS, KHJ and WMAL. Teddy Bergman (later known as Alan Reed) was featured in the part of the lead character, Meyer Mizznick. CBS publicists stressed the fact that Bergman, a well known radio actor, was best known for his portrayal of Joe Palooka, another comic strip character who made his way to the airwaves. They also called attention to the fact that Bergman had mastered some twenty different dialects.[4] Hershfield was credited with the character and may well have had a hand in writing the scripts. There is no indication of his having appeared on the program.

Adele Ronson of *Buck Rogers* fame (she played Buck's girlfriend, Wilma), portrayed Meyer's wife, Irma. Others in the cast included Ethel Holt as Meyer's secretary, Nick Adams as Uncle Ben, Dot Harrington as Beatrice and Geoffery Bryant as Milton, Meyer's son. Paul Douglas (who later became a featured Hollywood actor) rounded out the company as the announcer and doubled as a lawyer named Feldman. The program was set in New York City where Meyer, like so many other people at the time, was struggling to make a living during the Depression.[5]

The very first program aired on Thursday, August 25, 1932 at 8:30pm. In the 15-minute episode, listeners are introduced to Meyer and his wife. The latter has stopped putting on airs and has begun to focus her attention on keeping her family together in the midst of some of the worst days of the Depression. Listeners also learn that Meyer's son Milton is a student at "Coronell" College studying "horatory spicking" (Cornell College, studying oratory speaking), and that their daughter Beatrice attends "Wesser" (Vassar) and is in love with a cornet player from the ferryboat S. S. Benjamin Franklin. They also learn about Uncle Ben from Salt Lake City, Utica (Utah) who is in the habit of frequently dropping in for visits that could last up to twelve weeks.

As a sustaining program, the time slot for *Meyer's* next appearance one week later (September 1st) was changed to 6:30pm to make room in the evening schedule for a more profitable sponsored program. In this episode, the problems that had only been alluded to in the earlier broadcast begin to emerge. Uncle Ben arrives for one of his long visits, daughter Beatrice has a date with Sigmund Rappaport and poor Meyer continues to show stress. Listeners also learn that Meyer's former partner, a Mr. Kleinberg, made $1,000 in a crooked business deal and but didn't share the proceeds with him.

By the third episode of the series (September 8th), Meyer meets with lawyer Feldman, hoping to sue his ex-partner for half of the ill gotten gains referred to the week before. Adding to his woes, Meyer gets a collect long distance phone call from his son Milton. Listeners had to tune in the following week to find out what was so important that it necessitated an expensive phone call.

In the next episode (September 15th), the entire Mizznick family goes to the railroad station to meet Milton and discover the reason for his demanding $1,000 from his father. But when the train arrives, Milton is not aboard.

There was no mention of the program in the *Louisville Courier's* radio listings the following week (September 22nd) and it was not until an article appeared two days later, in the September 24th issue, that listeners learned the fate of the program.

> *Meyer the Buyer* with Ted Bergman (formerly Joe Palooka) in the title role has been shifted to 5:30 o'clock on Saturday afternoon. This dramatized Harry Hershfield comic strip was having great success when a new sponsored account interrupted its schedule, and the new hour will permit continuance of an unusual dialect comedy series.

Once again, the message was clear. As a sustaining program, *Meyer the Buyer* lacked the clout to be guaranteed a stable time slot; sponsors always had preference in selecting when their program would be broadcast.

Over the next few weeks, the intertwined stories of Meyer's pending lawsuit and his son Milton's troubles continued. Meyer's lawyer advised him on what histrionics would work best in court and Meyer rehearsed his pending court appearance with Uncle Ben acting as the judge. As for Milton, when he failed to show up or explain why he needed $1,000, Meyer decided that if his son would not come to him, he would make the trip to "Coronell" College to find out for himself.

The last known newspaper reference to the program that the authors are aware of appeared on November 12, 1932. Whether the program was re-scheduled to a different time and/or date or was cancelled is not known.

The Jewish Poker Game

Meyer the Buyer was not Hershfield's first foray into the world of radio broadcasting. At least one respected reference cites the existence of a 1926 series of broadcasts aired on station WGBS in New York City called *The Jewish Poker Game*.[6] Hershfield's fellow poker players were all masters of the Yiddish dialect and included Milt Gross, a fellow cartoonist whose cartoon characters spoke with a Yiddish dialect and whose book, *Nize Baby*, was written in English but with a Yiddish dialect, Max Fleischer, who was a successful cartoonist best known for his having turned to film where his studio produced the famous *Betty Boop* and *Popeye* animated films, and Jimmy Hussey, who despite being an Irish-American Catholic, achieved great success on stage and in vaudeville as a Jewish comedian.

Not enough is known about this program to comment further except to speculate that the four humorists probably would have spent their airtime *kibitzing* (talking) around a pretend poker table and exchanging jokes. A typical joke could have been:

> Six Jewish gentlemen were playing poker in the clubhouse when Meyerowitz loses $500 on a single hand, clutches his chest and drops dead at the table. Showing respect for their fallen comrade, the other five complete their playing time standing up.
>
> When the game is over, Finkelstein looks around and asks, 'Now, who is going to tell his wife?'
>
> They draw straws. Goldberg, who is always a loser, picks the short one. They tell him to be discreet, be gentle, don't make a bad situation any worse than it is.
>
> 'Gentlemen! Discreet? I'm the most discreet *mensch* (a good person, a stand-up guy) you will ever meet. Discretion is my middle name, leave it to me.' Goldberg *schleps* (defined alternately as to carry or to go somewhere unwillingly) over to the Meyerowitz apartment, knocks on the door. The wife answers and asks what he wants.
>
> Goldberg declares, 'Your husband just lost $500 in a poker game.'
>
> She hollers, 'Tell him he should drop dead!!'
>
> And Goldberg says, 'I'll tell him.'

Potash and Perlmutter

Potash and Perlmutter was an outgrowth of a series of popular short stories written by Montague Glass (1877-1934). The son of a successful garment manufacturer, Glass was 13 years old when he and his parents emigrated from England to the United States. Educated at the City College of New York and New York University, he decided to practice law rather than join his father in the family garment business. At the same time, he started writing humorous short stories that combined what he knew about the garment trade with the heavy Yiddish dialect used by its Jewish immigrant workers.

As Glass later recalled, "I began getting paid for writing in 1895 and sold my first Potash and Perlmutter story to the *Saturday Evening Post* in 1908."[7] It was not until 1910, however, that the first collection of his dialect stories was published as a book, *Potash and Perlmutter*. The stories centered on the activities of two Jewish business partners in the garment business, Abe Potash and Morris Perlmutter. It was at that time that Glass decided to give up the law entirely and devote the rest of his life to writing. In 1911, a second volume of stories, *Abe and Mawruss,* was published. Over the next several years, as the characters continued to grow in popularity, they were featured in a series of successful stage plays, four movies and a third volume of collected stories that was published in 1919.[8]

Following the path of other literary and cartoon characters of the day that made their way from the printed page to the airwaves, Potash and Perlmutter made their radio debut on June 26, 1933 on WJZ, the New York City flagship station for the NBC-Blue network. The program was initially heard at 8:30pm, most likely three days a week (Monday, Wednesday and Friday), but was switched to 7:30pm on October 23rd. The series remained on the air until May 18, 1934. For a portion of its relatively short run, it was sponsored by Health Products Inc., makers of Feen-a-mint, the laxative chewing gum.

The only audio recordings of the program known to have survived are three transcriptions, all dated February 9, 1933, some four months prior to the program's first broadcast. The recordings, a part of the NBC Collection at the Library of Congress, are identified as "Audition programs Nos. 1, 2 and 3," with each program 15 minutes in length. (Audition discs of this sort were generally used to tempt prospective sponsors to underwrite the proposed series or interest local stations in adding the program to their schedules.) Print material about the program is even more limited and consists of a few program cards in the NBC Collection and some publicity material from Glass himself.

In a two column puff piece, "Writing for Radio," that appeared in the November 12, 1933 radio section of *The New York Times*, Glass shared his insights about making the successful transition from writing for the printed page, movies and stage to the new medium of radio.

> It is not wise to try to crowd too much material in a short story, and that goes double for radio. The ideal number of characters is four or five, no more, and they should be made to speak slowing and distinctly, for the microphone is an ear, not an eye, to those outside who can only listen...The listener should not have to listen intently to get the thread of the story...Every situation, all substitutes for facial expressions, gestures and stage movements have to be adequately expressed in language or sound. Such writing must be done by persons who are familiar with telling stories in dialogue form...It is astonishing how one can convey by dialogue the part of a strong man, a weak man, the fleshy or thin person, by the type of voice the actor uses and the words he is given to recite...One of the cardinal principles of radio sketch-making is that the actors' voices must contrast perfectly to prevent listeners from being confused. And it's a good point to have the characters call each other frequently by their stage names. This keeps the audiences closely in touch with the action. When new characters are introduced this rule is especially significant.

As for the two Jewish entrepreneurs that he created two decades earlier, Glass concluded that:

> One would think Potash and Perlmutter could not find an appreciative new audience on the air. But such has not been the case. In radio I believe I have discovered an entirely new field for the characters which for years have been known only to readers and theatergoers. And so I am beginning to believe that thousands, until recently, have never heard of the characters I created so many years ago.

In the first of the three audition episodes, the two partners discuss the need to cut costs in their suit and cloak business due to poor economic conditions. Someone must be fired to save costs. Perlmutter, the tough partner, suggests a salesman who has not been productive. Potash, the more soft-hearted partner, reluctantly agrees, until he learns that the wife of the salesman selected to be dismissed has just been hospitalized. In the second broadcast, Potash visits the hospital and ends up underwriting the cost of the consultation by a specialist. While in the hospital waiting room, he meets a department store owner from Salt Lake City who is unhappy with the New York City manufacturers he has been doing business with. In the third episode, Potash's kindness is rewarded when the visiting department store owner, impressed by Potash's generosity toward an employee, gives the partners his business, thus solving their financial problems.

Joseph Greenwald, who portrayed Solomon Levy in the stage production of *Abie's Irish Rose*, played the part of Abe Potash. Morris Perlmutter was played by veteran stage actor Lou Welsh. Just in case listeners had any doubt regarding the ethnicity of the partners, both actors spoke with heavy Yiddish accents. The other cast members spoke without any identifiable accent.

Mama Bloom's Brood

In the 1930s, both Hollywood and network executives operated on the premise that it was far easier, and probably more lucrative, to replicate previous successes than to develop a brand new plot concept. Thus, given the success of *Amos 'n' Andy* and *The Rise of the Goldbergs,* two ethnic oriented programs, one can understand why, in 1932, CBS gambled on *Meyer the Buyer.* It may also explain why, a year later, NBC took a chance on *Potash and Perlmutter.* By 1934, another Jewish themed radio program was to surface. This time the program, *Mama Bloom's Brood*, was independently produced for syndication by a company called Transco (Transcription Company of America) which, at some point in time, was sold to Bruce Eells Associates. Both companies are long out of business and no records relating to their programs are known to have survived.

The good news about *Mama Bloom's Brood* is that as a syndicated program, multiple copies of each episode were prepared on transcription discs for distribution to subscribing stations. As a consequence, unlike other programs for which little or no audio is available, 76 out of the total of 78 episodes of this 15-minute series have survived. The bad news is that except for the labels on the transcription discs identifying Bruce Eells and Associates and Broadcaster Syndicate as the distributors of the series the second time around, little else is known about the program. Nothing, for example, is known about who wrote the scripts or what actors played the major roles. Nor is it known if the program aired daily, three times a week or weekly.⁹

During the 1930s and 1940s, it was not uncommon for some syndicated programs to be developed that were designed to run for a fixed number of episodes. In that way, they could be sold to local stations as a package, thus making it easier for stations to line up sponsors for a fixed number of episodes. *Mama Bloom's Brood* may well have fit into this pattern. In contrast, other syndicated programs were designed as open-ended series so that if they were well received by listeners, their story lines could go on and on. Some of the more successful opened-ended syndicated series were eventually picked up by the networks and become ongoing series.

There is some speculation that because *Mama Bloom* aired in 1934, the year in which *The Rise of the Goldbergs* left the airwaves for a year-and-a-half, Gertrude Berg may have been responsible for the program. Proponents of this theory point to the similarity between the name "Bloom" and Molly's neighbor of "Yoo Hoo" fame as well as the fact that Mama Bloom's husband was also named Jake. They also cite the episode in which Mama Bloom wants to change her first name from Becky (Rebecca) to Gwendolyn — which would have made her initials "G.B.," the same as Gertrude Berg.

However, as Berg used much of the time that she was off the air between 1934 to 1936 making personal appearances with members of her radio cast on the vaudeville circuit, the chances of her being behind *Mama Bloom* seem rather slim. Also, when one of the authors spoke briefly with Berg's son-in-law, inquiring about the possibility that his mother-in-law had written the *Bloom* program, the son-in-law replied that he had never heard any mention of the program.¹⁰ A final argument against the Berg connection is simply that the quality of writing in the *Bloom* series is vastly inferior to what Berg and the writers under her supervision were able to turn out, even on an off day.

The existence of all but two episodes of the entire run of this series provides today's listeners with the unique opportunity to follow the adventures of an immigrant family and its first generation offspring from their humble beginnings in New York's garment industry to the dream world of Hollywood. Each episode begins with an announcer intoning the words, "Well, well, well. Here's Mama Bloom's Brood." The opening lines are followed by a musical interlude designed to allow for the insertion of a local commercial.

In the very first episode listeners are introduced to Mama and her husband Jake. While some listeners — or readers — may view Mama's name "Becky" as an ethnic clue to her Semitic heritage, the name was a common one (having been used by both Mark Twain and Thackary for characters who were clearly not Jewish). Both parents speak with a heavy Yiddish accent and Mama is particularly prone to malapropisms, although some come across as forced and not nearly as witty as those mouthed by Jane Ace, the queen of the malaprop art. The scriptwriter, not one to plow new ground, also has Jake working in the garment industry, the same line of business as Jake Goldberg and the *Potash and Perlmutter* partners.

Following the pattern set by the generational differences in the Goldberg family, the speech patterns for the two Bloom daughters, Sarah and Yetta, were such that even Professor Henry Higgins would be hard pressed to identify them as the American-born children of immigrants. Also, following in the footsteps of Molly's daughter Rosalie, the Bloom daughters are not much different than those of other modern young women. The plot lines involving the daughters deal with clothes, dating and coming home late from parties, issues common to all parents regardless of religious or ethnic background.

In the initial episode, both girls want new dresses to wear for an upcoming social event. Although mama assures them of her support in their quest, when papa comes home, he rejects the idea. Mama, much to the dismay of her daughters, agrees with papa. But after mama tells her husband about a business rival of his who spoils his daughter, spending far too much on the young lady, listeners hear papa insisting that anything his rival does for his daughter, he too can do for his daughters. Needless the say, the episode ends with the girls getting their new dresses and the series establishes the pattern of the father sounding like a patriarch while it's mama's wit that wins the day. Mama also usually gets the last word.

By episode 13, Sarah declares her intention to marry Sidney Schiffbein, Yetta wants to change her name to Yvette and hire a maid, papa wants to purchases a new car and avoid being swindled and mama plans a party. Moving the story line ahead, by episode 25 Sarah's wedding has taken place but not before Sidney, who now works for papa, has made some interesting business deals and manages to make Sarah jealous. Not to be ignored, Yetta announces her own engagement (episode 26). Rather than go through with mama's wedding plans (episode 27), the couple elopes (episode 28) and upon their return from a honeymoon paid for by a reluctant papa (episode 29) Harold, the new son-in-law, is also given a job in papa's factory (episode 30).

By episode 42, life has changed for the Blooms. Both sons-in-law have made changes at the factory, papa's long time partner has decided to retire, an offer to buy the business has been substantially increased due to mama's intervention, mama and papa learn that they will soon be grandparents and they decide to follow Horace Greeley's advice and "go west."

Having developed the stereotype of Jews in the garment business to the hilt, the plot takes a twist when the family moves to California where a second Jewish stereotype is played out — what Henry Ford and Father Coughlin would call "the Jewish control of Hollywood." The two Bloom sons-in-law arrive in Hollywood and try to get papa Bloom to invest in the movie business. Much to their surprise, they find that the elder Bloom is way ahead of them, having already purchased his own movie studio.[11]

By episode 50, papa and Sidney have been feuding over studio decisions, but papa has control. Things appear to be going well until a temper tantrum by star Marsha Valle threatens to shut down production. Mama, as usual, comes to the rescue when she recognizes Marsha as the former Rachel Rabinowitz from the Bronx.[12]

By episode 65 the series is beginning to wind down. The usual studio ups-and-downs have been explored, as have been the usual rivalries and jealousies. Mama is growing homesick for New York. Sarah gives birth to twins. The next several episodes deal with deciding on names for the twins (Nathan and Rachel) and more monkey business at the studio. The final two episodes in the saga (episodes 77 and 78) have mama and papa attending a sneak preview of their movie following which they announce their retirement from the movie business.

Krausemeyer and Cohen

Krausemeyer and Cohen, another series in which at least one of the main characters was Jewish, is estimated to have been broadcast in 1936.[13] Like *Mama Bloom's Brood*, this series was also the product of syndication. With four episodes surviving in audio format, researchers and nostalgia buffs are able to gain a sense of the program's plot lines and character development. To date, the authors have not been able to find any print documentation about the program.

Each 15-minute episode begins with a musical interlude that sounds very much like *Auf Wedersehn* which allowed local sponsors the opportunity to promote their product. In the very first episode, the announcer introduces the new series to listeners:

> Ready everybody. Then let's go. We're now about to visit Krausemeyer's tavern for the first episode of the broadcast treat of the season. Krausmeyer and Cohen. A show that you'll love for its humor and humanness. A show that's kaleidoscopic and rapid-fire. Constantly changing situations. A show that's royally packed with comedy, drama, love, suspense, pathos. As we enter Krausemeyer's tavern...

The cast in each of the four surviving episodes consists of five stock characters. The comic braggart is Herman Krausemeyer who speaks with a thick German (or Dutch) accent bordering on Jack Pearl's rendition of Baron Munchhausen. Krausemeyer's partner, the unlikely Morris Cohen, is portrayed as the low keyed, thoughtful part owner, much like Amos is to the irascible Andy or the unscrupulous Kingfish. Cohen's Yiddish accent, which would rival the accent of Menasha Skulnik, clearly identifies his ethnicity. (Listeners familiar with the stereotypical notion that Jewish men are non-drinkers, may be surprised to find a Jew as a co-owner of a tavern — as well as partnered with a German.)

Another cast member is Percy, the tavern's headwaiter. A British emigré, Percy's very proper accent is much like that of the character actor Arthur Treacher. The lone female in the cast is Vivian, a Mae West sound-alike who digs for gold, but not in the Klondike. Rounding out the cast is Mr. Adams, a local alderman whose voice is without any trace of ethnicity.

In the first two episodes, listeners are introduced to the cast of characters and hear Herman being charmed by Vivian who has him eating out of her gloved hand. Not long afterward, Vivian convinces Herman to buy her several gifts but arranges for them to be delivered to the tavern via COD, (Cash on Delivery). That leaves Cohen in the position of having to lay out the money to pay for this partner's extravagances. By the end of the second episode, Herman is beginning to realize the cost of his new romance and Vivian talks herself into a job as hostess in the tavern.

In the remaining surviving episodes (numbers 39 and 40), listeners learn that Herman has been encouraged to run for alderman. Confident that he will win the election, he borrows money using his interest in the tavern to finance his campaign. Listeners also learn that in previous episodes he and Vivian had become engaged but that while the engagement was broken off, he was still making payments on the ring he gave to her.

The election returns come in and Herman loses by a landslide, with the unmistakable inference that Mr. Adams had set him up for the fall. Having lost his remaining interest in the tavern, Herman then sneaks away. He returns the following day to apply for Percy's old job as headwaiter as Percy, now a quarter owner of the tavern, is also the manager. Vivian, believing that Percy is related to royalty, enlists the help of Mr. Adams in her quest to snare the new owner. As listeners leave the premises of the Krausemeyer and Cohen Tavern, they learn that Percy left England some £40,000 in debt and that he is hoping to raise some cash by selling tickets to the upcoming sweepstakes. Herman, ever the optimist, says he will help him and perhaps buy a winning ticket himself so that he can regain his part ownership in the tavern.

Many questions about *Krausemeyer and Cohen* remain unanswered. In addition to the uncertainty regarding when the program was broadcast, it is also unclear how many episodes of the program were broadcast. As syndicated series were usually prepared in 13-week cycles, it is conceivable at least another 12 episodes of the program were prepared for distribution to local stations. But — it is also conceivable that the program came to an abrupt end because of events in Germany. If the Nazi Party was already in control of Germany and anti-Jewish measures were already in place when the series aired, audiences may have found it increasingly difficult to accept a humorous program about a Jewish-German business partnership, especially one that relied on stereotypical characters for its laughs.

The House of Glass

A somewhat less "forgotten" series was Gertrude Berg's *The House of Glass*, written after *The Rise of the Goldbergs* lost its sponsorship in 1934. Based on Berg's own experiences working at her father's summer resort, the program was set in a hotel owned by Bessie and Barney Glass in New York's Catskill Mountain region where mostly middle class Jewish families vacationed.[14] The weekly half hour program was broadcast from April 17, 1934 to December 25, 1935 on NBC's Blue-network. The series featured Berg as Bessie Glass and Joseph Greenwald as her husband Barney. Greenwald had earlier portrayed Abe Potash on the short-lived *Potash and Perlmutter* series. Others in the cast included Celia Babcock, Arlene Blackburn, Helene Dumas, Lea Penman, Roslyn Silber (Rosalie in *The Rise of the Goldbergs*), Paul Stewart, Bertha Walden and James R. Waters (Jake Goldberg on *The Rise of the Goldbergs*). Billy Artzt provided the music. The program was sponsored by Super Suds, a Colgate-Palmolive-Peet soap powder.

Initial reaction to the new series was positive, both from listeners and critics. *The New York Times* reviewer wrote that, "*The House of Glass* seems destined for a long run on the air...(Berg) has again developed a clever idea into a popular show on the air." Another critic noted that "The old Goldberg fans may be expected to love the series with the same devotion they lavished on *The Rise of the Goldbergs*."[15]

Given the program's positive reviews, one may wonder why the show was cancelled after only eight months. Two reasons, not necessarily mutually exclusive are possible. First, competition. Popular though the program may have been, it may have been no match against the long established and highly rated *Burns and Allen Show* that aired on CBS in the same time slot. A second and related reason was that old standby, money: the program's sponsor no doubt sensed that Molly Goldberg could generate more sales for its products than Bessie Glass. According to Berg's biographer, Glenn D. Smith, Jr., "there was no real attachment to *The House of Glass* for Berg, no lasting connection to Bessie Glass. At first opportunity, when Colgate executives agreed to sponsor a return of *The Goldbergs*, she did not hesitate to take them up on the offer."[16] Two weeks after *The House of Glass* went off the air, Berg returned to the airwaves with the newly renamed *The Goldbergs*.

In 1953, after the radio version of *The Goldbergs* had been off the air for four years, and with ratings for the televised version of the series declining, Berg decided to revive *The House of Glass* but with some modifications. In the new version, Berg changed her role to Sophie, the hotel cook and Joseph Bulloff, a stage, screen and radio actor, played the part of Barney Glass, hotel owner and worrier. Ann Thomas was heard as a waitress and Milton Katims provided the music. Sadly, the second effort, broadcast from October 23, 1953 to March 12, 1954, had an even shorter run than the original version.

Cohen, the Detective

Cohen, the Detective was a tongue-in-cheek comic take off on the antics of radio's respectable sleuths (Sherlock Holmes, Philip Marlowe, Richard Diamond, Nero Wolfe and scores of others) featuring a Jewish detective partnered with a "Dr. Wasserman." The series first aired as a sneak preview in the summer of 1943 on the NBC-Blue network. The program reappeared on August 10, 1943 but took its last breath on September 14th, having lasted only six performances (seven, if one includes the earlier preview).

If *Cohen's* radio career was short-lived, it was certainly not the fault of its cast that included the very talented John Brown, Pat C. Flick,[17] Sidney Stone, Natalie Cantor and Charme Allen, all talented and successful radio veterans. No audio copies of this program are known to exist. If one were to speculate on the actual contents, a comparison might be made with another long forgotten tongue-in-cheek take-off on the world of radio detectives, *Detectives Black and Blue*, a 15-minute syndicated daily program that was broadcast from 1932-1935. The program focused on the adventures of a pair of shipping clerks trying to be detectives. It may have been primitive, but it enjoyed a far longer lifespan.

All seven of these "forgotten series" experienced relatively short runs. Among the factors that may have led to their early demise were their heavy reliance on dialect, the use of few cast members and, sad to say, little in the way of originality.

May they all "rest in peace."

And a last minute addition of still another "forgotten series."

The Bronx Marriage Bureau

Himan Brown, who in the late 1920s appeared on at least two programs using the Yiddish dialect, appeared as a *shadkhen* (matchmaker) in *The Bronx Marriage Bureau*. The 15-minute serial was broadast twice a week on WOR at 7pm from 1932 to 1933 or 1934. The series was written by Julie Bernstein (a.k.a. Julie Berns) who appeared on the program as Brown's wife. No audio copies of the program are known to have survived.

Notes

1. http://www.midcoast.com/~lizmcl/earlyradio.html.
2. Gertrude Berg saved scripts, correspondence, scrapbooks and other papers, all of which are available to researchers at Syracuse University.
3. Four years later, in 1935, Hershfield signed a new contract with Hearst and the *Abie the Agent* comic strip was revived, running until 1940.
4. In later years, Bergman, by then known professionally as Alan Reed, portrayed the character of Pasquale in *Life With Luigi*.
5. One newspaper clipping says Meyer is in the "cloak and suit" business while another says he "presides over a clearing house for almost any sort of business."
6. Luther E. Sies, *Encyclopedia of American Radio 1920-1960* (Jefferson, NC: McFarland & Company, 2000), Citation #13203.
7. *The New York Times*, November 12, 1933.
8. Absent the discovery of a buried cache of long lost scripts or a significant run of transcription discs for the 70+ year old program, perhaps the easiest way for the reader to gain a sense of how Glass combined humor, the use of the Yiddish dialect and the every day problems facing clothing manufacturers during the first quarter of the 20th century would be to access a free download of one of his books at www.gutenberg.org. Copies of the books, although long out-of-print, are also available from many used book dealers at quite reasonable cost.
9. As a syndicated program, it was up to each station to decide how and when to broadcast the episodes.
10. A November 13, 2006 phone conversation with David Schwartz, Berg's son-in-law.
11. The writer may have taken a clue here from the real movie mogul, Sam Goldwyn, whose Yiddish accent was thicker than any dialogue written for radio or film and who was originally a glove manufacturer in New York before going to Hollywood.
12. Here again, the writer seems to have borrowed from real life Hollywood events, e.g., Thedosia Burr Goodman, the Jewish girl from Cincinnati who changed her name to Theda Bara.
13. The label on the surviving transcription discs provided David Goldin of radiogoldindex.com with a clue that led him to estimate that the programs were possibly released for broadcast in 1936.
14. On *Abie's Irish Rose,* the two fathers-in-law also owned a resort in the Catskills.
15. Glenn D. Smith, Jr., *Something on Own: Gertrude Berg and American Broadcasting, 1929-1956* (Syracuse, NY: Syracuse University Press, 2007), 65-66.
16. Ibid., 69.
17. Shown as "Patsy Flick" in some sources.

6
Funny, You Don't Sound Jewish

The Yiddish Dialect

There was a time (and perhaps still is) when people believed that Jews could be recognized by certain physical characteristics that were unique to them. It was not unusual, for example, for Jews to be portrayed on stage, in print and in general conversation in the stereotypical manner of a Shylock or a Fagin. Thanks to writers like Shakespeare, Dickens and others, the popular concept that Jews were recognizable by their long hooked noses, dark hair and other (no doubt unpleasant) features was generally acceptable. Indeed, a common response heard by many a Jew when being introduced to a stranger was: "Funny, you don't look Jewish."

Clearly, to radio audiences, physical characteristics did not matter. Radio created characters using "the mind's eye" and listeners "heard" their characters rather than "seeing" them. As an aural medium, radio required writers to come up with new ways to "identify" their characters and the use of language and dialect was the tool most often used for attaching an ethnic label to a person. When listeners used their imagination to *see* the characters they heard, two white men could portray two black men, and a skilled actor, no matter what his personal ethnic or religious background, could speak as if he were an Englishman, Irishman, Italian or Jew according to the dictates of the script.

Throughout most of radio's Golden Age, the primary way to identify a person as being Jewish was by having him speak in a Yiddish (a.k.a. Jewish) dialect.[1] In series such as *The Rise of the Goldbergs (*later renamed *The Goldbergs), Mama Bloom's Brood* or *Abie's Irish Rose,* typically the Yiddish dialect was used only by the "older generation" characters who had emigrated to the United States. The first generation offspring of these immigrants spoke without any trace of accent. On non-Jewish mainstream programs that featured a Jewish character such as Papa David on *Life Can Be Beautiful* or Mrs. Nussbaum on the Allen's Alley sketches on the *Fred Allen Show*, the character spoke with a heavy Yiddish accent.

In their 1943 book, *Foreign Dialects: A Manual for Actors, Directors and Writers*, authors Lewis Herman and Marguerite Shalett Herman explained that although there were geographic variations in the Yiddish dialect, there were some generally accepted rules or characteristics, including the sing-song "lilt" that they identified as the most important factor in the dialect, followed by the substitution of a few vowels and consonants and the use of a few variations in syntax.[2] The authors also noted that the pitch of Yiddish was higher than English, that falsetto was reached many times, especially under the stress of emotion, and that the "color" of the dialect was affected by sentence structure and phraseology. The authors also gave examples of several typical grammatical changes commonly found in the Yiddish dialect.

The authors went beyond dialect, however, and actually assigned specific traits to Jewish characters, although they did acknowledge that the Yiddish character was as varied as its speech. Fathers, for example were primarily good family men, and mothers were not the typical "drudges" found in German households. Jewish parents sacrificed everything for their children's welfare and education. Their children, in turn, seldom completely forsook their parents. Jews, the authors wrote, rarely drank liquor, but they did sip wine on holidays and almost never became intoxicated. Jews were warm-hearted and quick to make friends, extremely sentimental, and also relished argument for argument's sake (a tradition, the authors noted that dated back to early Talmudic scholars) and frequently answered a question with a question.[3]

Other stereotypes often associated with Jews not mentioned by the Hermans but which were used for other radio characters included their presence as workers or entrepreneurs in the garment industry and their image as being cheap. But just as the nuances of the Yiddish dialect varied, so did Jewish characterizations — from the wise and revered Papa David to the comic antics of Izzy Finkelstein on *Kaltenmeyer's Kindergarten*.

From the very earliest days of radio, continuing through the postwar period, the use of dialect to identify members of an ethnic group generated controversy. Radio historians Michele Hilmes and Susan J. Douglas both discuss the controversial relationship between language and cultural diversity that was very much on the minds of Americans in the 1920s and early 1930s.[4] As radio was establishing itself as the primary mass communications medium, there were two conflicting schools of thought regarding language. At one extreme, there were those who believed that radio should be used to "Americanize" the "tidal wave of immigrants" who some saw as a potential threat to the country's existing social balance. Radio, these people believed, could address this threat by helping to integrate the "us" and the "others" into a more unified "ourselves." To accomplish this goal, they believed that radio should adopt a standardized pronunciation and that English should be "forced" upon listeners. This school of thought is best summed up by the belief that the "universal leveling of dialects...will go far to promote sectional and national and international understanding."[5] In contrast, others accepted the reality of a diverse America and the idea that as long as dialect and malapropisms were permitted on the airwaves, radio would be used to define and reinforce class, ethnic, racial and gender differences, even when, as was generally believed, "dialects marked the speaker, rightly or wrong, as ignorant, stupid and low-class."[6]

The controversy continued throughout the 1930s and sponsors, networks and performers remained acutely aware of the criticism leveled against the radio industry for the use of dialect as a way of stereotyping characters. A February 1, 1938 article, "Drive Under Way to Stop Butchering of Yiddish by Radio Dialecticians," that appeared in the trade magazine *Broadcasting* reported the following:

> A widespread but subtly guarded campaign which has the cooperation of the believing Jewish comedians, organizations, and publications has been initiated to eliminate the butchering of Yiddish on radio programs. The movement, said to have originated in New York and Chicago, and now been taken up in Hollywood and in San Francisco, is not aimed to eliminate the Jewish dialect from radio entertainment business, it was said, but is pointed rather toward its elevation and refinement in a measure that will make Yiddish wholly intelligible while yet retaining its comedy values.
>
> Critics contend that the flagrant misuse of Yiddish on radio programs holds the Jewish people up to undesirable ridicule, misrepresenting their intelligence and intellectual attainments generally, thus creating a false impression of racial barriers. It is pointed out in old vaudeville days, the use of Yiddish on the stage caused little harm to Jewry generally.
>
> But the continuance of such routine on radio programs constitutes a current problem, which can be controlled only by the cooperation of Jewish leaders in the industry. They are being called upon to lend their

aid by encouraging the coherent types of routine, which are calculated to amuse without holding the race up to ridicule. following:[7]

In response to this criticism, NBC adopted the following guideline regarding ethnic humor in a July, 1938 final draft of its *Program Standards of the National Broadcasting Company*: "Statements and suggestions which are offensive to religious views, racial characteristics and the like must not appear in programs."[8] Even the Hermans' 1943 *Manual of Foreign Dialects* was sensitive to the dialect issue. In the book's Preface, Garson Kanin wrote that, "the superficial theatrical clichés must be abruptly discarded. Too often they tend to ridicule rather than represent. There is more than comedy in a foreigner's use of English. There is tenderness and beauty and pathos in the attempts of newcomers to express themselves in our tongue."[9]

The question that remained unanswered, though, was: who was to judge whether an ethnic characterization was malicious and demeaning or simply a laugh-getter, especially when the dialect was used by a character who was otherwise perceived of as warm and friendly. Fred Allen, for example, continued to use ethnic humor for nine years after the Standards were adopted and long after dialect humor had ceased to be the dominant comedic form in variety entertainment. He did, however, have to overcome some initial objections from NBC over the Mrs. Nussbaum character.[10]

After World War II, radio personality and newspaper columnist Walter Winchell picked up the anti-dialect issue and launched a campaign against comics he felt got their laughs at the expense of minority groups. While Winchell saw no problem with racial humor as long as it was performed with love and affection and didn't ridicule their subjects, he took issue with comedians who got their laughs by denigrating Italians, Jews, Negroes and others. In one of his columns, he made a point of singling out Jack Benny, noting that when the comedian used ethnic characters such as Rochester and Mr. Kitzel, he did so with dignity, love and affection. For comics he considered tasteless, he coined the word "vomics."[11]

From Vaudeville to Radio

Years before the 1927 film *The Jazz Singer* introduced moviegoers to the sound of Jewish voices, millions of Americans heard the thick dialect associated with Eastern European Jews on the stages of vaudeville houses and on inexpensive phonograph records.

One of the most popular series of phonograph recordings sold during the first quarter of the 20th century was known as the *Cohen on the Telephone* records. Because "Cohen" was a common name that could not be trademarked, as many as eight different comedians tried their hand at the routine.[12] Two of the eight, Joe Hayman, who made some 30 *Cohen* recordings (for Columbia) and Monroe Silver, who made 19 such recordings (for several labels including Victor, Banner, Emerson and Silvertone), are the best known and most remembered. Hayman's 1913 recording became the first comedy record that claimed to have sold over a million copies.[13]

Most, if not all, of the original *Cohen* recordings have been preserved and readers wishing to sample the humor and accent commonly heard in early 20th century America can obtain copies from dealers specializing in old sound recordings. Typical of the topics Cohen discussed during three minute recorded monologues were: his son, his tailor, his automobile, the radio, the gas company, the plumber and other quite mundane or otherwise ordinary subjects.

At least one of the *Cohen on the Telephone* routines was broadcast on network radio on March 14, 1935 when Monroe Silver appeared as a guest on Rudy Vallee's *Fleischmann's Yeast Hour*. In addition to his traveling vaudeville act, Silver also performed his *Cohen* skit in, of all things, an early 1920s short silent film. George Jessel also developed a successful, although slightly different, telephone routine in vaudeville that he later used in radio. But unlike Hayman or Silver, Jessel did not affect a Yiddish dialect when conducting these one-sided exchanges. However, the tone of his voice, the questions he asked and his repetition of his mother's supposed answers made it abundantly clear to audiences that Jessel, a first generation Jewish-American son, was paying respect to his traditional Jewish immigrant mother. Each of Jessel's telephone routines had the same opening: "Hello, Operator! Give me Fentingrass 3522. Hello, mama? Georgie!" Jessel would repeat some of these routines on his own radio program, *Thirty Minutes in Hollywood* that aired from 1937-1938. In 1946 he gathered a number of the routines into a 154-page book, *Hello, Momma*,[14] one of at least eight volumes of humorous recollections that he committed to print over the years.

In its formative years, radio borrowed extensively from the vaudeville circuits for both featured performers and for guests on variety-type programs. A number of vaudeville headliners, including many of the Jewish faith such as Eddie Cantor, Jack Benny, George Burns, Ed Wynn, Milton Berle and Al Jolson, would eventually star on their own programs. None of them, however, affected a Jewish persona or used a Yiddish dialect as part of their radio presence.

Although very few dialect comedians managed to do well enough on radio to sustain their own programs, several made periodic guest appearances on variety programs such as Jessel's *Thirty Minutes in Hollywood* or the more prestigious *Fleischmann's Yeast Hour*. Recordings of several of these guest appearances have survived, including at least five appearances that Willie Howard, a well known Yiddish dialect comedian, made between 1935-1944 and seven appearances by Smith and Dale (of the *Sunshine Boys* fame), including their 1935 appearance on the *Fleischmann's* show and their 1961 appearance with Mitch Miller.[15] Two Jewish dialect comedians who were featured on their own programs were Jack Pearl (Baron Munchausen) who used a Dutch or German dialect and Harry Einstein who adopted a Greek dialect for his character Parkyakarkas. Neither, however, would rival the popularity or longevity of the three "radio-born" dialect series, *Amos 'n' Andy, Lum and Abner* or *The Goldbergs*.

Still another example, but with a different outcome, of a Jewish vaudevillian-turned-radio performer was Fanny Brice (born Fania Borach, 1891-1951). Brice is remembered, of course, for her characterization of Baby Snooks, the precocious little girl who, week after week, drove her father (played by Hanley Stafford) to distraction on the *Good News Program, Maxwell House Coffee Time* and the *Frank Morgan-Fanny Brice Program*. But years before Snooks made her appearance, Brice (who spoke English with no more of a Yiddish accent than Gertrude Berg might have had when she wasn't playing Molly Goldberg) revived some of her Yiddish dialect successes from the Ziegfeld Follies on guest appearances she made on the *Fleischmann's Yeast Hour, Shell Château* and the *Ziegfeld Follies of the Air*. Brice's first known appearance on radio in 1930 was in a Yiddish dialect routine with another ex-vaudevillian, Henry Burbig (see "Burbig" section below). As a versatile singer, actress and comedienne, Brice had enough talent to easily give up her dialect routines.

Like Brice, Eddie Cantor (1892-1964), in addition to being a talented song and dance man on Broadway and in vaudeville, also engaged in comedy routines involving the use of the Yiddish dialect early in his career. In a stand alone scene about a couple of Jewish tailors in the 1929 musical comedy film, *Glorifying the American Girl,* Cantor and his partner, played by Louis Sorin, engaged in a typical Yiddish dialect exchange:

Vats der idea of calling me a damn fool in front off der customers? So it's a secret?

However, once Cantor began to appear on radio, beginning with the *Chase and Sanborn Hour* in 1931 and continuing until 1963, he did not personally engage in the use of ethnic dialect on his programs.[16] He did, nonetheless, engage the talents of three excellent dialect actors, including two who slaughtered the Russian language. When violinist Rubinoff was Cantor's orchestra leader, Teddy Bergman (a.k.a. Alan Reed), a master dialectician, would speak Rubinoff's lines. Years later, Bert Gordon, with hair trussed up and eyes popping, would show up in the middle of Cantor's program with his famous greeting, "How do you do" followed by Cantor introducing him as "The Mad Russian." Cantor's third dialect actor was Harry Einstein who played the Greek, Parkyakarkas.[17]

Although Cantor's Jewishness was not an integral part of his radio program, he did use his shows to express his concern over the growing anti-Semitism in the United States and the escalating crisis in Europe. In 1938, with Charles Lindbergh, Father Coughlin and Gerald L. K. Smith and others warning radio listeners against taking sides in the European conflict (with more than a hint that it was the Jewish-American lobby pushing for America's intervention in European affairs), Cantor inserted the following into the script for his Thanksgiving program: "(It was) wonderful to live in a country where on a day like this, the leader of the nation sits down to carve up a turkey, instead of a map." The words were never broadcast, though. In the 1930s, every broadcast was reviewed by the sponsor's advertising agency before it was aired and Cantor's program was no exception. The agency representing the program's sponsor, the R. J. Reynolds Tobacco Co. (Camel cigarettes), cut the remark for fear it might offend listeners who were isolationists or pro-Nazi. In an ironic twist, the censored remark ended up receiving even more publicity than if it had aired: Cantor shared the remark with his friend, President Franklin D. Roosevelt, and shortly thereafter the incident became a major news story.[18]

Cantor was also known for his efforts to rescue Jewish children from Germany and Eastern Europe, earning him threats from Nazi sympathizers.[19] In a speech made at the New York World's Fair Temple of Religion pavilion on June 13, 1939 he accused Father Coughlin of "playing footsie with the Nazis." He also attacked other pro-Nazi groups like the German American Bund, referring to them in as "the enemy within." His sponsor, not wishing to offend those elements sympathetic to Coughlin or the America First Movement lest they switch cigarette brands, declined to renew Cantor's contract. Except for an occasional guest appearance, Cantor remained off the air for a full year as possible sponsors were reluctant to underwrite a potentially controversial performer. When he returned to the airwaves the following season, sponsored by the Bristol Myers Company, Cantor credited his good friend, Jack Benny, with intervening on his behalf with the Young and Rubicam advertising agency.[20]

With the exception of *The Goldbergs* and *Abie's Irish Rose,* the two series that prominently featured Jewish themes and characters, several mainstream programs featured a Jewish character in a supporting role, either on an ongoing basis or as a frequent guest. In virtually every instance, the character was identified as being Jewish by his or her use of the Yiddish dialect, their name, and on some programs, their stereotyped behavior. The characters ranged from the wise and serious to the comedic and the programs they appeared on appealed to different audiences. For these reasons, it is difficult, if not impossible, to make generalizations as to what influence the characters might have had on middle America's overall perception of Jews.

Henry Burbig

A native New Yorker, Henry Burbig (1903-1980), honed his skills as a Yiddish dialect comedian in vaudeville, much in the mold of performers such as Willie Howard, Lou Holtz and others. His specialty was the retelling of popular poems and stories in which his use of dialect may well have generated more laughter than the cleverness of the actual content of the skit.

His earliest known appearance on radio was as a guest on a 1928 CBS variety program, *Vitaphone Jubilee Hour,* heard evenings at 9:30pm. Impressed with his burlesque-like routines, that same year he was hired by the CeCo Company, a manufacturer of radio tubes, to appear on its *CeCo Couriers'* program that aired at 8:30pm, also on the CBS network. When the company offered copies of Burbig's four minute "poetry" readings to listeners, the requests reportedly "poured in" and Burbig's success was assured.

A typical Burbig routine on *CeCo Couriers'* was the following rendition of the story of Robinson Crusoe.

> S'twas leeving ah lung time ago, s'twas leeving...ah man from de name Robinski Crusoe...he vas ha harring kippererer. So vun day vhile he vas out of his boat, trying to ketch ah copple harrings, ah terrible stumm came out from de nort end stotted to rock de boat...beck vid fro...pro vid con...horowertical vid prozontal. So Robinski got werry scarred, end geese peemples broke out all ower his goilish figger...so he stotted to sanding out hess ho hess singals to de rast ships, bot dey deen't hoid his singals, cuss dey vas too veek...he deen't have CeCo tubes, dot dope.

Burbig went on to host at least two of his own programs. During the 1930-31 season, he was heard on *Burbig's Syncopated History*, a CBS program on which he again presented fables in a Yiddish dialect along with musical interludes. On a second program broadcast on the NBC-Red network, *Burbig's Rhythm Boys*, (dates unknown), the comedian appeared with the music group, the Rhythm Boys. The program was sponsored by the Gillette Sports Razor Company.

Burbig also made guest appearances on several programs. In 1930, he appeared on the CBS network on the *Philco Hour* with Fanny Brice (in her first radio appearance) in burlesque-like skits, hamming it up in dialect as they retold the stories of Romeo and Juliet (February 5th) and Samson and Delilah (March 19th).[21] He also appeared on *Cheer Up America, The Hammerstein Music Hall* and *The Necco Surprise Party*, although the dates of these appearances are not known.

In 1929, taking a lesson from Milt Gross, the comic strip artist/comedian/radio performer who turned his Yiddish dialect skills into several volumes, including *Nize Baby*, Burbig wrote *Leffing Ges*, his own book of "leetle ferry jeengles."

The only audio containing Burbig's voice that the authors have been able to locate is an April 25, 1935 broadcast on which he appears in a brief walk-on part on the *Brad and Al* program that aired on WABC, the New York City CBS station.

In later years, Burbig continued to work for CBS as a director and producer. Sometime in the 1950s, he made a transition to television, and for an unspecified period of time, he followed Bob Keeshan (of *Captain Kangaroo* fame) as the host and performer on a children's television program, *Tinkers Workshop*, broadcast on WJZ/WABC, Channel 7 NYC.

Mrs. Nussbaum (Allen's Alley on the *Fred Allen Show*)

One mainstream comedian who infused his scripts with ethnic dialect throughout much of his radio career was Fred Allen.[22] Long before Allen ever strolled down the path known as Allen's Alley and Minerva Pious made her debut as Pansy Nussbaum, versatile cast members were heard speaking with Russian, German, Scottish, Cockney, Dutch, French, Yiddish and an assortment of other voices. Few listeners of Asian origin were likely to have appreciated the humor in Allen's frequent portrayal of the Chinese detective "One Long Pan" (Charlie Chan) first heard on May 1, 1935.

One of the earliest appearances of a Jewish character on a Fred Allen program was the March 21, 1934 broadcast of *The Hour of Smiles*. In the episode, actor Irwin Delmore was cast as the Jewish owner of a pet shop who, in a courtroom scene, accused someone of shoplifting a cat. In other episodes, the actor is identified as a Mr. Pinkbaum and speaks with a strong Yiddish accent.[23]

The very first Fred Allen program featuring Allen's Alley was broadcast on December 6, 1942. The earliest denizens of the Alley included Alan Reed who portrayed Falstaff Openshaw, Jack Smart as Senator Bloat, Pat C. Flick as Pablo Itthepitches, Charlie Cantor as Socrates Mulligan and occasionally as Pierre Nussbaum, John Brown as John Doe, and with the exception of Fred and Portland Hoffa (his wife), the Alley's longest surviving cast member, Minerva Pious, who played Pansy Nussbaum. Pious (1903-1979) had been providing the voices of Jewish women in comedy sketches since joining Allen's cast in 1933. In the years that followed, all but Pious were replaced as residents of the Alley. In addition to Nussbaum, the other most remembered cast members of the Alley were Peter Donald as Ajax Cassidy, Parker Fennelly as Titus Moody and Kenny Delmar as Senator Claghorn. Allen's Alley remained a staple of the *Fred Allen Show* until the program's final broadcast in 1949.

Initially, NBC executives expressed concern over the Nussbaum character, fearing that the heavy Yiddish accent might offend Jewish listeners. They relented, however, after Allen and his representatives pointed out that Jewish dialect comedy had been used in vaudeville and burlesque for thirty years without offending anyone.[24] In his book *Treadmill to Oblivion*, Allen described the Nussbaum character: "Her Jewish housewife was never the routine, offensive burlesque caricature. Mrs. Nussbaum was a human being, warm, honest, understanding and — 'you should pardon the expression' — very funny."[25] The character was also seen in a positive light by Jack Gould, the radio critic for *The New York Times,* who described Nussbaum as "...a rich characterization in the first place, to be sure, but it is executed with faultless timing and a magnificent sense of appreciation. Miss (Minerva) Pious is providing a comic cameo that shouldn't be missed."[26]

The positive reception notwithstanding, at least one listener denounced Mrs. Nussbaum in a 1948 letter to the president of NBC.[27] "Mrs. Nussbaum is no longer funny — she is merely a grievous racial stereotype in an age where too many graves attest to the evils of racial stereotypes." The letter writer went on to complain about the characterization of Ajax Cassidy, the Irish resident of the Alley.

While there were variations in Mrs. Nussbaum's weekly appearances on Allen's Alley, she is best remembered for those sketches in which Allen's knock on her door elicited gems of wit worthy of being repeated and remembered. The first three lines of the Allen/Nussbaum exchange followed a set pattern: Allen would knock, Mrs. Nussbaum would respond, "Nuu," and then Allen would reply, "Ah, Mrs. Nussbaum." The laugh-line usually came next with Pansy Nussbaum's sarcastic response:

1/31/43:	You were expecting maybe Becky Davis?
10/7/45:	You were expecting maybe Emperor Shapiro Hito?
10/14/45:	You were expecting maybe the Smiling Irishman?
10/28/45:	You were expecting maybe Dinah Schnorer?
11/11/45:	You were expecting maybe Lauren Bagel?
11/25/45:	You were expecting maybe Katharine Schlepburn?
12/2/45:	You were expecting maybe Cecil B. Schlemiel?
12/16/45:	You were expecting maybe Rosalyn Yussel?

Other Nussbaum moments were equally memorable, such as:

- When she gave up eating mincemeat because she didn't want the butcher to kill "a little mince" just for her.

- When the soap powder she had purchased to wash her husband's shirt turned out to be baking powder, she told Allen, "One sleeve is a strudel."

- When she told Allen that she had read the story of *Schmo White and the Seven Schwartzes* to a neighbor and had enjoyed reading the poetry of Heimie Wadsworth Longfellow and Rudyard Kaplan.

Shlepperman (*The Jack Benny Program*)

Jack Benny, Fred Allen's pretend feuding partner, became a regular on radio in May, 1932, five months before Allen's first broadcast. Like Allen, Benny got his start in vaudeville where he was exposed to the dialect comedy routines common in those days. He also employed several talented dialect performers during his long radio career, including the well known Mel Blanc whose single syllable "Si, Sy, Sue, Saw" routine in a Mexican dialect remains a classic. The same could said of Blanc's painful French accent as Benny's violin teacher, Professor LeBlanc. Benny's vocalist, Dennis Day, was also a talented mimic and Eddie Anderson, popularly known as Rochester, had simply to be himself in order to be representative of the African-American community. Over the years Rochester's character underwent several changes, beginning with his employment as a Pullman porter to becoming Benny's chauffeur, valet and butler, and generally holding his own against his boss.

Always looking for fresh talent, Benny met Sam Hearn (1900-1964) at a Friars Club meeting where Hearn was entertaining the members with a Yiddish dialect routine featuring a Mr. Shlepperman.[28] Impressed by Hearn's performance, Benny invited the comedian to appear on his program, although he initially used Hearn not as Shlepperman but in small roles in a series of ever changing sketches. In his first appearance on the program on June 2, 1933, for example, Hearn played Watson opposite Benny's portrayal of Sherlock Holmes in a comic detective routine.[29]

After appearing on Benny's program 19 times in a series of bit roles, Hearn's Yiddish speaking Shlepperman character debuted on August 3, 1934 in another detective comedy sketch, "The Stooge Murder Case." The routine may well have earned Hearn the distinction of having created the first continuing Jewish character to appear on a regularly scheduled prime time mainstream broadcast.[30] When Shlepperman appeared in subsequent sketches, his persona varied according to the dictates of the routine, but two characteristics remained constant: his Yiddish dialect and his trademark opening, "Hello, stranger."

Eight weeks elapsed before Shlepperman appeared again on the Benny program on September 28, 1934, although Hearn had appeared twice in other roles during that time. Four broadcasts later, on November 4, 1934, Hearn was back again in the role of Shlepperman. He appeared as Shlepperman on six of the final eight broadcasts of 1934, clearly suggesting that listener reaction to the character was positive. During the 1934 broadcast season, Hearn made a total of 26 appearances on the Benny show, eight of them as Shlepperman. In 1935, all but three of his 16 appearances on the Benny program occurred during the first three months of the year and eight of his 16 appearances, or one half of them, were as Shlepperman. In 1936, 12 out of 19 of Hearn's appearances were as Shlepperman. As the Yiddish speaking character grew in popularity, Hearn made occasional guest appearances on other radio programs such as *Glamour Manor* and *The Great Gildersleeve*.

After 1936, the number of Hearn's appearances on subsequent Benny programs slowly diminished. Milt Josefsberg, one of Benny's gag writers and the author of a biography about the comedian, speculated that the reason the Shlepperman character faded away may have been related to the rise of Hitler and the subsequent increase of anti-Semitism.[31] Hearn's last regular appearance on the Benny show in the guise of Shlepperman occurred on January 31, 1943. While he appeared on Benny's radio programs some 21 times between December, 1946 and February, 1955, he was heard again as Shlepperman only one more time, on December 22, 1946.

What follows is an example of Hearn as Shlepperman. In the scene from a May 31, 1942 broadcast, he plays the part of the High Lama in a take-off of the film, *Lost Horizon*. Benny plays the Ronald Colman part.[32]

Jack:	Your Excellency!
Hearn:	Hello, stranger.
Jack:	Shlepperman!
Hearn:	Quiet, I'm a lama now.
Jack:	A lama?
Hearn:	And I thought I was joining the Elks.
Jack:	Well, tell me Shlep, how are you doing in Shangri-La.
Hearn:	Oye, Jackie-boy, am I making money...everybody here lives to be three hundred years old, four hundred, five hundred, there's no limit...I tell you Jackie, I'm cleaning up.
Jack:	What do you do?
Hearn:	I sell birthday candles.
Jack:	Birthday candles? You must be making a fortune...Say, is your wife here with you?
Hearn:	How else could I get nine hundred years so quick?
Jack:	Oh, that's right.

Hearn:	Well kiddies, I got to toodle along now to the Shangri-La airport.
Jack:	Oh, do you have an airport here?
Hearn:	Yes, that's where the bombers leave for Tokyo.

Mr. Kitzel (*The Jack Benny Program*)

Artie Auerbach (1903-1957), another talented Yiddish dialectician who enjoyed performing at private parties, was originally a successful photographer for a New York tabloid, but gave up the newspaper business for a career as an entertainer.[33] Long before he appeared on the Benny program, he was heard, at one time or another, in different roles on *The Goldbergs*, the Eddie Cantor program, *The Great Gildersleeve*, Jack Haley's *Log Cabin Jamboree,* and in 1937 on *Al Pearce and His Gang*.

Although Auerbach's Yiddish dialect character, Mr. Kitzel, is generally associated with *The Jack Benny Program*, the character's first known radio appearance was on the January 24, 1940 broadcast of *Al Pearce and His Gang*. (Auerbach's first known use of the Yiddish dialect was earlier, on November 6, 1937 when he played a bit part on *Log Cabin Jamboree*. In a sketch, Jack Haley played an officer in the French Foreign Legion who engaged in conversation with Auerbach portraying a Sergeant Lafayette.) Mr. Kitzel also made at least one known guest appearance on *The Kate Smith Hour* on May 7, 1943 and several on *The Abbott and Costello Program* in 1944 and 1945.

Mr. Kitzel did not appear on the Benny program until January 6, 1946, some six years later.[34] The character's name was not used — but by then, it is likely that audiences were familiar with the voice and the character and no introduction was needed. The sketch had Mary and Jack at the Rose Bowl game on New Years Day.

Jack:	Hey mister! Four hot dogs, please...
Kitzel:	Yes sir (sings) "Pickle in the middle and the mustard on top, just the way you like 'em and they're always hot... Four puppies. Coming up!
Jack:	How much are they?
Kitzel:	Three cents apiece.
Jack:	Three cents???
Kitzel:	Uh-huh...
Jack:	Why do you sell them so cheap?

Kitzel:	Taste 'em!
Jack:	Oh...say, they do look...they do look like pretty tough weenies.
Kitzel:	Tough? Hoo hoo hoo! What suitcase handles they would make.

Two weeks later, on January 20th, Mr. Kitzel was back on the program, still selling hot dogs, still without a name and still singing the "pickle in the middle and the mustard on top" jingle that went on to become a popular phonograph record. News reports of people around the country singing the little ditty about the "pickle in the middle" made it clear to Benny and his writers that after three years without a Yiddish dialect character (Sam Hearn's Shlepperman character having made his last appearance in 1943) it was now okay to bring back a Yiddish sounding cast member as a regular guest.

Between 1946-1955, Auerbach made more than 100 appearances on the Benny program, primarily, but not always, as Mr. Kitzel. At one time, he tried to create a spin-off program using the Kitzel character but the idea was never picked up. When Sam Hearn asked Benny if he could return to the program, he had to assure the host that he would portray another continuing character as there was no possibility that Shlepperman would replace Kitzel who was by now the regular Jewish voice on the Benny show. As a result, when Hearn occasionally appeared on the program, his new persona was that of a "rube" from Calabasas County.

Papa David Solomon (*Life Can Be Beautiful*)

While the comedic characters portrayed by Minerva Pious, Sam Hearn and Artie Auerbach (Mrs. Nussbaum, Shlepperman and Mr. Kitzel) may be the most memorable of the continuing Jewish characters on mainstream radio, a fourth Jewish character from a different program genre was equally memorable and presented a very different Jewish image to the listening audience.

One of the most listened to soap operas during radio's Golden Age was *Life Can Be Beautiful* (September, 1938-June, 1954). With dozens of soaps for housewives and other stay-at-homes to listen to, *LCBB* (the shortened title that was frequently used when referring to the program) was popular, in part, because of its inspirational theme. Following the opening

Life Can Be Beautiful: Left to right: Ralph Locke, Alice Reinheart, John Holbrook

Sam Hearn (Shleppermann)

Minerva Pious (Mrs. Nussbaum)

George Jessel

Kaltenmeyer's Kindergarten: Left to right: Bruce Kamman, Thor Erickson, Marian Jordan, Merrill Fugit, Jim Jordan, Johnny Wolf (Izzy)

commercial for Procter & Gamble soap, the announcer would read a quote from author John Ruskin to the effect that: "Whenever money is the principal object of life, it is both got ill and spent ill, and does harm both in getting and spending. When getting and spending happiness is our aim, life can be beautiful."

One year before the program's final broadcast on June 25, 1954, a victim of the rise of television, *Time* magazine, on September 7, 1953, carried a brief article, "This, Too, Will Pass," that summarized the essence of the program: "One September day in 1938, Papa David Solomon of NBC's *Life Can Be Beautiful* gave shelter in his secondhand bookstore to a teen-aged slum girl named Chichi and put her to bed on a pallet in the rear of his shop. This week, 15 years later, Chichi is only about five years older and she's still camped in Papa David's back room." The article went on to tell the running plot of the soap opera with Chichi facing the problems of a young girl trying to survive in the inner city and her love interest, Stephen Hamilton, a young cripple who also lived with Papa David.

The cement that held the entire series together — and what made it unique in radio's portrayal of Jews — was the character of Papa David, the owner of the Slightly Read Bookshop, a clever name for a used bookstore (unless some cynic were to translate "read" to "red," meaning communist). Although he owned a bookstore, Papa David was not well off financially. He was kind. He was charitable. He was wise. Above all, the advice he gave Chichi and others was such that listeners could nod their heads to and say "Amen." When a respondent in a survey of daytime serial listeners was asked if the program helped her in any way, she responded: "I think Papa David helped me to be more cheerful when Fred, my husband, comes home. I feel tired and instead of being grumpy, I keep on the cheerful side."[35]

The role of Papa David was played by Ralph Locke (188?-1954), a successful stage actor who began his radio career in 1935. Although he is credited with having appeared in scores of other programs, including *Second Husband, Big Sister, Death Valley Days, Gang Busters* and *Young Dr. Malone*, Locke is best remembered for his portrayal of Papa David, a role he played for the entire 16-year run of the series. In sharp contrast to the squeaky, sing-song, comedic Yiddish accent of radio's other Jewish "David" (Uncle David on *The Goldbergs* played by Menasha Skulnik), Locke's accent kept the traditional lilt and pronunciation but the words were delivered in a quiet calm voice that exuded wisdom and age. Both actors were masters of their trade: if one voice led to laughter, the other, most assuredly, led the listener to thoughtful contemplation, which for soap operas of that period, was quite an achievement.

If there was a lesson to be learned from the *LCBB* scripts written by Don Becker and Carl Bixby and the vocal performance of Ralph Locke, it was that a mainstream soap opera with a clearly identified Jewish character playing a pivotal role could sell the sponsor's product. What is not known is what portion of the program's listeners accepted the Papa David characterization as being representative of the Jewish community. However, the fact that the program enjoyed such a long run on both CBS and NBC does indicate that listeners responded well to the character of a kindly old gentleman, regardless of his religion or ethnic background.

In addition to the dozen or so regular *LCCB* episodes that have survived, a special series of five programs broadcast as part of the World War II era program *Victory Front* is also extant. *Victory Front* was a government sponsored program in which the casts of a number of popular programs used their radio personas in special scripts designed to build national unity and help the war effort.[36] The *LCBB* broadcasts, which were introduced by Conrad Nagel, presented a serialized dramatization of what life in America would be like under Nazi rule. The plots were presented as a series of dream sequences, or more like nightmares, experienced by Chichi. In each episode, the listener was given a taste of how the loss of freedom would affect Americans. In one, almost surrealistic episode, Papa David was engaged in an argument with a Nazi official concerning the books he could sell in his shop. In the "new" world, Papa David would have been arrested, shot or sent to a concentration camp and the shop long since closed. In the episode, Papa David, perhaps reminiscent of the famous speech in the *Merchant of Venice* in which Shylock speaks of having the same characteristics as other humans, makes a poignant argument that Americans are all alike. By reminding the listener that the Nazis would not put up with cripples like Stephen, the back-talk of gentiles like Chichi or the lack of loyalty shown by the neighborhood butcher who happened to be a German Catholic, Papa David was saying that all Americans were facing the same threat. Clearly the government was doing all it could to enlist the radio industry to send a message to listeners: in time of war, we were all Americans, regardless of our ethnicity or religion and we must not give in to divisiveness.[37]

Abe Finkelsein (*Houseboat Hannah*)

Other than *The Goldbergs* and *LCBB*, the authors have been able to identify only one additional Golden Age soap opera with a recurring Jewish character: *Houseboat Hannah*. The series was about the life of Hannah O'Leary, her husband Dan and their family and friends, including Abe Finkelstein. Abe was involved in a business venture with Hannah and his daughter Becky stayed with Hannah while he was away on business. Besides his name, Finkelstein's Yiddish accent clearly identified him as being Jewish. His daughter, however, as a first generation American, spoke without a trace of an accent.

The series originated in 1936 in Chicago as a Frank and Anne Hummert syndicated program, initially sponsored by Procter & Gamble's Lava soap. The program was carried by Mutual on a sustaining basis during the 1937-1938 season, and from September 26, 1938 to April 25, 1941, the program aired on NBC, again sponsored by Lava soap.

The story dealt with the struggles of an Irish-American family to overcome hardships while living on a houseboat anchored on what was called Shanty Fish Row on San Francisco Bay. In the three 1939 episodes that the authors have heard, the heroine Hannah has been endowed with friends and acquaintances of several ethnic backgrounds, including one named Pasquale (portents of the *Life With Luigi* series yet to come). The program's musical theme was, quite appropriately, the Irish ballad, *The Last Rose of Summer*. Both Henrietta Tedro and Doris Rich played the part of Hannah while Norman Gottschalk portrayed Dan O'Leary. Other cast members included Lester Damon, Nancy Douglas, Virginia Dwyer, Don Gallagher, John Larkin and William Rose.

The following exchange between Abe and Becky, taken from an episode broadcast on June 16, 1939, takes place at the train station where Abe is on his way to the city to try to sell the lobsters trapped by the O'Leary clan.[38]

Becky:	Papa, papa, don't rush around so.	
Abe:	Nuu, she tells me not to rush and will you look at the clock yet. Becky darling, you think that my train is going to wait for me?	
Becky:	But you have ten minutes and all that remains is for you to walk across the track.	
Abe:	Dots all, and how long does it take to carry the suitcase and the samples? Becky, please don't walk so slow.	

Isadore (Izzy) Finkelstein (*Kaltenmeyer's Kindergarten*)

Another, much younger radio Finkelstein, was Isadore (a.k.a. Izzy) who appeared regularly in the early comedy-variety show known as *Kaltenmeyer's Kindergarten*. The program debuted on October 14, 1932 from Chicago's WMAQ. The series was created by Bruce Kamman who portrayed headmaster Kaltenmeyer, the teacher whose task it was to keep order among the zaniest group of students one could imagine. The cast represented a virtual League of Nations with Kamman affecting a German or Dutch accent, Izzy Finkelstein, played by Johnny Wolfe, speaking with a true-to-form Yiddish dialect, Harold Peary (of *The Great Gildersleeve* fame) playing a student with an Italian accent and Thor Ericson as a Swedish student. The program's best known alumni were Jim and Marian Jordan, each of whom would play several roles (one of Jim's roles was Mickey Donovan).[39] During the 1936-1937 season, the program was ranked fifth in popularity for daytime programs.[40]

Among the repeated gags used to poke fun at Izzy was his reputation for trying to sell the famous Finkelstein two-pants suit while in class or hearing Kamman repeat the admonition: "Wake up Izzy, wake up." These traits did not quite make Izzy a character that listeners were likely to admire.

Early in 1940, as war in Europe became a reality, the idea of a German headmaster, humorous or otherwise, in charge of Izzy and his classmates was reason enough to result in a change of program title and theme. The renamed series became *Kindergarten Kapers* and Kamman was renamed Professor Ulysses S. Applegate. The change proved insufficient, however, to rescue the program beyond September 14, 1940 when it went off the air for good.[41] At least one episode of the program is known to have survived, along with several scripts.

In this excerpt of a typical headmaster/Izzy exchange taken from the December 12, 1936 broadcast, Kaltenmeyer is calling the roll and comes to Izzy (Isadore).

> Izzy: Teacher, here I am and I'm wide awake. Oh. I can't sleep for thinking about the Christmas bargains at Finkelstein's store.
> Kalt: Isadore. Please. No advertising.
> Izzy: Well, teacher. For this week only, if you buy a two pants suit, we sew your initials in it free.
> Kalt: Initials. That's very nice Isadore, albie you know it ain't

Kalt:	the initial cost. It's the upkeep. Ha. Ha. Ha. Laugh children. That's my joke.
Chldrn:	Ha. Ha. Ha.
Izzy:	All right then. For the upkeep we'll throw in a pair of suspenders

(LAUGHTER)

Kalt:	Never mind all that.

(LAUGHTER)

Kalt:	The question is: Are you here?
Izzy:	Absolutill. Positivall. And certaintude. And besides that, I'm sure of it.
Kalt:	Oh. One positivill, absolutill and certaintudel in the book for Isadore. And how is your papa and mama getting along, Isadore?
Izzy:	Oh, they're all right teacher. But mama never sits in papa's lap anymore.
Kalt:	Oh, that's too bad. I suppose that means their romance has disappeared.
Izzy:	No. It's papa's lap that disappeared.

(LAUGHTER)

Kalt:	Quiet please in the classroom. Isadore, you tell your papa that he should ought to reduce his weight.
Izzy:	Oh, you mean he should mark himself down from 250 to 198?
Kalt:	Well, something like that. Your papa ought to exercise more. Why don't he take up golf?
Izzy:	Oh, he tried that teacher but he can't play golf.
Kalt:	No. Why not?
Izzy:	Well, because when he puts the ball where he can see it, he can't hit it. You see, and when he puts it where he can hit it, he can't see it.

(LAUGHTER)

Harry Hershfield (*Can You Top This?*)

Harry Hershfield, the creator of the *Meyer the Buyer* series discussed in Chapter 5, was far better known as one of the three raconteurs on *Can You Top This?* Their job was to come up with jokes that were funnier than those submitted by members of the listening audience. The program enjoyed a 14-year run, from December 9, 1940 to July 9, 1954, and was heard at various times on the Mutual, NBC and ABC networks.

The program's format was simple but effective. A half-dozen or so jokes were selected from the literally thousands that were sent in each week by listeners. These were told by versatile dialectician Peter Donald (of Allen's Alley/Ajax Cassidy fame) who would enhance the submission by giving each joke just the right touch of voice and emotion. A laugh meter (named after the current sponsor) would measure studio audience response to the joke at which time Hershfield and his co-panelists, "Senator" Ed Ford and Joe Laurie Jr., were each challenged to come up with a joke in the same general category that scored higher on the laugh meter. Monetary awards given to listeners whose jokes were selected were insignificant by today's standards, $5.00 initially and later $10.00, and were enhanced by an additional $2.00 each time the panelists were unable to top the listener's joke.

The program attracted listeners who enjoyed hearing three old codgers put a fresh spin on jokes, some of which were old enough to have appeared in *Joe Miller's Joke Book*. At a time when dialect was being used less and less on the radio, listeners could still hear Harry Hershfield delivering one of his jokes in a strong Yiddish dialect. Other panel members, when appropriate, would tell the jokes using Irish, German, Cockney and plain old-fashioned English. Laurie, a former vaudevillian, was also known to match or exceed Hershfield in the number of jokes featuring people with Jewish sounding names. He also added a touch of Yiddish dialect when the joke was about a person named Bloomberg, Epstein, Weinstein and the like. Many a listener could be heard the following day repeating the jokes heard on the program. As the program originated in New York City and its studio audience was made up primarily of New Yorkers, it may not be stretching a point to suggest that the frequent use of both the Yiddish and Irish dialect by members of the panel was motivated more by a desire to please the audience than the need to tell an otherwise simple joke. But, as performers were likely to say, "That's show business!"

A typical Hershfield joke, told in a Yiddish accent, went something like this:

> Little Pinkus was on the witness stand. One of those tough lawyers was giving him a rough questioning and every time Pinkus answered, the lawyer would sneer at him. What do you do for a living? snapped the lawyer. I'm a calciminer,[42] answered Pinkus and not a very good one at that. Oh a calciminer, eh? sneered the lawyer. What do you think your status is in society? Well, admitted

Pinkus, I couldn't get in the Four Hundred, that I know, but I still feel that I'm doing better than my father did. What was your father? snapped the attorney. A shyster lawyer, answered Pinkus.

Its popularity notwithstanding, the program did come in for criticism from at least some Jews. In 1944, four years into the series, Samuel H. Flowerman, the Executive Director of the Jewish Community Relations Committee of the Essex County (New Jersey) Council of Jewish Agencies, wrote to the American Jewish Committee expressing his concerns:

> Jewish-dialect stories which portray the Jew as a sharp, unethical, cunning character — even when told by Jews — in my opinion serve to reinforce the stereotypes of the Jew which is held by Christians. Harry Hershfield, Lou Holtz and others are excellent raconteurs, but when their stories go out over a nationwide hook-up, they may be doing a good deal of harm.[43]

The letter went on to give an example of how stereotype jokes could backfire. At a school fire prevention assembly, a fire department official told a joke about an Irishman, Scotsman and Jew. In the story, the Jew got the better of the other two. After delivering the punch line, the official said: "Some people are always trying to take advantage of others."

Mr. Horowitz (*Life With Luigi*)

The trip from kindergarten to night school, at least on the radio, took eight years; the time span between *Kaltenmeyer's* last broadcast (1940) and the debut of *Life With Luigi* (September 21, 1948). Carried by CBS, the program remained on the air until March 3, 1953, a five-year run that ended when it could no longer compete with television.

Radio writers had no hesitation borrowing script ideas or themes from other sources. The standard opening for *Life With Luigi* drew heavily on both George Jessel's routine of calling his mother on the phone and the even earlier *Cohen on the Telephone* recordings in which Cohen recited his many frustrations. Every week, the program started with Luigi writing a letter to his mother back in Italy. A typical letter would begin with "Dear Mama Mia," followed by a brief sentence or two explaining Luigi's latest experience in America which then became the story line of that particular episode.

Unlike *Kaltenmeyer's Kindergarten*, which to a large extent was slapstick in style, Luigi Basco, portrayed lovingly by versatile actor J. Carrol

Nash (who was born in Ireland and often played villains), provided audiences with inspirational themes in addition to laughter. Its premise was such that it would have been a perfect follow-up to the 1938-1939 series, *Americans All, Immigrants All*. Luigi, initially referred to as, "The Little Immigrant," was brought to America by a family friend, Pasquale (played by Alan Reed), whose goal in life was to find a husband for his overweight daughter, Rosa. While the hero was Italian, the plots could apply to almost any immigrant group. In many episodes, Luigi, intent on becoming an American citizen, attended night school where he enjoyed the friendship and camaraderie of his classmates Horowitz (a Jew played by Joe Forte), Schultz (a German played by Hans Conried), and Olsen, a Swede (played by Ken Peters). Luigi shared his problems with his night school classmates and all-American teacher, Miss Spaulding, and in return, received both sympathy and advice in the individual style and dialect of each classmate, as illustrated in the following exchange from the December 27, 1949 episode.

> Luigi: Excuse-a me, Miss Spaulding (the teacher), but soona is gonna be New Year's Eve and ...I'm a no have enough-a money to call my Mamma on the telephone...
>
> Miss S: Aw...
>
> Olsen: Oh, poor Luigi...he is homesick...
>
> Schultz: Schtop, Olsen...Luigi iss here mit us...how can he be homezick? Schmile, Luigi...I'm just trying to sheer you up...
>
> Horw: Luigi...Luigi, how much would it cost to make a telephone call from Chicago to Italy?
>
> Luigi: Well, uh...how much is-a cost to make-a the call?
>
> Horw: Yes, how much?
>
> Luigi: I was-a ask long distance operator...she's-a tell me she's-a cost with-a government tax, fifteen dollars-a first three minutes...five dollars each-a next minute...
>
> Schultz; Ach! If you give a hiccup by mischtake you lost *three dollars*!
>
> Miss S: Yes, it is quite expensive...if you should speak to your mother for only ten minutes it would cost about fifty dollars...
>
> Olsen: Gee, that's a lot of money for a phone call...
>
> Horw: True, true...but when you wanta talk to your mother,

Horw:	a t'ousand dollars ain't too much…wait, Luigi, I got an idea for you…why don't you lend the fifty dollars from your friend Pasquale?
Miss S:	Mr. Horowitz, it is not *lend*…it is *borrow* fifty dollars from Pasquale…
Schultz:	What's the difference? Either vay he ain't gonna get it…Luigi, I got an even better idea…go into Pasquale's schtore ven he's not dere and make the call on his telephone…
Luigi:	No…no, thanks-a Schultz…but-a now I know what I'm-a do…it's-a hard to get-a money from-a Pasquale…but maybe he's-a gonna let me use-a his telephone and when-a the bill has-a come, I'm-a gonna pay off-a little by little…
Horw:	That's a good idea!
Schultz:	Oh, Luigi, are you a schmartkopf! Schmile…and vat if you don't pay him back zo quick? Vat can Pasquale do to you? Can he zue you in court? Can he take avay your schtore? Can he make you marry his daughter Roza?
Luigi:	(Timidly) Schultz-a, can he?
Schultz;	About the zuing and the house, I don't know…but about Roza…on dat I can giff you my guarantee!

Millie Bronson (*Meet Millie*)

Meet Millie was a late comer to radio, making its debut on CBS on July 2, 1951. Its plot line was much like that of *The Adventures of Maisie* (1945-1947) and *My Friend Irma* (1947-1954), both CBS comedies about single young secretaries (so much for originality). Millie Bronson, played initially by screen actress Audrey Totter and later by Elena Verdugo, was a secretary who lived with her mother, played by Florence Halop. Marvin Kaplan was featured as friend and neighbor Alfred Prinzmetal, the poet laureate of Brooklyn. The program made its final radio appearance on September 23, 1954, although it enjoyed an overlapping career on television (October 1952 to March 1956), a respectable double run.

Enough episodes of this series have survived to give today's listeners the opportunity to hear the voices of its main characters. Millie, her mother and Alfred did not speak with the Yiddish accents typically heard in the 1930s and 1940s. Therefore, some listeners might have simply recognized their accent as being from New York or Brooklyn. There was, however, a distinct difference between their 1950s-style Yiddish sing-song lilt and the New York/Brooklyn accents of William Bendix's Chester Riley (*The Life of Riley*) or Shirley Booth's Miss Duffy (*Duffy's Tavern*). To listeners in the midwest, south or far west, the differences may not have been apparent. But listeners along the east coast were not to be fooled; their voices belonged to Jewish characters.

Sam Lapidus (Lou Holtz)

Lou Holtz (1893-1980) was a talented and versatile performer whose professional career began, as it did for so many other comedians, in vaudeville as early as 1914. Holtz actually began his career as a singer and was discovered by Elsie Janis, a popular vocalist who brought him to New York as a member of her trio. Holtz's early career was summed up in a September 25, 1944 *Time* magazine article that observed: "On Broadway, as a song and dance man, Holtz was a flop. He flopped again as a comic until he got the idea of telling his Jewish stories in blackface, clicked in vaudeville and climbed to George White's Scandals."[44] Holtz went on to play the Palace Theater, recorded some of his routines and appeared in two long-forgotten films made in the 1930s, *School For Scandal* and *Where Do We Eat?*

Holtz's most successful routines involved a character he called Sam Lapidus, a name he saw on a building sign in 1924. An early Lapidus laugh getter, spoken in heavy Yiddish dialect, would have Holtz saying, "In shoes I take a size eight, but size nine feels so comfortable I wear a size ten."

Once vaudeville began to fade in popularity, Holtz turned to radio where he became a frequent guest on Rudy Vallee's program. A typical Lapidus exchange had him telling the audience that he and a friend from Tzicagi (Chicago) having finished a stylish dinner together were confronted for the first time in their lives with finger bowls:

Lapidus: For vhat good is it for vhat? It kent be soup. Soup ve already hed it. It kent be vawter. Vawter is in the glesses, and vith lemon on the side has got me beffled complittly. I theenk I vill ask the vaiter.
Friend: Pliz dawnt hoomiliate me.
Lapidus: Vaiter, excuse the introoson, but for vhat are thiz two articles?
Waiter: These are to wash your fingers in.
Friend: See, you esk a foolish question you're entitled to a foolish enswer.

Vallee invited Holtz back to his program several times and at least nine of those programs have survived. Holtz was also a guest on a number of other high profile network programs such as the *Good News, The Trommers Troupers Show, The Kraft Music Hall,* and *The Radio Hall Of Fame.*

In addition to his many guest appearances, Holtz was also the star on the *Chesterfield Show* in 1933 and *Time Out For Laughs.* He also appeared in a syndicated series of five-minute programs, *The Lou Holtz Laugh Club.* While the Sam Lapidus character was used sparingly in many of his appearances, it was never completely discarded. Years after television overtook radio as America's most popular form of entertainment, the Lapidus character was revived when Holtz appeared on television with Merv Griffin, Jack Parr and Ed Sullivan. Today, many consider Holtz as the inspiration for a later generation of Jewish comedians, including Myron Cohen and Sam Levenson.

Notes
Abbreviations
AJC   American Jewish Committee Radio Department Archives at Yivo Institute, New York, NY.

1. Yiddish, a German based language, was the linga franca of the Eastern European Jews who immigrated to America in large numbers from the late 19th century and first two decades of the 20th century. By the time these immigrants began arriving, the German Jews who had immigrated in the mid 19th century were already assimilated into American culture and spoke without a "foreign" accent.

2. Lewis Herman and Marguerite Shalett Herman, Foreign Dialects: A Manual for Actors, Directors and Writers (Chicago: Ziff-Davis Publishing Company, 1943) 392-415. Writing in 1943, more than a decade after many Jewish characters had already become a fixture of popular radio shows, it is hard to know if the authors were simply documenting speech patterns that had already been established or were issuing prescriptions for what was to follow. Their description of pitch and nasality, for example, sounds very much like the voice of Menasha Skulnik who appeared on both *The Goldbergs* and *Abie's Irish Rose.*

3. Ibid., 393.

4. Michele Hilmes, Radio Voices: American Broadcasting, 1922-1952

(Minneapolis: University of Minnesota Press, 1997) and Susan J. Douglas, Listening In: Radio and the American Imagination (New York: Random House, 1999).

5. Douglas, Listening In, 368 (n4).

6. Ibid., 103.

7. Broadcasting, February 1, 1938, 60.

8. Alan Havig, *Fred Allen's Radio Comedy* (Philadelphia: Temple University Press, 1990), 192-193, 266 (n18).

9. Herman, *Manual of Foreign Dialects*, Preface.

10. Havig, *Fred Allen's Radio Comedy*, 192.

11. Milt Josefsberg, *The Jack Benny Show* (New Rochelle, NY: Arlington House, 1977), 85. As for Winchell's motivation, theater critic Henry Popkin wrote in "The Vanishing Jew of Our Popular Culture, *Commentary*, 14, #1, July, 1952, 47: "Walter Winchell, who used to print dialect jokes featuring one Max Mefoofsky, has since 1947 been campaigning against dialect stories with all the virtuous intolerance of a fallen woman reformed." Also Bob Thomas, *Winchell* (Garden City, NY: Doubleday & Company, 1971), 239, recounts that Jewish comedian Myron Cohen protested Winchell's use of the term "vomics," pointing out that much of his material came from what Winchell himself had printed as Mefoofsky jokes. Winchell, Thomas wrote, was not dissuaded, and some comedians lost their livelihoods because they were considered "vomics." See also page 99 for an example of Winchell's earlier use of the Jewish dialect that some Jews at the time considered to be anti-Semitic.

12. Michael Corenthal, *Cohen on the Telephone: A History of Jewish Recorded Humor & Popular Music, 1892-1942* (Milwaukee, WI: Yesterday's Memories, 1984).

13. Scripts of the Cohen routines are available in three publications which, though long out-of-print, are available from used book dealers. Joe Hayman, *Twenty Different Adventures of Cohen on the Telephone and Other Samples of Hebrew Humor* (New York: George Sully & Co., 1927); Joe Hayman, *Cohen on the Wireless* (London: Austin Rogers, 1920s); and Monroe Silver, *Monroe Silver's Famous Cohen on the Telephone: Over 100 Original Jokes, Stories, Monologues and Parodies As Recorded By the Author In His Popular Series of Phonograph Records* (New York: Irving Berlin Standard Music Corporation, 1927).

14. George Jessel, *Hello Momma* (Cleveland: World Publishing Company, 1946).

15. For details about these surviving programs, check the Internet site, www.radiogoldindex.com, a well respected reference that identifies more than 90,000 old time radio broadcasts. Despite their rare radio appearances, in the spirit of audiences that never tired of Abbott and Costello's "Whose On First" routine, Smith and Dale continued to revive their classic "Dr. Kronkeit" routine

to enthusiastic audiences. Neil Simon's stage and film hit, *The Sunshine Boys*, was based on the Smith and Dale story.

16. Sources differ on the details of Cantor's first appearance on radio. James Fisher in *Eddie Cantor: A Bio-Bibliography* (Westport, CT: Greenwood Press, 1997), 129, "presumes" that his first appearance was in 1921 as a guest on an unnamed WJZ radio program. Gregory Koseluk in *Eddie Cantor: A Life in Show Business* (Jefferson, NC: McFarland & Company, 1995), 351, says "it is generally believed" that Cantor's first broadcast occurred sometime either in late 1921 or early 1922 over WDY.

17. If there was ever a mainstream American entertainer of the Jewish faith who put principles over profit, it was Eddie Cantor. His reputation in this respect extends to his strong friendship with the black vaudeville comedian Bert Williams to his decision in 1945 to hire the black vocalist Thelma Carpenter.

18. Koseluk, *Eddie Cantor*, 365-366. Cantor's anti-Hitler remarks were to cause trouble again on March 27, 1939. In an informal post-broadcast session with the audience, Cantor entered into a fictitious dialogue involving a rabbi and Hitler. This led a naturalized American citizen born in Austria to heckle Cantor and yell out, "I'll fix that Jewish so-and-so" before leaving the theater. A few minutes later, the heckler and his wife were beaten outside the CBS studio and the man cited Bert Gordon, the Mad Russian, as one of the assailants. While not condoning the beating, Cantor is reported to have said, "My jokes about Hitler and Nazism aren't any different than jokes I've made about other prominent people in the public eye — like Roosevelt and Hoover, for instance." Cantor also denied that Gordon had been involved in the beating.

19. In addition to his regular network programs, during the 1930s-1950s Cantor appeared on a number of special radio broadcasts in support of Jewish causes including: 10/20/36 for Youth Aliyah; 11/28/40 for the Jewish Philanthropic Societies; 7/9/43 for Young Aliyah; 12/28/48 on a Jewish Theological Seminary program; 7/3/50 on "Israel, The Promised Land" for the United Jewish Appeal; 3/21/51 on "One Foot In Tomorrow," another United Jewish Appeal program; 10/31/55 on "Religion In American Life"; 4/7/57 on "Children of Light," part of *The Eternal Light* series; plus many appearances in support of other charities, particularly the March of Dimes and other wartime and refugee causes. Fisher, *Eddie Cantor*, 129-142.

20. Koseluk, *Eddie Cantor*, 366-367.

21. Brice originally contracted to do three skits for the program. It is not known if Burbig was to be in the third skit. The first program was not reviewed, but when Brice repeated the skit three days later as part of her routine at the Palace Theater with a different Romeo, *The New York Times* described the routine as "hilarious." When the second radio program received negative reviews (it is not clear from what source/s), the third program was cancelled. Barbara W. Grossman, *Funny Woman: The Life and Times of Fanny Brice*

(Bloomington, IN: Indiana University Press, 1991)185-86, 262 (n98). Brice repeated the Romeo and Juliet sketch on the January 12, 1933 broadcast of *The Fleischmann's Yeast Hour*. The actor who played Romeo is not identified. Copies of that program have survived.

22. It may well have been Allen's years in vaudeville as a juggler envying the laughs that the dialect comedians received that influenced the direction his radio humor. For additional insights into Allen's early radio career see Robert Taylor, *Fred Allen: His Life and Wit* (Boston: Little, Brown and Company, 1989); Alan Havig, *Fred Allen's Radio Comedy*; and Allen's own autobiography, *Treadmill to Oblivion* (Boston: Little, Brown and Company, 1954).

23. As the name Delmore does not appear in any of the many reference books dealing with the history of radio programming, media historians may speculate that the name really belongs to Kenny Delmar, the actor comedian who later created the character of Senator Claghorn on Allen's Alley.

24. John Crosby, *Out of the Blue: A Book About Radio and Television* (New York: Simon and Schuster, 1952), 275.

25. Allen, *Treadmill to Oblivion*, 193.

26. Jack Gould, "Mr. Allen's Comeback," *The New York Times*, October 14, 1945, sec 2, 5 cited in Havig, *Fred Allen's Radio Comedy*, 266 (n19).

27. Havig, *Fred Allen's Radio Comedy*, 193. For additional insights into Allen's use of ethnic humor on Allen's Alley see Chapter 8, "Allen's Alley," 183-209.

28. In Yiddish, to "schlep" means to carry, or alternately to move slowly and unwillingly.

29. Mary Livingston, Hilliard Marks and Marcia Borie, *Jack Benny: A Biography* (Garden City, NY: Doubleday, 1978), 66-67.

30. Although the Shlepperman character was given a first name, Irving, in this episode, in subsequent broadcasts no first name was used. In a later 11/25/34 broadcast the character is referred to as "J. Shlepperman Smith." For the most part, though, the singular name of Shlepperman was used. Laura Leff, *39 Forever*, 2 vols, (Piedmont, CA: The International Jack Benny Fan Club, 2004, 2006). Also, see Leff to identify the specific episodes on which Hearn appeared as Shlepperman.

31. Josefsberg, *The Jack Benny Show*, 109.

32. The sketch was a revised shorter version of a *Lost Horizon* routine first broadcast November 21, 1937. The reference to Shangri-La airport, added in this updated version, was a morale building salute commemorating the first American bombing raid on Tokyo on April 18, 1942 led by Jimmy Doolittle. The planes took off for the raid from the deck of the aircraft carrier, U. S. S. Hornet, which in the interest of wartime security was labeled "Shangri-La."

33. According to Milt Josefsberg, Benny's biographer, Auerbach worked for the now defunct *New York Daily Mirror*. However, an Auerbach obituary

stated that he worked for the New York *Daily News*. Considering that Josefsberg was writing scripts for Benny from 1943 onward, including those in which Auerbach appeared, the authors cast their vote for the *Daily Mirror*.

34. For the dates of Mr. Kitzel's appearance on the *Jack Benny Program* see Leff, *39 Forever*.

35. Paul F. Lazarsfeld and Frank N. Stanton, *Radio Research 1942-1943* (New York: Essential Books, 1944) 27.

36. The broadcasts was quite similar to the *Nazi Eyes on Canada* series broadcast by the Canadian CBC and was also reminiscent of the earlier effort of the United States government to foster a sense of national unity among different ethnic groups in the 1938-1939 series *Americans All, Immigrants All*.

37. The government's wartime goal of promoting inclusiveness recalls the 1945 statement by the Lutheran Pastor Martin Niemoller who died in a concentration camp:

> In Germany, they first came for the Communists and I did not speak out because I wasn't a Communist; then they came for the Jews, and I didn't speak up because I wasn't a Jew. Then they came for the Trade Unionists, and I didn't speak up because I wasn't a Trade Unionist. Then they came for the Catholics, and I didn't speak up because I was a Protestant. Then they came for me and by that time no one was left to speak up.

38. The practice of setting a scene on a train or at a railroad station was fairly common during radio's Golden Age as rail was the major means of long distance travel. *The Railroad Hour,* a long running program that featured an abbreviated operetta and starred Gordon MacRae, was sponsored by the Association of American Railroads. Jack Benny's writers made frequent use of a railroad setting as Benny traveled cross-country. Rochester made his very first appearance on *The Jack Benny Program* as a railroad porter. And who, after once hearing it, could forget the voice of Mel Blanc announcing stops at "Anaheim, Azusa and Cucamonga." Molly Goldberg said goodbye to her son Sammy on his way to war at a railroad station (see Chapter 2) and one of the few *Meyer the Buyer* episodes that anything is known about takes place at a train station (see Chapter 5). *Grand Central Station*, an otherwise quite ordinary half hour dramatic anthology, is best remembered for its powerful opening sequence in which "shining rails in every part of our great country are aimed at Grand Central Station, crossroads of a million private lives." Only train buffs would know, however, that the sound effect was of a steam locomotive, despite the fact that only diesel and electric-powered locomotives were used in the "real" Grand Central Terminal.

39. The Jordans, of course, would go on to star in their own program, *Fibber McGee and Molly*, a comedy series known for its use of dialect-speaking

walk-on characters.

40. CAB Ratings. *Variety Radio Directory, 1937-1938* (New York: Variety, 1938), 30.

41. Another wartime character that had to undergo an ethnicity change was the *Green Hornet's* Japanese valet Kato who, after December 7, 1941, almost overnight became a Filipino valet.

42. The word "calciminer" appears in the joke as it was reprinted in "Senator" Ed Ford, Harry Hershfield, Joe Laurie, Jr., *Can You Top This?* (Garden City, NY: Blue Ribbon Books, 1945), 102. There is no explanation of what a "calciminer" is or does. The three panel members authored a second book of jokes from the program, *Cream of the Crop* (New York: Didier, 1947).

43. Letter from Samuel H. Flowerman to Dr. Solomon Andhill Fineberg, November 28, 1944. AJC. Box 238, Folder Radio-TV Programs, 1940-1944.

44. At one point, Holtz was hired by the Schuberts as an understudy for Al Jolson to remind Jolson that he could always be let go. S. D. Trav, *No Applause, Just Throw Money* (Faber and Faber, 2005), 180.

7
Abie's Irish Rose: From Stage to Film to Radio

Long before environmentalists popularized the concept of recycling, the radio industry discovered the value of "borrowing" plots and concepts from films, plays, novels, magazine stories and even comic strips for material needed to fill the hundreds of hours of airtime. Often the recycled material made a successful transition to radio. Just as often, it did not. While the efforts of Harry Hershfield (*Meyer the Buyer*) and Montague Glass (*Potash and Perlmutter*) to bring their characters to radio failed to win the interest and loyalty of listeners, this chapter focuses on one of radio's more successful recycling efforts: Anne Nichols' popular play, *Abie's Irish Rose*. It also examines some of the more contentious aspects of how Jewish characters could be or should be portrayed on radio.

The Play

Who would have thought that a young woman, born in Georgia in 1891 and raised as a Baptist would write a Broadway play about a Jewish-Catholic marriage that, despite unflattering reviews at the time, went on to become the quintessential model of mixed marriages of its day?

Anne Nichols ran away from home at age sixteen, quite naively seeking a part in a play. Although lacking experience, she nonetheless managed to land a role in the chorus of a biblical play. She eventually married Henry Duffy, a Catholic actor/producer in either 1913 or 1915 (depending on which reference is cited), had a son (Henry), toured with her husband in vaudeville, and turned to writing when the couple needed money to purchase new material for their stage routines. Several of her plays were produced, including one co-written with Adelaide Matthews called *Just Married* that broke stock company records in three cities. After 10 years of marriage, Nichols divorced Duffy. At some point in her life (the date is uncertain), she converted to Catholicism.

Abie's Irish Rose, Nichols' story of a mixed marriage between an Irish Catholic girl and a Jewish boy, was staged initially in San Francisco and Los

Angeles where it was enthusiastically received. While the theme of romance between two individuals with different cultural backgrounds and feuding families was hardly a novel idea, it certainly was a popular one that dated back to Greek and Roman times. It was also the theme of Shakespeare's *Romeo and Juliet*. In 1908, 13 years before *Abie's Irish Rose* was written, theatergoers in New York and other major cities flocked to Israel Zangwill's play, *The Melting Pot*, the story of a love affair between an immigrant Jewish violinist, David Quixano, and Vera Revendal, the daughter of a Russian nobleman who years earlier was responsible for the pogrom that had massacred David's family.

Despite *Abie's* west coast success and the enthusiastic response to Zangwill's earlier play, when Nichols tried to bring her play to New York she received a less than enthusiastic reception. Much to her surprise and dismay, she discovered that the story of a mixed marriage did not appeal to the Broadway producers whose financial backing would be required for any production on the Great White Way. One producer is reported to have turned down the opportunity to purchase a half interest in the play's profits for $5.000.[1]

Undaunted, and believing enough in the merits of her own work, Nichols decided to produce the play herself. In order to raise the necessary funds, she mortgaged her house and went as far as borrowing money from the notorious gambler Arnold Rothstein. At the time, she was the sole female producer on Broadway, an establishment not only dominated by men, but mostly Jewish men. And, as they say, "The rest is history."

Abie's Irish Rose opened at the Fulton Theater on May 23, 1922. Despite almost unanimously negative reviews, the play became an overnight hit as word spread, especially among Jews, the Irish and other ethnic groups, about the hilarious and authentic new play about intermarriage. Ticket sales grew to the point that a theater with a larger seating capacity was needed and the play moved to the Republic Theater where it remained for five years. By the time it closed on October 1, 1927, the play had run for 2,327 performances — a box office record that held for the next 14 years.[2]

Foremost among the critics who panned the play was humorist Robert Benchley. Not satisfied to have dismissed the play when it opened, he returned numerous times during its long run to poke fun at his own judgment, the taste of theatergoers and the play itself. It was Nichols, however, who enjoyed the last laugh as after the play's record-breaking run on Broadway, it went on to enjoy equal success on the regional theater circuit and was even seen abroad in translation. When critic Alexander Woollcott called her play "unquestionably the most prosperous enterprise the world has ever known,"[3] he may have had in mind the $5 million dollars that the play had generated in revenue or the 11 million patrons who had seen it.

The plot is about Abraham Levy, a wounded World War I army pilot, who falls in love with and secretly marries (thanks to the services of a Protestant minister) Rosemary Murphy, a nurse he met while recuperating. As second generation Americans, the couple's religious and ethnic differences do not interfere with their romance. Both know, however, that their respective fathers who are widowers and who expect their children to marry within their own faith will be crushed when they find out what their children have done.

In the opening scene, highly reminiscent of the old *Cohen on the Telephone* phonograph records, the audience sees Solomon Levy, Abie's father, speaking on the telephone with a heavy Yiddish accent: "Hello! Who iss it? Yes Vot? Me! Yes. It's me. Who am me? Say who am you? What number? I don't know the number. I didn't get the phone to call myself."

As the play continues, Abie and his bride arrive at the Levy residence and Abie, hoping that his father will think that his wife is Jewish, introduces Rosemary as Rose Murpheski. As soon as Abie and his father are alone, the scene shifts to what some might view as a less than positive aspect of the Jewish character: Solomon inquires about Rosemary's financial status and then proceeds to give thanks for her being Jewish.

Shortly thereafter, Rabbi Samuels marries the couple for a second time, following which Rosemary's father Patrick and his priest, Father Whalen, arrive from California. When the two fathers meet, it doesn't take long before they discover the true religious identities of Abie and Rosemary, causing each father great displeasure. In a statement, quite impressive for the mid-1920s, Father Whalen reminds the two disappointed fathers:

> Shore they all had the same God above them. And what with the shells bursting and the shrapnel flying, with no one knowing just what moment death would come, Catholics, Hebrews and Protestants alike forgot their prejudices and came to realize that all faiths and creeds have about the same destination after all.

By the end of the play, the fathers are reconciled after Rosemary gives birth to fraternal twins who are named for Rosemary's Irish father and

Abie's deceased Jewish mother and both families sit down to a Christmas dinner that includes kosher food as well as a ham.[4]

In 1928, Hollywood released the first of what were to be two films based on the play. The silent film featured Charles "Buddy" Rogers, Nancy Carroll, and Jean Hersholt and was directed by Victor Fleming. Its plot was identical to that of the play. For those who couldn't get enough of the story, Grosset and Dunlap, a publishing firm that specialized in printing novelizations of popular movies, came out with a 324-page hardcover version of the story written as a novel. The book included illustrated scenes from the photoplay of the Paramount film. (See below for information about the second film.)

Nichols' popular story of a mixed marriage was even exploited by others while the play was still appearing on Broadway. In 1926, Universal Pictures began filming a series of comedy films about the Cohens and the Kellys that featured a Jewish groom and his Irish bride. Nichols sued, claiming the concept was hers, but the court ruled in favor of Universal finding that, "copyright protection cannot be extended to the characteristics of stock characters in a story whether it be a book, a play or a film."[5]

The Radio Version

In 1942, millions of Americans who had never seen the play or film or read the novel were introduced to Abie and Rosemary via radio. The theme of a mixed marriage was particularly relevant during wartime when it was important to demonstrate that people of different religious and ethnic backgrounds, facing the same problems, could live and work together in harmony. The program began as part of the *Knickerbocker Playhouse*, an anthology program. When the *Playhouse* went off the air, *Abie's Irish Rose* remained in the time slot as an ongoing series. The initial episodes closely followed the play: the couple repeated their wedding vows in two additional ceremonies; Rosemary gave birth to twins; and the fathers-in-law, while initially demonstrating hostility towards one another, slowly grew to appreciate each other. After the plot of the original play had been exhausted, future episodes followed the typical soap opera formula of a running story line that left the listener waiting to see how things turned out the following week.

As new plot lines were developed, the relationship between Abie and Rosemary continued to be the focus of the series. The program's humor, however, came from the interaction of the fathers-in-law as well as that of

Mr. and Mrs. Cohen, two characters who were carryovers from the play. Isaac Cohen, referred to as "Papale" (pop-ah-leh), was a friend of the family and Solomon's attorney. His overbearing wife, Mrs. Cohen, was affectionately known as "Mamale" (mam-ah-leh).

The program's three older generation Jewish characters, Solomon Levy and the Cohens, all spoke with a Yiddish accent and Yiddish expressions were sprinkled throughout their dialogue. When the first names of characters were used, for example, it was always Abiele (abe-ah-leh), Rosele (rose-ah-leh), Isassicle (eyes-ah-kul) and Patrickle (pat-reh-kul). Common Yiddish expressions were interwoven into the script without any explanation such as "Oi, vey ist mir," (Oh, woe is me), shlemiel (a clumsy bungler or an inept person), shmendrik (a nincompoop, or an alternate term for a shlemiel) and gantseh macha (a big shot). The scripts also made use of malapropisms (another technique used in the past to identify Jewish characters) such as the following example from a 1944 script when Solomon, talking about his great-great grandchildren-to-be refers to them as "your springoffs."

    Patrick: You mean offspring, Sol.
    Solomon: That's what I said — they will say it's my great great grandma — she was one of the FFB.
    Abie: FFV? — that's First Families of Virginia.
    Solomon: So I said FFB — First Families of the Bronx.

Or, when Solomon, complimenting Mrs. Cohen on her dinner tells her, "I loved your stuffed neck," and she replies, "So sometimes I'll stuff it again."

The series ran for 119 episodes, from January 24, 1942 through September 2, 1944. It was broadcast on the NBC-Red network at 8pm Saturday evening and was sponsored by Drene Shampoo. Nichols wrote the scripts with assistance from Morton Friedman and Alford Van Ronkel. Nichols was also credited as producer and director of the series although scripts in the authors' personal collection name James Haupt as the person in charge of the production. A September 13, 1942 newspaper clipping noted that Carlton Alsop was replaced by Axel Gruenberg as the program's director.

Radio fans are aware of the importance of memorable openings such as the announcer cautioning listeners, "Don't touch that dial. Listen to BLONDIE." Similarly, the opening of *Abie's Irish Rose* was designed to capture the attention of the listening audience. Each episode began with the sound of Solomon Levy's hearty laughter (the script called for chuckles building to laughter) followed by Patrick Murphy's Irish brogue asking, "What are you laughing at?" And Solomon responding, "What am I laughing at? I'm just laughing. What's the matter, there's a law against that?" Corny? Perhaps, but radio in the mid-1940s had more than its fair share of corn, most of which listeners seemed to enjoy.

If the program's opening was consistent week after week, so was its inspirational closing that was reminiscent of the speech that Father Whalen gave in the play when he tried to bring the two warring parents together by reminding them that during the midst of battle (World War I in the play) people of different faiths could come together. Each episode ended with the following sign-off: "Abie's Irish Rose is dedicated to the spirit of freedom and equality which gives to this nation the greatness that is America."

Sydney Smith was originally cast as Abie but when rumors regarding a possible film deal began to circulate, the part was given to Richard Coogan. Coogan, in turn, was replaced by Richard Bond who was replaced by Clayton Collyer. The part of Rosemary also went through several cast changes. Betty Winkler, the first Rosemary, was replaced by Mercedes McCambridge, who in turn was replaced by Marion Shockley who was replaced by Julie Stevens.

Solomon Levy was portrayed for most of the run by Alan Reed (who, as Teddy Bergman, played Meyer Mizznick on *Meyer the Buyer* and would later, as a skilled dialectician, play the part of Pasquale on another ethnic radio series, *Life With Luigi*). For a brief time, Alfred White and Lou Sorin also portrayed Solomon Levy. Patrick Murphy, the crusty Irish father with a heart of gold and temper that he occasionally controlled, was played throughout the entire series by Walter Kinsella.

The part of Isaac Cohen was played by Menasha Skulnik, an actor whose voice, once heard, was not likely to be forgotten. Skulnik's delivery was such that regardless of what he said, the audience was likely to respond with laughter. A veteran of the Yiddish stage, Skulnik was also heard as "Uncle David" on *The Goldbergs* during the same time period. Mrs. Cohen was played by Anna Appel, also a long time veteran of the Yiddish stage. There was little question that when the couple was together, it was Mrs. Cohen who would have her way. Over time, the character of Mrs. Cohen, as well as the way she was portrayed by Appel, became controversial and may have been a contributing factor in the program's cancellation. (See below.)

The only other continuing characters in the series were Lily, the Levy's maid, played not surprisingly by an actress who specialized in that type of role, Amanda Randolph. Radio audiences also heard Randolph as the battleaxe mother of Sapphire, Kingfish's long-suffering wife on *Amos 'n' Andy*. She was also one of the several actresses who portrayed Beulah, another radio maid, and Aunt Jemima, all of which says something about the casting problems faced by African-American actors in the 1940s, even when, on radio, they were heard, not seen. (Randolph's youngest sister, Lillian Randolph, also portrayed a maid on radio; in her case, putting up with the Great Gildersleeve.)

Other actors who appeared on this program from time to were: Carl Eastman (David Lerner), Ann Thomas (Casey, the secretary), Bill Adams (Father Whalen), Dolores Gillen (the Levy twins), Paul Douglas (J. Harrison Leonard, an artist) Florence Freeman (Marsha Brown, an interior decorator), Florence Williams (Nancy Johnson, a lodge guest) and Johnny Myers (John Call, Nancy's love interest).

The program's first announcer was Howard Petrie who was later replaced by Richard Stark. When Stark left the program on July 1, 1944 to join the Marine Corps, he was replaced by Dwight Weist. Stark's departure was treated quite dramatically when, at the conclusion of the program, listeners heard the following announcement:

> Folks, this is Walter Kinsella, better known to you listeners as Patrick Murphy. I just wanted to tell you that with tonight's show we're losing our fine announcer, Richard Stark, who is leaving Abie's Irish Rose, to be free to accept a commission in the United States Marine Corps. Having been a Marine myself in the last war, I know Dick has picked a great outfit. And when the Marines get Dick, they'll be getting a fine young fellow. Good luck to you, Dick, from the entire cast and the listening audience of Abie's Irish Rose.[6]

The program's musical opening began with a few bars of "My Wild Irish Rose," followed by a few measures of a Jewish melody and then additional bars of the same Irish theme. The closing music was simply "My Wild Irish Rose." The music was under the direction of Joe Rines with Jack Ward at the organ and Joe Stopak conducting the orchestra. Harry Hiller was the studio engineer and Robert Prescott provided the sound effects.

On February 8, 1942, after listening to the first three episodes of the program, *The New York Times* critic, John K. Hutchens, gave the new series a less-than-encouraging review. After savaging the 1922 play in several paragraphs, he went on to say that the radio version was at least better than its stage predecessor. The show's writing and acting, he added were:

> ...a bit more brisk on the air then they were on the stage. The humor is not yet what you would call subtle, but it is not dismally obvious. The hearts of the Levys and Murphys still beat with sentimental fervor, which, however, is less cloying than, if memory serves, it used to be. Although all of the original characters seem to be on hand, they do not talk so much — or rather they talk at less length — because there are more episodes. This is all to the good, and has an air of progress, though it scarcely adds up to what a cheerful announcer describes as 'a modern Romeo and Juliet.'

Hutchens then went on to speculate about what Nichols would do for a plot once she exhausted the material from the original play.

> The answer is simple enough. 'Abie' will be a soap opera played once a week at night, instead of every afternoon, as most soap operas are. Indeed, that may be the solution to the whole mystery of the original long run of 'Abie's Irish Rose.' Perhaps it was a sort of soap opera all the time, before people knew what soap operas were. Because, as everybody knows, a soap opera can be pretty bad and yet run forever.

The program's humorous segments took two forms: the friendly and light-hearted give-and-take that occurred between the fathers-in-law and the more contentious exchanges between the Cohens. Typical of the kind-hearted competition between the two fathers is the following dialogue from the June 3, 1944 episode. In the previous episode, the two men had decided to go into business together and had purchased the Loony Lake Lodge, a 600-room resort hotel in New York's Catskill mountains, a popular resort areas for Jews. As the scene opens, Solomon tells Patrick that he has ordered new stationery for the hotel.

Patrick: You've ordered them — well, so have I.
Solomon: You ordered some, too — why didn't you tell me.
Patrick: Because you didn't ask me.
Solomon: I'll bet you'll like what I picked — on the top a beautiful picture of the hotel — and the name, "Looney Lake Lodge" — and underneath — Levy & Murphy, Proprietors.
Patrick: Levy & Murphy — mine says Murphy & Levy.

Solomon: Patrick Joseph Murphy, why do you always try to get ahead of me.
Patrick: Because if I don't I always wind up behind you.
Solomon: It's Levy & Murphy.
Patrick: It's Murphy & Levy.
Solomon: Levy.
Patrick: Murphy.
Solomon: Patrickle, you talk like a mule.
Patrick: And you bray like a donkey.

The argument finally ends when Mrs. Cohen joins the partners. But it doesn't take long for the two men disagree again — this time when they introduce themselves to the hotel's meat chef and each tries to tell the chef how to cook roast beef.

Patrick: Hey, what are you doing to that roast beef there?
Chef: I am wiping it with ze damp cloth — of course.
Patrick: Never wipe it with a cloth — do you think you're cleaning up the floor — Wash it off with running water.
Chef: M'sieur, nevaire — nevaire — could I wipe it off with running water.
Solomon: The chef is right — and you're wrong, Patrickle — did you ever see a cow taking a shower?
Patrick: No, did you?
Solomon: A roast of beef should be soaked in vinegar for one hour.
Chef: Aaaaah — M'sieur — soak ze beautiful boeuf in vinegaire — you are murdering me — and murdering ze boeuf.
Patrick: Wash it in running water.
Solomon: Soak it in vinegar.
Patrick: We'll be around later to see that you've followed instructions — come on, Sol.
Solomon: Sure — let's go.
Chef: (Off) Water — vinegaire — sacre bleu — nom d'un nom — sapristi.
Solomon: What's he yelling about?
Patrick: Oh, he's so happy about the helpful cooking hints we gave him — he's jumping with joy.

In contrast to the mild, good-natured humor of the fathers-in-law, the exchanges between Papale and Mamale received more laughs — but they also generated controversy as some Jewish organizations saw the characters as negative images of Jews. (See below). The following dialogue is from the May 27, 1944 episode. As the scene opens, Papale is worried.

Cohen	Do you realize Solomon and Mr. Murphy have been gone a week and we haven't had a word from them?
Mrs. C:	That's a pleasure — but stop worrying, darling — they can look after themselves.
Cohen	They can't, Mamale — every time they go off together, they get in trouble — unless they have me to guide their footsteps.
Mrs. C:	So what are you — an Indian guide — Look at him. Little Chief Patch-in-Ponum (slap-in-face) — Who guides you?
Cohen	So all right — but I'm still worried.
Mrs. C:	Stop worrying, Tootsele — put on your coat and go to your office — already you're late.
Cohen	Okay — but first I got to stop at the bookstore.
Mrs. C:	Why?
Cohen	Because I want to buy a book — what else?
Mrs. C:	You want to buy a book? — What did you do with the book I gave you last year?
Mrs. C:	I read it.
Mrs. C:	Read it again — it's not worn out yet.
Cohen	But, Mamale, don't you understand — a book is like an egg.
Mrs. C:	Like an egg?
Cohen	Sure — you don't have to eat an egg twice to know what it taste like — I want a new book.
Mrs. C:	Oi, Isaacle, I got a much better idea.
Cohen	What?
Mrs. C:	Write your own book — it's cheaper.
Cohen	How could I write a book.
Mrs. C:	How? You got a pencil — so write.
Cohen	A man has to have the time — it reminds me of what my grandmother told me once.
Mrs. C:	So what did she tell you?
Cohen	She said in order to write a book you must have lots of time — if you have lots of time you can't be working at a job — if you're not working at a job, you're a bum — how can a bum write a book? — Get it?
Mrs. C:	If you mean the bum — I got him thirty years ago.

Cohen	Oi, Honya.
Mrs. C:	I'm only kiddling you, tootsele — but I'm also serious — why don't you write a book — I'll be so proud of you.
Cohen	When would I have time?
Mrs. C:	In the summer — courts are closed until fall — you can rest from being a lawyer by writing a book.
Cohen	Mamale, I just wanted to rest period.
Mrs. C:	Isaacle, you are writing a book this summer — I've decided.
Cohen	But what shall I write about?
Mrs. C:	About 300 pages — that's enough.

During its first year on the air, *Abie's Irish Rose* was one of the more popular programs. According to a May 3, 1943 issue of *Time* magazine, the program was one of the top 20 programs in the U.S., was broadcast coast-to-coast on 125 stations and was heard in some 5 million homes. The magazine also noted that the story of *Abie's Irish Rose* had indeed been a money-maker for its author, having earned more than $2 million in royalties, plus approximately $500,000 from the movie version. Not bad for a play that was dismissed by the critics when it opened back in 1922. In 1943, it was voted number 10 of the top 11 dramatic serials by radio editors and critics.[7]

Praise for the program came from both Jewish and non-Jewish individuals and organizations. Two of the gentile sources took special note of the program's message of tolerance of different groups, an issue that was a major concern during World War II. The Reverend Norman Vincent Peale of the Marble Collegiate Church in New York City wrote, "The radio presentation of *Abie's Irish Rose*, beloved story, is rich in the fine entertainment and the delightfully tender human qualities for which the play is noted. Beyond that, however, and with a natural simplicity, the great American principles of tolerance and understanding are emphasized. All of us, Jew, Catholic and Protestant, are bound together by common spiritual ties, and our love for America makes us one. *Abie's Irish Rose* reminds us of this essential unity."[8]

Another non-Jewish testimonial for the program came from the Reverend Daniel A. Poling of The Baptist Temple in Philadelphia who wrote, "It (the program) is a significant contribution to the morale of America and to that unity of all our ways and faiths without which we cannot win this war." In his capacity as the editor-in-chief of the *Christian Herald*, Poling

Richard Coogan and Mercedes McCambridge as Abie and Rosemary Levy

Anna Appel and Menasha Skulnik as Mr. and Mrs. Cohen (Mamale and Papale)

Walter Kinsella as Patrick Murphy

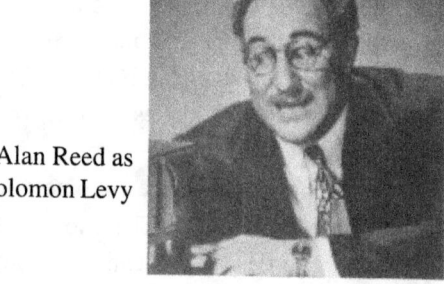

Alan Reed as Solomon Levy

also wrote to Procter & Gamble, the program's sponsor, calling the program "side-splitting entertainment, but it is significantly more. It is American unity — it is freedom on the march. Nothing on the air, Sir, is doing a finer job in building morale at a time when morale is a first imperative."[9] The National Conference of Christians and Jews also paid tribute to the program.

But the program also generated its share of complaints. In an echo of the controversy among some African-American organizations and newspapers regarding *Amos 'n' Andy* that dated back to the 1930s, there were some Jewish individuals and organizations that objected to the program and its portrayal of Jews. One such complaint was from Rabbi Harry Z. Zwelling of New Britian, Connecticut who wrote that he was:

> ...in turn surprised, humiliated, nauseated and infuriated by the program. I had imagined that the 'vaudeville Jew' had died and was given the indecent burial which he deserved. But compared to the portrayal referred to above, the vaudeville Jew was 'innocent' fun. For here we were subjected to a most vulgar caricature of Jewish life, which perhaps not legally, but in fact was libelous. I am intolerant of Jews who indulge in such so-called 'Jewish humor.' I am insulted when non-Jews broadcast such trash. The sponsors close their program with something to the effect that their program is dedicated to freedom. Does this include the freedom to humiliate?[10]

In examining these objections, it should be remembered that the program aired during World War II when Jewish secular groups were doing all they could to fight anti-Semitism and the die-hard anti-Semites who were still blaming Jews for having gotten the United States into the war. Whereas some vaudeville and theater audiences in the 1920s might have considered the stereotyped dialogue and characterizations of Jews amusing and acceptable, by 1942, concerned Jews saw these same negative stereotypes as being outdated and weakening their efforts to portray Jews as being no different than other Americans.

In October, 1942, after *Abie's Irish Rose* had been on the air for 10 months, Richard C. Rothschild, the American Jewish Committee's (AJC) Director of Public Relations, wrote to the public relations counsel for Procter & Gamble that, "As a whole the programs are well-meaning and entertaining," adding that, to date, "I have found no scenes which showed the Jew as a sharp trader or sly schemer." The part of the program the AJC found objectionable, however, was the accent of the Levy[11] family and "the poor taste in using expressions (supposedly to evoke laughter) such as 'oy, yoi yoi' and 'oy gevalt' which are repeatedly groaned throughout the dramatization." Rothschild went on to contrast *Abie's Irish Rose* with *The Goldbergs*, citing the Goldberg family as "a fine, loyal Jewish family" always trying to help their neighbors and make life happy and joyful for their friends. Molly Goldberg speaks with a Jewish accent, he wrote, but the accent isn't "too ugly to listen to as those in *Abie's Irish Rose*."[12]

The October letter apparently had no impact on the program's creative team as five months later, in a March 23, 1943 internal memo, Milton Krents, head of the AJC's Radio Department, cited even more complaints about the series.[13] This time, Krents noted that, "The subject of money plays a prominent part in a number of the scripts with much price haggling." Taking note of the fact that Procter & Gamble continued to take the position that the program was doing a positive service and indeed had received very few complaint letters, Krents outlined a strategy for dealing with the issue. He suggested: 1) an organized letter writing campaign to P&G and 2) a "sit down" with the sponsor to try to improve the objectionable Jewish characters.

Krents' memo was followed up with an April 19, 1943 letter that Rothschild sent to the Biow Company, most likely was the sponsor's advertising agency.[14] The letter stated the Committee's two underlying concerns relating to its ongoing efforts to combat anti-Semitism:

1) the idea that the Jews are basically different from other people, not only in their mannerisms, but in morals as well; and
2) the idea that the Jews are given to sharp practices and shady business dealings.

Rothschild then proceeded to cite very specific objections to two programs that he said were chosen at random. A week later, an internal AJC memorandum summarized specific objections to the April 24th program.[15] However, when the AJC's complaints about these episodes are compared with the actual scripts, it is clear that most of the Committee's comments were taken out of context and dialogue was attributed to the wrong character. (See Appendix 2 for a side-by-side comparison.)

The last available AJC document relating to *Abie's Irish Rose* is a brief note in a general report on the Committee's public relations work from February to May, 1943. Under the heading "Abie's Irish Rose," the report noted: "Series of interviews with Public Relations Director, advertising agency executive and script writer of this program (Anne Nichols) in an attempt to eliminate undesirable features. Considerable but not complete success."[16]

The Anne Nichols Papers offer a different perspective on the controversy. The earliest correspondence regarding the issue is a letter dated January 13, 1944 from Ted Mertz of the sponsor's Chicago advertising agency to a Virginia Smith.[17] (Smith's relationship to Nichols or the program is not known.) In the letter, Mertz reminded Smith that as a result of earlier meetings (with the AJC), Anne (Nichols) had made the suggestion that Menasha Skulnik meet with Rothschild so that Menasha could convince Rothschild "that he doesn't understand his own people." Mertz then laid out four key problem areas that Smith and Nichols should examine:

1) The role of Mrs. Cohen (Mamale) as well as the way she is being portrayed by Anna Appel. He suggests that Appel has to be "watched closely," as she's an "unpredictable character" and will often give an entirely wrong expression to a soft line. "I think we would all feel better if Mamale were as highly regarded as Papale and always left the audience with the definite impression that in spite of her irascibility, she's a loveable character with a heart of gold."
2) The need to reduce the use of Jewish dialog and expressions.
3) The possible need to add more Irish characters.
4) The possibility of making Patrick the innocent butt of more jokes as it might tend to "even things up between the Irish and the Jew and possibly relieve us of some of this snipping."

"It would be desirable," Mertz continued, "to eliminate any possibility of those ever present Jew baiters being given the chance of saying, 'What do you expect from one of those kikes.' Certainly making Mamale more loveable wouldn't seem to take anything away from the show and might automatically silence whatever complains there are."

Mertz concluded the letter by advising Smith that while he waited for more documentation regarding specific complaints, "As I told you, we don't take these complaints too seriously but feel that we would be better off if by one means or another we could eliminate them. Don't get concerned about it yourself or allow Anne to be upset until we're able to obtain more actual and specific information."[18]

In her February 7, 1944 response to Mertz,[19] Smith wrote that both she and Anne were "considerably amazed that any such situation existed, particularly in view of all the requests, praises and what have you that we get here from Jewish groups and especially high schools. But as you know too, if any such feelings do exist in whatever minority, however slight, we certainly want to make every effort to alleviate them." She then proceeded to challenge Rothschild's credentials to comment on a Jewish program. Noting that Rothschild "says anybody listening to the program would think that the Jews don't know the English language," she added, "I could be facetious and say that judging by the contents of his letter, Mr. Rothschild, as a Jew, doesn't even know the Jewish language since he has used an entirely different euphonious method of spelling in some of the Jewish expressions."[20]

In the February 7th letter, as well as in two follow-up letters later in the month, Smith detailed the steps she and Nichols planned to take to address each of the concerns, especially minimizing and softening the role of Mrs. Cohen "until the memory of that harsh, shouting voice has become less evident in the minds of listeners."

On balance, taking into consideration the time period in which the series was broadcast, the documents in both the American Jewish Committee's archives and the Anne Nichols Papers, access to some 68 scripts, and recordings of the four episodes known to be available, the authors have come to the following conclusion: While there was merit in some of the AJC's complaints, the organization appears to have been overly sensitive to other aspects of the program. On the other hand, it appears that Nichols and her team failed to carry through on changes that even they recognized needed to be made. Also, the controversy was likely heightened by generational and class differences between the involved parties.

The AJC's objections to the characterization of Mrs. Cohen appear to be on point. Depending on one's frame of reference, she could, at times, be construed as an unpleasant person. Her voice had a harsh quality and she was frequently nasty, vindictive and argumentative towards her husband. In one of the recordings, she's angry at Papale because he remained at the Levy apartment long after she left. When Papale gets home, he finds the front door locked and he's forced to sit outside for a while. The next morning, he has a cold, but Mamale is clearly not sympathetic to his plight: had he listened to her the night before, he would not have gotten sick.[21] As Rothschild pointed out in his March 13, 1943 letter, Mamale was the antithesis of Molly

Goldberg, the warm, kind, wise Jewish matriarch. The Mertz/Smith letters notwithstanding, listening to Mrs. Cohen on two programs broadcast one year apart, there did not appear to be much change in the character. With the exception of one line in the 1944 dialogue cited above ("I'm only kidding you, Tootsele — but I'm also serious") delivered in an almost loving voice, there hardly seemed to be any "softening" of either the character or the voice. As Mertz pointed out in his letter, part of the problem lay with Appel who could even change the intent of a "soft" line. Nichols may have wanted Mamale to be viewed as being "loveable," but that was not the way she came across, due to the writing, the delivery, or a combination of both.

The character of Papale, although less of a problem than Mamale, could also be looked upon as a negative stereotype of a Jewish male. Despite his being a kind-hearted person and at times providing sound advice as an attorney, because he was continually henpecked by his wife, he came across as being meek and weak. When Mamale would get the best of him and Skulnik, in his trademark whining voice would respond, "Oi, honya," the audience may have laughed, but there was no doubt that the man could not stand up for himself. In contrast, Skulnik's "Uncle David" on *The Goldbergs* was also portrayed as a meek person, but he was treated with respect by Molly. In making the role of Mr. Cohen more comedic, Skulnik, either intentionally or inadvertently, portrayed a less than positive Jewish male character.

It is important to remember that both Appel and Skulnik were veterans of the Yiddish Theater, an entertainment form that appealed primarily to immigrant and first generation Jews and which reached its heyday in the 1920s-1930s. While the characterizations of Mamale and Papale may have been acceptable in that venue, and to that audience, an argument could be made that the same stereotypes may not have been appropriate for a radio program beamed to millions of mainstream Americans in the middle of the war. It is also possible that "assimilated" Jews from a different economic or social class were not familiar with the comic traditions of the Yiddish theater.

The AJC's objections to the constant arguing and negative business practices of the Jewish characters appear to have less merit. The arguing between Patrick and Solomon was part of the show's humor and it was always clear that it was good natured bickering, not much different than the tit-for-tat exchanges between the married couple on the popular program, *The Bickersons*. As for the undesirable business practices, as documented in Appendix 2, the instances cited by the AJC appear to be based on a misunderstanding of the series' plot lines and/or which character was speaking.

Too many Jewish expressions? That's a matter of taste, class and one's exposure to the Yiddish language. But it is also a stretch on the part of the AJC to argue that the use of the expressions gave the impression that Jews did not understand English. Obviously the audience didn't seem to have a problem with them. Nor did Patrick Murphy who used some of them. When some expressions needed an explanation, one was given. Others simply didn't need explaining given the context of the line or the way the phrase was spoken.

As noted earlier, *Abie's Irish Rose* was broadcast at a time when Jewish organizations were especially sensitive to negative stereotypes about Jews. That concern was evident when, in 1944, another Jewish organization, the Anti-Defamation League (ADL), raised an objection to a phrase being used in a revival of the 1922 play that was being staged in San Francisco. In June, 1944, Nichols received a letter from Herbert Lizt, the ADL Publicity Director, objecting to the phrase "You Shylock" that Patrick Murphy used when he addressed Solomon Levy in a moment of anger. Acknowledging that it might seem strange to raise the issue in 1944 after the play had already been seen by millions of theatergoers, Lizt added, "were it not for the fact that certain propaganda machines and interests which are hostile to the American way of life are concentrating their barrages against Jewish citizens in order to accomplish division in American life, we probably would not even approach you on this subject." In a short response, Nichols indicated that the offending word would be changed.[22]

The January-February, 1944 letter exchange between Mertz and Smith also called attention to the program's uncertain future. While the parties agreed that it made sense to plan for a summer season with a new plot line, Smith expressed concern that it would be difficult to develop a new story line without knowing whether there would be a fall season.

Smith's worries about the program's future were borne out when Procter & Gamble cancelled the program in September, 1944. What factors influenced P&G's decision? Was it pressure from Jewish organizations and letters from Jewish consumers? A drop off in listeners? A combination of both? We may never know. What is known is that *Abie's Irish Rose* was not up against stiff competition for listeners from rival networks.[23] Also, the only evidence that the complaints were a factor in the show's cancellation is a November 6, 1946 article in *Variety* that states that the program was "forced off the air" because of organized listener protests to Procter & Gamble.[24]

An argument can also be made that listeners were tiring of the soap opera-like format that relied on a continuing plot. Whereas daytime serial listeners (mostly housewives) had no problem with the continuing story format when the program was broadcast five days a week, it was more difficult to retain audience interest and loyalty when the program was heard only once a week and listeners may have missed the previous week's episode. As noted in Appendix 2, some of the AJC's objections to the program were possibly due to coming into a program in the middle of a plot and not understanding the context of what was being said. In hindsight, would the program have survived longer if, like two other longer running play-to-radio series, *The Aldrich Family* and *Meet Corliss Archer*, each *Abie's Irish Rose* broadcast had been a self-contained story and listeners could have enjoyed the series even if they missed an occasional episode?

In the final broadcast on September 2, 1944, Dwight Weist announced at the close of the program: "With this episode the makers of Drene Shampoo bid a fond farewell to Abie's Irish Rose." And over the musical theme, *My Time Is Your Time*, he continued, "Next Saturday night at this time, Drene Shampoo brings you a new show starring one of your all time screen and radio favorites." Listeners then heard the voice of Rudy Vallee saying, "Hi, ho, everybody. I hope you'll all be on hand for the gala opening of my new series…

After Procter & Gamble dropped its sponsorship of the program, Colgate-Palmolive took an option on the series that was never exercised. Efforts in 1949 to bring *Abie's Irish Rose* to television were also unsuccessful.

In 1946, two years after the program went off the air, a second film version of the original story was made with Bing Crosby as the producer and Joanne Dru and Richard Norris in the title roles. The movie was sharply criticized by Jewish organizations as well as the National Conference of Christians and Jews on the grounds that it riveted the negative stereotype of Jews in the mass mind, included distortions and did incalculable damage.[25]

Not long after Nichols passed away in 1966, two former cast members of the radio series, Betty Winkler and Carl Eastman, appeared on Richard Lamparski's popular nostalgia interview program, *Whatever Become Of?*[26] The actors described Nichols as a very strong woman who would bask in the limelight of success when things were going well but who retreated to her home, remaining out of sight for long stretches of time when her subsequent stage efforts flopped. They made it quite clear that Nichols participated to a major extent in the broadcast series.

The play version of *Abie's Irish Rose* was revived on Broadway at least three times; in 1937, 1944 and 1954. All had short runs.[27] It was reprised again in 1999 in a limited run Off-Broadway production.

To this day, Samuel French, Inc., the publishers of plays, reports amateur and professional performances of the play are occurring somewhere in America.

Notes

Abbreviations

AJC   American Jewish Committee Radio Department Archives at Yivo Institute, New York, NY.

ANP   Anne Nichols Papers, New York Public Library for the Performing Arts, Billy Rose Theater Collection, New York, NY.

1. Moss Hart, *Act One, An Autobiography* (New York: Random House, 1959) 56-57, cited in Ted Merwin, "The Performance of Jewish Ethnicity in Anne Nichols' Abie's Irish Rose," *Journal of American Ethnic History*, 2001, Vol. 20, # 2.

2. The box office record was broken by *Tobacco Road* that ran for 3,182 performances.

3. *Philadelphia Inquirer*, May 17, 1925, cited in Merwin, "The Performance of Jewish Ethnicity."

4. See the Merwin article for additional insights into the play.

5. See www.coolcopyright.com/cases/fulltext/nicholasuniversaltext.htm for the full court decision in the lawsuit, Nichols v. Universal Pictures Corporation et al.

6. Script for July 1, 1944 broadcast, 18.

7. Jack Alicoate, ed. *The 1944 Radio Annual* (New York: Radio Daily, 1940), 93.

8. ANP, Box 1, Folder 6.

9. Ibid. Poling also suggested to P&G that the company might be interested in sponsoring a radio version of the movie *One Foot In Heaven* that was about a Methodist minister and his family.

10. March 12, 1943 letter from Rabbi Harry Z. Zwelling to the American

Jewish Committee. AJC, Box 235, Folder Abie's Irish Rose.

11. Various documents in the AJC files regarding the program refer to "Mr. & Mrs. Levy." From the context of the documents, however, it is clear that, in most cases, they are referring the Papale and Mamale, or Mr. and Mrs. Cohen, and only occasionally Solomon Levy, Abie's father. It is not clear why this error was repeatedly made. For the sake of clarity, when the authors' refer to an AJC document that specifies "Levy," they note when they believe that the writer meant one of the Cohen characters.

12. October 29, 1942 letter from Richard C. Rothschild to Edward L. Bernays. AJC, Box 235, Folder Abie's Irish Rose.

13. March 23, 1943 "Abie's Irish Rose" Memo from Krents to Rosenblum. Ibid.

14. April 19, 1943 letter from Rothschild to Milton Biow. Ibid.

15. April 27, 1943 memo from Esther Schulman to Richard C. Rothschild. Ibid.

16. "Public Relations Work February to May, 1943," 15. No author. Available online at www.ajcarchives.org. In a May 14, 1943 letter to W. M. Ramsey, Director Radio at Procter & Gamble, Rothschild wrote that he had met with Anne Nichols for about one hour, had tried to explain the Committee's position and that, "I think she understood." Ibid.

17. ANP, Ibid., Box 1, Folder 7. In the letter Mertz, specifically mentions Rothschild but erroneously refers to him as being with the Anti-Defamation League, another Jewish secular organization.

18. In light of the AJC's earlier correspondence, it is difficult to accept Mertz's contention that more specific details were needed. Also, one wonders if the Nichols team pointed out the misunderstandings in the AJC's earlier objections.

19. ANP, Box 1, Folder 7.

20. Smith's challenge of Rothschild's spelling of Jewish words does seem petty, especially as it is common for foreign words to be spelled differently when translated into English.

21. Program #42 broadcast January 16, 1943.

22. ANP, Box 1, Folder 7.

23. Programs that aired opposite *Abie* included *Mr. Adam & Mrs. Eve, Roy Porter News,* the *Boston Symphony, Crumit & Sanderson, The Ford Program,* and *Blue Ribbon Town.*

24. The main focus of the article was the opposition of Jewish groups to the 1946 movie version of "Abie's Irish Rose." The reference to the cancelled radio program was just a single line. Although Krents suggested in March, 1943 that one way of handling the *Abie* problem was organizing a protest letter writing campaign (see footnote 13), there are no other documents in the AJC radio files indicating that such a strategy was ever implemented. Also, a March

31, 1943 letter from the manager of P&G's Division of Public Relations to Rothschild states that the company has "come to the conclusion that the program is definitely contributing to the happiness of the public and greater understanding and tolerance of all people." Without additional documentation, it is therefore difficult to state definitively that it was an organized letter writing campaign, and not other factors, that led to the show's cancellation.

25. *Variety,* November 6, 1946 and AJC, Box 235, Folder Abie's Irish Rose Folder.

26. A December 1966 program broadcast on WBAI, New York.

27. The 1937 version lasted for 46 performances. *The New York Times,* February 8, 1942, 12. Prior to the 1944 opening, two touring companies were staging the play. One troop had a 47 week run in Ventura, California and a second company played for 63 weeks in Washington state. *The New York Times,* July 9, 1944, Drama, Recreation News Section, X1. Also, in the February 28, 1944 letter referenced above, Smith told Mertz that Nichols was working on a sequel to *Abie's Irish Rose* that would focus on the young couple but which would also include the two fathers. Nichols, Smith wrote, was delaying the publication of the sequel until she had completed adapting it for radio.

8
Judaism Aired: Religious Oriented Programs

Religious broadcasting is as old as radio itself. One could trace the first transmission of a religious message (although admittedly not wireless) to the year 1837 when Samuel Morse sent the message, "What hath God wrought?" demonstrating that his invention worked. For the record, it should be noted that the message was non-denominational.

In the very early years of radio, it was not uncommon for those experimenting with the new wireless method of sending messages to fill the airwaves with prayers, hymns and bible readings. Station KDKA, owned by Westinghouse in Pittsburgh, Pennsylvania, the first station to broadcast presidential election returns, was also the very first station to broadcast a complete religious program. On January 2, 1921, a mere two months after the station had begun its regular schedule, the services at Calvary Episcopal Church were broadcast via a remote hook up from the church.[1]

Over the next several years, numerous religious organizations went on the air to deliver a variety of messages, some strictly inspirational, others more zealous in their efforts to "save souls." The fact that the vast majority of these broadcasts represented the efforts of Protestant, Catholic and several evangelical groups should come as no surprise as this was simply a reflection of the religious affiliation of the vast majority of the general population. There were, however, isolated examples of one-time-only Jewish religious broadcasts such as a March, 1922 program aired on station WJZ in New York that featured a radio chapel service that included a talk by Rabbi Solomon Foster and music by Cantor Maurice Cowan.[2]

At a time when many radio stations began, and often ended, the day with a brief prayer, spoken almost exclusively by members of the Protestant or Catholic clergy, a few stations serving communities with substantial Jewish populations would, on occasion, invite a rabbi to participate in this activity. In 1923, station WNAC in Boston invited Rabbi Harry Levi of Temple Israel, a Reform congregation, to offer the daily prayer. Listener response was such that the station offered the rabbi a return engagement, and beginning in January, 1924, the station arranged to broadcast his temple's services twice-monthly.³ Two years later, Levi told a newspaper reporter:

> ...in every way the radio is proving a blessing...Work has been found for the unemployed, contributions have been secured for community projects. Members have been secured for the temple...people of every shade of opinion, frankly confessing to prejudices against (Jews), have as frankly given assurance of a fairer, juster [sic] and more religious attitude henceforth.⁴

Years later, Levi appeared as a frequent guest on the *Message of Israel* program.

By 1923, some 12 different religious organizations (none Jewish) were licensed to operate radio stations. Faced with the possibility of losing a segment of their potential listeners to church affiliated stations, the owners of secular stations decided to follow the example of KDKA and made room on their schedules for religious broadcasts. In 1926, the year that NBC came into existence, the network's Committee on Religious Activities recommended that free or sustaining time be allotted to Protestant, Catholic and Jewish organizations under the condition that they, and not the network, underwrote the cost of production. The Council also recommended that the programs be limited to preaching and that they avoid controversy.⁵

One of the earliest Jewish organizations to use radio was the United Synagogues of America which represented Conservative Judaism. On August 30, 1923, the group broadcast a service from a synagogue that was heard on WEAF in New York City. In 1928, the organization's Women's League sponsored a second program, also aired on WEAF, although no details regarding that program have survived.

In March, 1926, some 19 years prior to ABC's popular daytime program, *Bride and Groom* (1945-1950),⁶ listeners in New York City heard Rabbi Josef Hoffman marry Winnie Gordon and Julius Goldberg in a ceremony broadcast over station WRNY. And between February 10, 1929 and January 1932, the *Jewish Art Program* was heard on an irregular basis on WABC. The program featured a variety of Jewish artists whose Yiddish presentations were translated.⁷

By the late 1920s, a growing number of Reform congregations began to explore using radio to broadcast their services to shut-ins as well as Jews living in small communities without synagogues. While these programs were not broadcast under the auspices of the Union of American Hebrew

Congregations (UAHC), the umbrella group for Reform Judaism, the organization did collect information about the broadcasts, and between 1929-1930 it distributed a weekly broadcast schedule to Jewish newspapers.[8]

In 1932, *The American Israelite*, a leading Jewish weekly newspaper, surveyed all rabbis affiliated with the UAHC and the Central Conference of American Rabbis on their use of radio. The study found that while many of the rabbis believed that radio had "vast possibilities...for creating good will between themselves and those of other faiths," only six of the rabbis who responded to the questionnaire were still broadcasting their services. Many cited the lack of funds as the reason they had stopped broadcasting; others explained that an advertiser had purchased their time slot.[9] Of the 110 survey responses, 17 rabbis had been, up to the time of the survey, broadcasting on a regular basis; 20 reported occasional broadcasts such as holiday services and sermons; 11 broadcast regularly, but not religious services, and 62 had never done any broadcasting. Of the six synagogues with ongoing programs that broadcast their services, only one of the programs originated from the synagogue.

The 11 rabbis who broadcast regularly, but not religious services, reported that their programs dealt with ethnical and social issues, current events, books reviews and Jewish history and literature. "They all feel that programs of this nature are the means of creating a very sound sort of good will for the Jew and the Jewish community on the part of the non-Jewish listeners."[10]

Considering the old adage that whenever several Jews gather there will always be several different opinions on an issue, it was not unusual that there were differences of opinion among various Jewish organizations as well as individuals concerning the wisdom of using radio to disseminate information about Jews. In a theme that would be heard time and again over the next two decades, some thought that calling attention to Jews on the radio could actually lead to more anti-Semitism. These differences notwithstanding, independent stations in several larger cities did air one or more Jewish religious programs, either on a continuing basis or as special one-time broadcasts. The nature and content of these early programs was dictated by which branch of Judaism, Orthodox, Conservative or Reform, was responsible for the production. While this distinction may not have been significant or understood by non-Jewish listeners, it was a concern for some Jews.[11]

According to Zev Zahavy, the author of the doctoral dissertation, "History and Survey of Jewish Religious Broadcasting," during radio's early days, both the Orthodox and Reform branches of Judaism were heard on the airwaves while Conservative Jews had less of a presence on radio until the mid-1940s.[12] Over time, however, the balance between the three branches of Judaism changed. In his analysis of programs in the postwar period, Zahavy concluded that Conservative Judaism, as represented by the Jewish Theological Seminary, dominated NBC's Jewish programming, while the *Message of Israel* heard on ABC (but originally heard on the NBC-Blue network) represented Reform Judaism. In contrast, the Mutual network took a more balanced view in its two programs, the *Sunday Radio Chapel* (a.k.a. *Radio Chapel of the Air)*[13] that was sponsored by the Synagogue Council of America, an umbrella group that represented the three branches of Judaism, and *Minute of Prayer* about which no additional information is available. Zahavy listed several Jewish organizations that were heard on CBS, but he did not identify either specific program names or the affiliations of the groups.[14]

Based on his research into programs broadcast during the 1940s-1950s, Zahavy, an Orthodox rabbi, expressed concern that because Orthodox Judaism was not represented on an equal footing with either the Reform or Conservative branches, listeners may have been given an erroneous impression of American Judaism.

> In their desire to get on the air, some Jewish religious broadcasts have lost their efficacy. They have been impelled by a self centered motivation to promote themselves rather than a worthwhile message. As a result, the listening audience may have been disappointed by some of these Jewish presentations...When the Jewish religious spirit is lacking in a broadcast, it is hardly possible to gain anything of lasting meaning through such a broadcast.[15]

The religious programs described in the following pages appear in the order in which they first aired.

The Lamplighter

Rabbi Jacob Tarshish began airing brief messages of inspiration on radio stations in the Cincinnati area as early as 1926. His reputation as a speaker who connected with listeners, regardless of their religious affiliations, eventually resulted in programs on WOR in New York, WGN in Chicago and WXYZ in Detroit, all Mutual affiliated stations. Sometime during the late 1920s, Tarshish began using the title *The Lamplighter* to identify his broadcasts. Radio historians may never know if that decision was his or the network's, nor is it likely to ever be known if the decision was influenced by the hope that listeners would not identify Tarshish as being Jewish. The program was carried on the Mutual network until April 1941, after which time Tarshish's talks continued to be carried on a regional basis on the west coast until sometime in 1942.

During the 1930s and 1940s, it was a common practice for certain types of programs to make printed copies of their "scripts" available to listeners who requested them. These booklets served both as a measure of listener support and also as a means of further advertising for both the program and its producers. Tarshish made use of this promotional device and several of his booklets are in the authors' collection. Three volumes of Tarshish's radio talks were also published. The first volume, *Half Hours,* ran some 111 pages and was popular enough to lead to a second 128-page volume, *Little Journeys with the Lamplighter*, that was published in 1935. A third 108-page volume, *Prelude to Happiness,* was published in 1937. While Tarshish is scarcely remembered today, either as a radio performer or for any influence he may have had as a spokesman for Jewish beliefs, he clearly had a substantial audience, most of which accepted his advice and precepts to live by.

Jewish Hour

According to NBC program logs at the Library of Congress, the *Jewish Hour* debuted on November 3, 1929, just two-and-a-half weeks prior to the very first appearance of *The Rise of the Goldbergs*.[16] Although *The Lamplighter* pre-dated the *Jewish Hour* by three years, because it was more of an inspirational program (even though it was hosted by a rabbi) rather than a religious broadcast, the *Jewish Hour* is considered to be the earliest Jewish network religious program. Stations that carried the program as part of the NBC-Red network included: WEAF, WTAG, WCSH, WGY, WWJ, WLS, WHO, WOW, WJAX, KSD and KSL. The program consisted of religious services arranged by Orthodox Rabbi Samuel Cohen and is described in NBC program index cards as "very high-class music characteristic of the Jewish race and religion and at least one speaker besides Rabbi Cohen, frequently Rabbi Nathan Krass, and a question and answer session." The program was broadcast Sundays from 3pm to 4pm and remained on the air until June 1, 1930.

During the *Jewish Hour's* final months of broadcasting, listeners heard from Dr. David de Sola Pool of New York's Spanish and Portuguese Synagogue, Professor Adele Bildersee, Dr. Jonah B. Wise, Dr. Elias Margolis, Felix M. Warburg, Dr. Israel Goldstein, Dr. Stephen S. Wise, Dr. David Goldfort, Dr. Leo Jung, and several other eminent speakers, both religious and lay. The subjects of their talks ranged from morality and marriage to religious education, worshiping idols, superstition, etc. Responsibility for the program's weekly content was under the jurisdiction of the Committee on Jewish Religious Radio Programs.

When the series ended, several local stations serving communities that included a substantial number of Jewish listeners adopted the name *Jewish Hour* for their own programs. Zahavy, for example, refers to a 1934 *Jewish Hour* program that aired on WJZ in New York City that featured talks by prominent speakers. And during at least 1936 and 1937, WCNW in Brooklyn, New York broadcast a program by the same name. The WCNW program, which was broadcast weekly in a 60-minute time slot, was hosted by Madame Bertha Hart and was more of a Jewish and Yiddish variety show than a religious program. An Internet search reveals the existence of several additional regional programs that used the same *Jewish Hour* name although there was no connection between the programs.

"The Poet Prince"

Abraham Feinberg served as a rabbi until 1930, at which time he became a professional singer. He adopted the stage name of Anthony Frome and was successful enough to be featured on his own radio program from 1932-1935 where he was dubbed, "The Poet Prince of the Air Waves." Though his broadcasts were not reflective of Jewish programming, his decision to abandon his career as a radio entertainer and return to his rabbinical duties in response to the rise of Hitler and Nazism in Germany may be viewed as reason enough to acknowledge him as a conscientious Jew whose religious principles outweighed ambitions of a career in show business. Feinberg devoted the rest of his life to supporting peace movements throughout the world and was saluted by many and reviled by others as being far too radical.

Church of the Air[17]

In 1931, after canceling Father Coughlin's controversial broadcasts, CBS decided to adopt a different approach to religious broadcasting. Instead of airing multiple religious programs, it created the *Church of the Air,* a series that featured different speakers representing the three major faiths. Programming for the Jewish segment was arranged by the United Jewish Laymen's Committee, a constituent group of the Union of American Hebrew Congregations that represented the Reform branch of Judaism. The half-hour program, which was aired twice a day on Sundays so that it could be heard by different faiths, was broadcast until 1957. Initially, the Protestant segment was aired at 10am while the Catholic and Jewish broadcasts were heard at 2:30pm.

Based on his review of the program's speakers, Zahavy concluded that between 1931 and 1957, the *Church of the Air* featured a total of 238 Jewish broadcasts, or approximately ten percent of the programs.[18] While the speakers represented all three segments of Judaism, the largest number of talks (142) featured rabbis from the Reform movement. Among the Reform rabbis heard on the program were Abba Hillel Silver, Solomon Freehof, Stephen Wise, Jonah Wise, Samuel Goldenson, Louis Mann and Louis Newman. The Orthodox branch of Judaism was represented at times by David deSola Pool and Herbert S. Goldstein and the Conservative branch was represented at times by Israel Goldstein.

The program consisted primarily of a sermon. In his analysis of the Jewish sermons from 1931-1938, Zahavy found that the themes ranged from the self-help advice (26 sermons), brotherhood (23 sermons), politics (20 sermons) and marriage and other domestic problems (5 sermons). The remainder dealt with the Bible and Jewish history and holidays. In 1938, as the situation for Jews in Europe worsened, an increasing number of programs dealt with political issues.[19] After the war, in a January 26, 1946 sermon entitled "Immortality on Earth," Rabbi Pool reminded listeners:

> Hitler is living and will live on endlessly in human misery. His malignant life is still at work in hundreds of millions of stories of human sorrow, bereavement, frustration, hatred, homelessness, hopelessness and utter misery.[20]

The program's first tribute to Jewish music was on February 15, 1948 and was a presentation by the National Jewish Music Council of the National Jewish Welfare Board in celebration of the fourth National Jewish

Music Festival. The program featured the cantor and choir of Manhattan's Mount Neboh Temple, a Reform synagogue, and a portion of the service was led by Rabbi Ira Eisenstein. Similar music celebrations were broadcast annually in 1950, 1953, 1955 and 1956.[21] In recognition of these special programs, the National Jewish Music Council awarded a special citation to both the *Church of the Air* and CBS, lauding them for their "...consistent efforts over the years on behalf of the Jewish Music Festival (which) have fostered wide appreciation and understanding of the role of Jewish music among Americans of all faiths."[22]

In a theme repeated in his examination of other religious broadcasts, Zahavy, while praising *Church of the Air* for its "fine array of speaking talent," took the United Jewish Laymen's Committee to task for the over-representation of Reform rabbis, particularly, he notes, as the Reform group represented a much smaller proportion of American Judaism than the Orthodox group. "It may incite dismay amongst Orthodox and Conservative circles to note the utilization of this free radio time on a program of great fame, for the personal benefit and welfare of their Reform brethren. Having been given the key to its time dispensation, the Reform group doled out sermon opportunities to the other segments on a very penurious scale."[23]

Message of Israel

The *Message of Israel* has the distinction of being the longest-running Jewish themed program on radio, broadcasting more than 2,500 programs over a period of more than 50 years, from November, 1934 to July, 1986. It also ranks as one of radio's longest-running radio programs, together with the *Mormon Tabernacle Choir* and the *Grand Ole Opry*. Considering its historic run, it is surprising that so little has been written about the program; most books about broadcasting history and/or religious radio programs include only a paragraph or two about the program.[24]

The program debuted on November 2, 1934 and was carried by WJZ, the NBC-Blue network's flagship station in New York.[25] It was produced under the auspices of the United Jewish Laymen's Committee. Rabbi Jonah B. Wise of New York's Central Synagogue, part of the Reform branch of Judaism, hosted the program.[26] In the mid-1940s, when NBC was forced to give up one of its two networks, the program continued to be carried by the newly created American Broadcasting Company (ABC) until 1986.

The *Message of Israel* was created in part as a response to the growing anti-Semitism of the 1930s as well as the unsettling events in Germany. In a 1964 sermon recalling the program's early days, Rabbi David J. Seligson, Wise's successor at Central Synagogue, said of Wise:

> "(he) felt that an instrumentality had to be created which would present in dignified and effective ways, who the Jew was and what he stood for. This was not for purposes of polemics or apologetics, but to enlighten and inform, to substitute knowledge for ignorance, understanding for prejudice, love of fellowman for the hatred and deviceifness [sic] that was the prevailing theme of the Hitler racial theory."[27]

The half hour program was initially broadcast on Friday evenings, but switched to Saturday evenings at 6pm as of March 2, 1935, a time that Wise's biographer, Sam Cauman observed, "was almost the best on the air. Time of that order was a rarer gift than gold."[28] On December 5, 1943, the program switched to Sunday mornings at 10am where it remained until it went off the air in 1986. In later years, its airtime was reduced to 25 minutes and then to 23 minutes. During the program's early years, Rabbi Saul Applebaum, an assistant rabbi at Central Synagogue and also the radio manager for the United Jewish Laymen's Committee, assisted Wise with many of the administrative details associated with each broadcast. In the mid-to-late 1940s, Wise's son David became the program's producer/director in charge of arranging for speakers, getting sermons prepared on time, assembling program components, responding to "fan" letters and keeping in contact with the program's affiliated stations.[29] At one point, the program was carried on 200 stations as well as over the Armed Forces Radio Service and was heard by millions of listeners throughout the United States and on six continents.

In 1949, when the Union of American Hebrew Congregations became the co-producer of the program, the *Message of Israel* became the official radio voice of Reform Judaism.

With a few exceptions, the program originated from the sanctuary of Central Synagogue in New York City. When the broadcast time was switched to Sunday morning, a sign was placed outside the Synagogue inviting people to attend the special Sunday radio service. "Few visitors, if any at all, ventured into the Synagogue during the broadcast. It gave the program a ghost-like background, to note the preacher speaking into a radio microphone on a pulpit which faced an audience of empty benches, and yet, at the same time was being heard by one of the largest congregations in the world."[30]

In a 1985 article celebrating the series' 50th anniversary, David Wise described the program as a "creative worship service" that was built around a central theme, such as a holiday or commemorative occasion that combined music, usually in the beginning and end of the program, with a sermon and some prayers. The program was designed for Jews who couldn't attend regular synagogue services as well as non-Jews. As Cauman noted:

> In a country that had more than thirty times as many Christians as Jews in it, the *Message of Israel*, not unnaturally, had many more Christian than Jewish listeners. Jonah had his non-Jewish listeners very much in mind when he shaped his broadcasts, for it was important as never before that American Christians see their Jewish neighbors for what they were.[31]

Indeed, on the very first program, Wise discussed the churches of Christendom as the children of the synagogue and quoted the thirteenth chapter of Acts that describes Paul, Barabbas and John as visiting synagogues in Salamis and Antioch. The program also included a brief reference to American synagogue history and Jewish prayer. "Next to the Bible, he (Wise) stated the prayer book for the Jews is their oldest spiritual heritage."[32]

Subsequent broadcasts during the program's first month on the air analyzed Jewish prayer, including two of Judaism's most sacred prayers, the Shema and Kaddish, and discussions of the Ten Commandments and the Sabbath. On the November 23rd program, Wise called the Bible "a handbook of human rights," a textbook of social duties and a code of humane and enlightened laws. The following week, he spoke about the influence of the Bible (referring to it as the "Old Testament") on the Pilgrims, Jesus, Mohammed, Martin Luther and Oliver Cromwell.[33]

Many of the program's sermons were delivered by guest rabbis (sometimes by a remote hook-up) who typically delivered a series of four or five consecutive weekly sermons. Most represented the Reform branch of Judaism, but from time-to-time Conservative and Orthodox rabbis were invited to appear on the program.[34] Christian clergyman also delivered guest sermons, including Reverend Ralph Sockman[35] of Christ Church (Methodist) in New York City and Reverend Henry Knox Sherrill (Episcopal). In a memorandum that David Wise prepared for Cauman containing recollections about his father, the son recalled that when it came to choosing guest rabbis, his father had his favorites, who were usually his "best friends" but that he also invited others because of their ability as speakers without regard to their personality. But, David Wise added, "He was not above asking men whom he considered to be in a position to raise sums of money for the program from their congregations."[36] He also wrote that his father "was always the star of his own show, to the extent that this was possible. This was the attitude he maintained even at the risk of sacrificing one or two musical selections on each broadcast or limiting guest speakers in the amount of time devoted to sermons."[37]

According to Cauman, the most popular speaker, as measured by both the amount of mail and contributions that were received, was Rabbi Joshua Loth Liebman of Temple Israel, Boston, and author of the best-selling book, *Peace of Mind*. Liebman appeared on several occasions during the 1940s His talks focused on the relationship between religion and psychology with sermons on issues such as: "Making Life Worth Living," "Finding Serenity In An Insecure World," and "Wise Rules For A Happy Marriage." In 1936, Wise also invited laymen to give addresses, including the philosopher, John Dewey, (December 19th, "The Promise of America"), Dr. Mary Woolley, a peace advocate and president of Mount Holyoke College (December 19th, "The Field of Liberalism in America") and Dr. William H. Kilpatrick of Columbia University (December 26th, "Education and Liberalism"). Listeners were invited to write in requesting free copies of the sermons.[38]

In February and March, 1938, a series of four sermons was delivered by Boston Rabbi Harry Levi whose topics were: "Why Believe in God," "Why We Suffer," "Why Pray," and "After Death What?" In a portion of the "Why We Suffer" sermon that has survived in audio format, the rabbi asks the very same question that continues to be asked almost 70 years later: If God is good, why does he allow people to suffer? The "Why Pray" sermon discussed prayer as it applied to all religious groups.

A December 2, 1939 sermon reflected a very different theme. On that broadcast, the guest rabbi was Rabbi Morris S. Lazaron of the Baltimore Hebrew Congregation, a frequent speaker on the program. Lazaron devoted his talk to speaking out in opposition to a planned visit to the United States by Chaim Weizmann, former president of the World Zionist Organization. His rationale, shared by several others at the time, was that certainly Jews, in good conscience, could support the establishment of a homeland for the Jewish people. Such support however, if carried out openly could, in addition to doing harm to Arab-Jewish relationships in Palestine, also encourage anti-Jewish elements in the United States.[39]

A 1950 study on the popularity of the program's sermons concluded that the two most popular categories were the relationship between Judaism and Christianity and the religious approach to life. Of the five most popular sermons, as measured by receiving at least 3,000 or more letters, the top four sermons fit into the first category while the fifth fit into the second grouping. In descending order, the five most popular sermon were:

- The Jewish Jesus and the Christian Christ (5,000 letters)
- Christianity's Debt to Judaism
- The Jewish Position on Jesus
- Judaism's Debt to Christianity
- Wise Rules for a Happy Marriage

In his analysis of 266 programs broadcast between 1950-1959, Zahavy concluded that 55 had self-help themes, 42 were political, 36 were devoted exclusively to expounding the advantages of Reform Judaism, 31 were on either brotherhood or Christianity, 18 dealt with sociological subjects, seven on science, six on home life, sex and marriage, four on Israel and 61 on various religious discussions.[40]

The music for the program was initially under the direction of bass-baritone Frederick Lechner, who also performed as a soloist on the program. The choir was under the direction of Lazar Weiner and Alexander Richardson was at the organ. Over the years, the works of several Jewish composers were featured, including Ernest Bloch, Herbert Fromm and Darius Milhaud. According to David Wise, music never played an important role on the *Message of Israel* during his father's lifetime. Cauman noted that whereas Lechner saw music as an end in itself, for Wise, music was a means to an end — a difference of opinion that led to occasional clashes between the two men. In his desire to keep the program popular, Cauman wrote, "He (Wise) was not in the least averse to homely touches, such as common hymns or choral offerings by the children of the synagogue." One such clash resulted in Lechner telling Wise, "If you are going to stoop so low as to schedule that moronic hymn you want me to sing, I'll sing it, but you'll have to get right down there with me and cheapen your sermon, too."[41]

Despite his concern that the program, like the *Church of the Air,* did not provide sufficient balance between the three branches of Judaism, Zahavy considered the Reform oriented program to be, "one of the most renowned Jewish religious radio programs of our times. Its national scope and character made the host (Rabbi Jonah B. Wise) a figure known throughout the land."[42] David Wise also reflected on the program's diverse audience when he observed, "Our faithful listeners include the homebound and those who live in remote areas, as well as many Christians who (tune in) while en route to church. In addition to the letters from our Jewish friends, we have received many from nuns, priests, and other non-Jewish listeners, all of whom are afforded a unique opportunity to see how rabbis think about a wide range of social and personal issues that affect Jews in every land."[43]

As examples of the program's interfaith focus, Cauman cited two letters from non-Jews written sometime in the 1950s:[44]

> It was the singing of that choir that first attracted me to the program. Off and on for weeks, months, I had twisted dials on Sunday morning in hope of finding some 'satisfying music' but no luck; then suddenly, there it was — exactly what I had been searching for and missing probably by seconds. I was slightly amused to learn that it was a 'Jewish service' — expecting to hear a lot of informative ritual — but it could have been a service from my own church...I have grown to love the voice of Rabbi Jonah B. Wise and miss him greatly when he is away. Many of the anthems sung by the Temple choir are sung by our own choir...

The second letter was written in response to a comment Wise made during a broadcast indicating that he was not certain about the size of the listening audience or its reaction to the program.

> I listen regularly and we have discovered much to our surprise that several of our friends also listen. I speak of it as a surprise because, you see, none of us are Jewish. Now when you are a Scotch Presbyterian it is a little awkward to casually refer to what Rabbi So-&-So said on the Message of Israel, and yet that has happened, and it happened because what is said on your program is not only applicable but quotable.
>
> What is it that we like? The reasoned, almost intellectualized approach. The short description of Jewish holidays, what they are and why (which have always been a mystery before). The happy relief from 'hell fire and damnation' and the raving and/or groaning of preachers. In short you and your special speakers are worth listen-

ing to, for information, guidance, and, if you like, for understanding. And more than that, the program is stimulating.

An unanticipated negative consequence of the program's success was that its name was appropriated by an evangelical minister, Coulson Shepherd, who, in 1945, initiated his own program, *Message To Israel*, that was designed to convert Jews. The program was broadcast in New York City on Sundays at 10pm over WINS and elsewhere by transcription. Wise, Cauman wrote, decided not to take any legal action against Shepherd for possible copyright infringement on the grounds that such action would only have called more attention to the new program.[45] The American Jewish Committee, acting on a complaint from Mrs. Felix Warburg, the wife of one of the founders of the *Message of Israel*, also looked into the matter but there are no records indicating that the AJC took any action to stop the program.[46]

When Jonah B. Wise died in 1959, his successor at Central Synagogue, Rabbi David J. Seligson, became the program's host. David Wise continued as the program's producer and later became its host. In the late 1950s when free air time was no longer made available to religious groups, the program began to experience financial difficulties and appeals for funds went out to listeners. The program remained on the air, however, for almost 20 more years, broadcasting its last program on July 8, 1986.

Copies of some of the sermons delivered on the *Message of Israel* are in the Central Synagogue Archives. Additional sermons can be found in the American Jewish Archives that houses the personal papers of some of the rabbis who appeared on the program. The only known sound recordings of the program broadcast earlier than 1960 are portions of three programs from 1938 and 1947. Tapes of later programs are available in the Central Synagogue Archives and at the American Hebrew Archives in Cincinnati.

Sunday Radio Chapel

Like CBS's *Church of the Air*, the *Sunday Radio Chapel* heard on the Mutual network in the 1940s gave air time to the three major faiths on a rotating basis.[47] The Jewish segment was under the auspices of the Synagogue Council of America and, according to Zahavy, time was allotted to all three branches of Judaism on an equal footing. The 30-minute program consisted of an opening and closing prayer as well as a sermon that generally ran for about 16 minutes. The themes of the Jewish sermons included self-help topics, Jewish holidays, the role of religion in America as well as

political subjects. A May 2, 1943 sermon marked an interfaith day of prayer and intercession for Jews who had been murdered at the hands of the Nazis.

Faith in Our Time

During the 1940s, Mutual carried a second religious program, *Faith in Our Time*, that also provided air time to the three major faiths on a rotating basis.[48] In 1949, the program was heard over 133 stations in 36 states. The Jewish segment was under the auspices of the Synagogue Council of America, the same group responsible for the network's *Sunday Radio Chapel*. The program allotted equal time to all three branches of Judaism.

Unlike other religious programs that consisted primarily of sermons, the focus of these 15-minute broadcasts was how religion could be applied to the listeners' daily lives to help them solve their problems.

The Light of the World

Conducting research for a chapter focusing on broadcasts that reflected Judaism as a religion presented the authors with interesting challenges. Should the chapter be limited to programs that were created entirely by Jewish religious institutions — or perhaps include broadcasts that reflected Jewish issues? Would a program heard by millions of listeners every day that focused on biblical themes with an emphasis on the Old Testament, qualify for inclusion? *The Light of the World* was just such a program. Considering that the Old Testament provides much of the basis of the Jewish religion, the authors decided that a daily broadcast reminding listeners, Jew and gentile alike, of the trials and tribulations experienced by the Jewish people, was indeed an appropriate program to include in the chapter.

Produced by Frank and Anne Hummert, the team responsible for introducing probably more successful soap operas and prime time series than any other entrepreneurs in the business, the idea behind the program was that the Old Testament provided enough drama and religious inspiration to appeal to people of all faiths. Despite the Hummert's remarkable track record, Hal Erickson, in his book on religious broadcasting, observed that, "in 1940 most of the radio community thought that NBC and General Mills were a little gone in the head to attempt a daily program serializing the stories of the Old Testament."[49] The couple's faith in their idea was, however, well founded. The program remained on the air, mostly on NBC's

Red network, for a decade, from March 18,1940 until June 2, 1950, with only a brief hiatus (August-December, 1946) due to a shortage of flour, the sponsor's product.[50] During the time it was off the air, there was an unprecedented flood of letters demanding that the program be brought back. When General Mills did resume its sponsorship, the number listeners increased by some 50 percent.[51]

Jim Cox, in his excellent book, *The Great Radio Soap Operas,* wrote that the series appropriately began with a multi-part retelling of the story of Adam and Eve featuring Philip Clark and Eleanor Phelps in the titleroles.[52] In the weeks, months and years that followed, other chapters of the Old Testament were played out in daily segments, with some events requiring more air time to flesh out than others. By the time the series celebrated its first anniversary, the March 31, 1941 issue of *Time* magazine reported that the program was number eight in popularity among daytime radio serials. The article went on to report that the show was currently dramatizing the story of Moses after having scored a hit with six weeks of broadcasts on the adventures of Joseph. The article noted that in the Bible, the story was told in just 14 versus in the Book of Genesis.

The writer and critic Max Wylie thought enough of the program to include a script of one of its broadcasts in his prestigious book, *Best Broadcasts of 1940-1941.*[53] The program's traditional opening, which followed the opening musical theme played by organist Clark "Doc" Whipple, featured a voice coming from an echo chamber intoning: "The Light of the World...the story of the Bible, an eternal beacon lighting man's way through the darkness of time!" More organ music was heard, then a commercial and more organ music and finally an announcer who introduced the program as follows:

> This is our day to day story of the holy Bible, presented as a living monument to man's faith in God, reverently portrayed. The story is told in the language of today for clarity and understanding and to bring the greatness, the humanness of the Bible and its people to everyone, and to make those people as much alive today as the book which houses them. And now, we continue the story of Joseph, a character from the book of Genesis, chapter 44, verse 4.

The following dialogue illustrates how the biblical verses were "translated" to meet the demands of a daytime soap opera. The setting: Joseph's brothers have been brought into the Pharaoh's great reception hall and

Joseph is waiting to see if his brothers will sacrifice Benjamin as they had sacrificed him several years earlier:

Simeon: (Anxiously) Judah...
Judah: Yes, Simeon?
Simeon: (Low) Do you think we'll all be put into prison?
Judah: (Low) I hope not. But...why couldn't the silver cup have been found in my grain sack...instead of in Benjamin's!
Simeon: Judah...we know Benjamin didn't take that cup!
Judah: Of course he didn't. (Sighs) Simeon...I...I don't understand it...but...I'm sure that this is our punishment for what we did to...Joseph.
Simeon: (Hopelessly) Yes. I've always known that someday we'd be punished for selling him to the slave traders ...and for lying to father...telling him Joseph was dead . . .

An example of how the writers[54] managed to relate biblical times to every day events was evident in the story of Moses that aired on June 6, 1944. During that broadcast, the actor who played the role of the Pharaoh used a voice that sounded much like that of Germany's Fuhrer, ranting loudly with sounds from the crowd cheering him on in responses that could well have been imagined to sound like, "Sieg Heil." Dramatic license aside, the producers of this program proved that an ecumenical approach to religious broadcasting was possible.

The Eternal Light

While the jury may still be out regarding what effect, if any, the programs cited above may have had on the listening public's attitude towards Jews, there can be little doubt that *The Eternal Light* played a positive role in gaining understanding and goodwill for Jews from a significant portion of the entire listening public.

The authors wish to express their appreciation to Eli Segal, author of *The Eternal Light* and Jeffrey Shandler and Elihu Katz for their chapter, "Broadcasting American Judaism" in *Tradition Renewed*, a two-volume history of the Jewish Theological Seminary, the organization that created the program.[55] Segal's book, in addition to being authoritative, is more personal in its approach as he is the son of Robert Segal, one of the program's two cantors, and he frequently accompanied his father to the NBC studio when the program was broadcast. His book also includes a log of the program from 1944 through 1982. The more historically oriented Shandler/Katz chapter is based on documents in the Seminary's archives and interviews with people who had been associated with the program.

To gain a full understanding of how and why *The Eternal Light* came about, one must know something about the Jewish Theological Seminary. Founded in 1886 for the purpose of training rabbis in the Conservative Jewish tradition, the Seminary began producing broadcasts as early as the 1930s under the guidance of its then president, Cyrus Adler. On March 15, 1937, a program celebrating the Seminary's 50th anniversary was broadcast on WEAF in New York. Also in the late 1930s, the Seminary produced *The Women's Hour*, a weekly half hour program that aired on New York's WHN.

Rabbi Louis Finkelstein, who became president of the Seminary in 1940, also recognized radio's value, both in terms of explaining Judaism to the American public and of giving Jews a better appreciation of their own heritage. Early in his tenure, Finkelstein expressed an interest in the possibility of initiating a network series that would reveal Judaism as, "the world's best-kept secret."[56] Planning for the new series began to take shape in 1943 when Finkelstein met with NBC president David Sarnoff. The network was interested in airing a new Jewish program as it had recently lost the *Message of Israel* to ABC when it was forced to divest itself of the Blue network.[57] At the meeting, it was decided that NBC would provide the facilities for a weekly broadcast organized by the Seminary with the understanding that the broadcasts had to reflect Judaism as a whole, not merely the Conservative movement.

With NBC committed to the new series, the Seminary hired Milton Krents on a contingency basis to develop the new still unnamed program. The head of the American Jewish Committee's Radio Department, Krents had earlier produced some radio programs for the Seminary on a freelance basis. It was during this early planning stage that one of the key factors that led to the program's eventual success was decided: Krents suggested to Finkelstein that the new program should consist of dramatizations, a sharp departure from the traditional format of religious broadcasts that featured devotional services, concerts of sacred music and sermons. In support for this new format, Krents argued that radio drama could effectively present topics of serious social concern to general audiences.[58]

Krents then persuaded the Seminary to contract with playwright Morton

Wishengrad to develop several scripts for the proposed series. A former staff member of the International Ladies Garment Workers Union's Education Department, Wishengrad had already written several scripts for radio, including the *NBC University of the Air* series *Lands of the Free*. An avowed agnostic, Wishengrad was reported to have found it hard to maintain his skepticism about religion after an extended lunch with Finkelstein.[59]

The overwhelmingly positive public reaction to one of these early scripts, "The Battle of the Warsaw Ghetto," may well have been the deciding factor that convinced the Seminary's divided Board of Directors to support the proposed new series. Broadcast on Yom Kippur, October 3, 1943, Wishengrad's powerful drama recounted the events that had happened only six months previously when the inhabitants of the ghetto had battled Nazi troops for over a month.[60] Prior to the Board's vote, members opposed to the series had argued that limited funds should not be used for a questionable project.[61] They also raised the often heard argument about the wisdom of keeping a low profile: a weekly series, they believed, would bring too much attention to the Jews and could be damaging.

Once the decision was made to proceed with the series, the Seminary was given the responsibility for script development while NBC assumed responsibility for providing production and technical staff for each program. The network also assigned Max Jordan, its director of religious programs, to work with Krents who became the program's producer, a position he occupied throughout the program's entire run. Marjorie Wyler of the Seminary's Public Relations Department was also closely involved with the program and at some point was also given the title of producer. To facilitate the development of scripts, Krents worked with NBC staff members, advisers from the Seminary, Wishengrad and a small department at the Seminary, today known as the Radio and Television Department but initially known as simply the Eternal Light Department. He also encouraged and received input from a number of biblical and historic scholars. Moshe Davis, a dean of the Teachers Institute of the Seminary, was appointed program editor and was responsible for hiring Seminary students as research assistants to provide supporting data for script ideas. An outside advisory committee representing the various major religious movements of American Jewry was also created to provide input on script development. One of Krents' first acts as producer was to change the proposed name of the weekly series from its original title, *Synagogue of the Air,* to the name that listeners would become familiar with for the next four decades. According to Shandler and Katz, the name change was motivated by a desire "to present something other than conventional American religious programming rooted in some aspect of public worship...(The name) also invokes an image of Jews as a timeless moral 'light unto the nations.'"[62]

To prepare the listening public for the new series, the Seminary's Public Relations Department drafted a series of press releases that stressed that the program was designed "to show Judaism as a moral force in important moments of history."[63] Follow-up press releases highlighted the series' basic precepts: "to extol all who sanctify God's name; to emphasize the sanctity of the human personality; to demonstrate the fundamental character of the democratic impulse in a good society; to define the place of Palestine in Jewish religious aspiration; and to introduce, elucidate and interpret Jewish ritual, ceremonial and folklore."[64] It is interesting to note that only two of the five precepts mention Judaism; the other three would fit comfortably into any Christian statement of faith.

The mix of Judaism and general ethical/moral principals was equally prominent in a 1940s promotional poster for the program that described *The Eternal Light* as "dramatizing the ideals of Judaism" but also "attacking apathy and ignorance." The poster featured the Seminary's Institute for Religious and Social Studies that provided educational programs for clergymen of all faiths.[65]

Clearly, what set *The Eternal Light* apart from other contemporary religious programs — and which most likely contributed to its popularity among non-Jews — was its emphasis on humanism as distinct from theology. Shandler and Katz cite two major studies of religious broadcasting that highlight the major differences between *The Eternal Light* and non-Jewish religious programs. While Christian programs were generally concerned with theology, Jewish programs, the studies found, were motivated more by historical and pragmatic issues. Also, *The Eternal Light* "affirmed the dignity of all human beings" and did not consider men as puppets of either God or the devil.[66]

In its inaugural season, the program was carried by 33 of the network's affiliates as well as Canada's CBC network. While the program was always aired on Sunday, its time slot changed from 11:00-11:30am to 12-12:30pm to 12:30-1pm in 1946. The program was broadcast for over four decades, including more than three decades during which it was on both radio and television, although at different times and with different scripts.[67]

As discussed in earlier chapters, during radio's golden age, program openings often served as a signature for a favorite program. Even today, listeners familiar with the old programs recall some of radio's most memorable openings: the "William Tell Overture" on *The Lone Ranger*, Ferde Grofe's "Grand Canyon Suite" that introduced Johnny calling for a Philip Morris cigarette, and the sounds of marching feet and the rat-a-tat of machine guns on *Gang Busters*. The opening for each episode of *The Eternal Light* series would likewise become memorable for years to come and consisted of a cantor[68] chanting the Hebrew song "Shomer Yisrael" and the narrator solemnly intoning the words from Leviticus:

> And the Lord spake unto Moses, saying, Command the children of Israel that they bring unto thee pure oil olive, beaten for the light, to cause the lamps to burn continually in the tabernacle of the congregation, and it shall be a statute forever in your generations.

In his analysis of the episodes broadcast between 1944-1982, Segal grouped the programs into six broad and sometimes overlapping thematic categories: Instruction, Social Problems, Biography/Historical Events, Holidays, Biblical Stories, and Palestine/Israel. He noted, however, that all the programs "served to educate a general listening audience in the ethics and values relevant in any day."[69]

The format for most of the programs consisted of a mix of narrative and dramatization, followed by a brief talk delivered by either a religious leader or a secular person, including public figures such as New York's Mayor Fiorello H. La Guardia.[70]

At the suggestion of Finkelstein, it was decided that the first 13 episodes would dramatize the importance of the synagogue in Jewish history. But when Wishengrad translated the suggestion into actual scripts, the results were radio dramas that focused more on the stories of individual Jews and Jewish communities throughout history and throughout the world than on actual brick and mortar buildings. The first episode, for example, that aired on Sunday, October 8, 1944, "A Rhode Island Refuge," was about the Jews of Newport, Rhode Island during the Revolutionary War and the Touro Synagogue, the first Jewish house of worship in the United States. During the war, most of the congregation supported the colonists' cause. But, when a member of the congregation who supported the Loyalists was killed by a mob, the congregation nevertheless mourned his death as a man who died for loyalty's sake. The program also included a reading of the letter that George Washington sent to the congregation after the war in which he wrote: "For happily the Government of the United States, which gives to bigotry no sanction, to persecution no assistance, required only that they who live under its protection, should demean themselves as good citizens."[71] The program's underlying message was clear — and a repeat of the message broadcast on the 1939 Jewish episode of *Americans All, Immigrants All*: Jews were loyal Americans and their values were compatible with traditional American values.

Subsequent episodes in the pilot series dealt with a Jewish scholar who became a frontiersman, demonstrating that Jews could fit in anywhere ("Jacob and the Indians," October 22, 1944[72]), how the Jews in 14th century Europe were blamed for the plague ("The Black Death," November 5, 1944), and how a 17th century Chinese Jew who was both a scholar and a soldier saved his community ("The Temple of K'ai-Feng-Fu," November 26, 1944). In this last episode, after the dramatization, a guest rabbi explained that the Jewish community in China dated back to the 11th century and that its original synagogue had been destroyed several centuries later.

The second series of 13 programs focused on Jewish personalities (Louis Brandeis, Rebecca Gratz, Cyrus Adler, Emma Lazarus, etc.) but also used history to tell the story of the Jewish struggle. This group of programs included: "Mr. Lincoln and the Rabbi," (February, 11, 1945) about President Abraham Lincoln and a Baltimore rabbi who confronted the issue of slavery, "A Second Exodus," (March 25, 1945) about the expulsion of the Jews from Portugal in 1492, and a rebroadcast of "The Battle of the Warsaw Ghetto," (January 28, 1945).

While a considerable number of the early programs in the series focused on historical events, the Seminary did not hesitate to address important current issues such as the struggle faced by some of the displaced persons in Europe following the end of World War II, U.S. efforts to assist Japanese women scarred by the atomic bomb, and a dramatization of Anne Frank's diary. When the General Assembly of the United Nations convened for the first time, the October 20, 1946 episode, "Isaiah and the United Nations" had the prophet Isaiah addressing the Assembly's opening session. The series also included biographical stories about prominent non-Jews such as George Washington Carver (February 2, 1949) and Mahatma Gandhi (January 1, 1950).

Judaism Aired: Religious Oriented Programs 179

Rabbi Jonah B. Wise hosted the *Message of Israel* from 1934 to 1956. (Photo courtesy of Joan Wise Kaufman.)

Cast of *The Eternal Light* during a fundraising performance, ca. late-1940s, early-1950s. Left to right: Roger DeKoven, unidentified, Cantor Robert Segal, Norman Rose, Dan Ocko and Bernard Lenrow. Isidor Geller at keyboard. (Photo courtesy of Eli Segal.)

Not all the episodes dealt with serious subjects, however. In "The Wise Men of Chelm," (July 7, 1946), writer Milton Wayne borrowed from Jewish folklore and told the tale of the legendary town where bread always fell to the floor buttered-side down. And in the comedy "The Would-be Pauper," (August 11, 1946), a formerly wealthy man is unable to convince his friends that he is no longer rich.

Within a year after its premiere broadcast, the number of NBC affiliates carrying the program more than doubled.[73] And by 1946, the Hooper ratings suggested that the program was drawing as many as five million listeners and was almost as popular as *The Catholic Hour* which had been running for 15 years and which enjoyed a better time slot.[74] Commenting on the program two months after its debut, *The New York Times* radio critic Jack Gould wrote:

> Technically, it is listed as a 'religious program,' but that is to do it a gross disservice. More accurately, and perhaps primarily, it should be described as a series of fine and sensitive dramas which stand very much on their own merit as radio plays. Coincidentally, it provides rich stimulation of the spirit of brotherhood among all men and an opportunity for renewal of the individual's faith, be it Jewish, Protestant or Catholic.
>
> This blend of dramatic and religious aims is believed unprecedented in a religious group's use of radio but patently has not been unwanted. Letters from all races and creeds, numbering among them newspaper editors, ministers, teachers, lawyers and housewives, have poured in on the seminary's office...in appreciation of the broader appeal inherent in a dramatic presentation as opposed to the more conventional sermons and hymns....
>
> Despite the chosen setting, 'The Eternal Light' is nonsectarian in its appeal. Through each week's program are woven certain basic thoughts which are applicable to all faiths...Mr. Wishengrad underscores another point worth stressing in all faiths. It is the importance of being one's self, whether Jew or Gentile, for to compromise one's faith for immediate expediency is to compromise one's own dignity as a human being.[75]

By the 1950s, even though more than 100 stations across the United States carried the program, the size of the audience declined from a peak of six million to two-and-one-half million, largely due to the advent of television. The Seminary received an average of 500 letters a week from listeners and mailed printed scripts of the programs to 900 regular subscribers at a cost of ten cents each.[76]

The program also won dozens of awards, including one in 1946 from the National Conference of Christians and Jews. Accolades for the program came from many sources, including the trade paper *Variety* that praised both the program and its production values, a 1948 manual on how to produce religious programs that cited *The Eternal Light* for being "not only one of the best religious programs on the air, but also one of the leading dramatic shows in all radio," and *The New York Times* that praised the program for its "fundamental new approach...to religious broadcasting." Even Eleanor Roosevelt mentioned the program in her daily newspaper column, "My Day."[77]

Several factors contributed to the popularity of *The Eternal Light*. In addition to the universality of its content as discussed above, the series attracted a group of talented writers and some of the finest radio actors in the business, including Alexander Scourby, Roger DeKoven, Ralph Bell, Louis Van Rooten, Norman Rose, Raymond Edward Johnson, Karl Swenson, Juano Hernandez, Bryna Raeburn, Leon Janney, Guy Repp, Santos Ortega and Berry Kroeger. For the program's first 13 years, the actors performed at the American Federation of Radio Artists (AFRA, later renamed AFTRA) union scale minimum salary, which at one point in time was $42 per program. While Morton Wishengrad is the writer most closely associated with the program, other writers included Joseph Mindel, Irv Tunick, Marc Siegel (no relation of the authors), Sylvia Berger, Ernest Kinoy, Arnold Perl, Erik Barnouw, Shimon Wincelberg, Norman Rosten and Irwin Gonshak.[78]

A number of well known and talented directors also participated in the series, including, Anton M. Leader, Walter McGraw, Frank Papp, George Voutsas, Ira Avery, Ed King, Dan Sutter, Kenneth MacGregor. Prominent NBC staff announcers who introduced the program included Tex Antoine, Arthur Gary and Mel Brandt. The program's music was under the direction of conductor Milton Katims.

From the outset, *The Eternal Light* was designed to appeal to both non-Jewish as well as Jewish audiences. For non-Jews, the series was designed to "demystify Jewish history, beliefs, and practices, and, by eradicating ignorance about Jews, eliminate anti-Semitic prejudice." For Jews, the Seminary saw the program as a way to "provide a point of entry for the unaffiliated, isolated or culturally illiterate members of the community."[79] An estimated 60 percent of the program's mail came from non-Jews.[80]

In their research, Shandler and Katz had an opportunity to read some of the letters from listeners that were used by the Seminary's public relations office for publicity purposes. Although they caution that the letters may have been selected by Seminary staff because they conformed to the Seminary's expectations, they nevertheless included the following excerpts of undated letters from both Jews and non-Jews in their chapter.

From a non-Jew in South Carolina:

> I always make it a point to listen to your Sunday morning program, "Eternal Light." I am a Gentile who is finding it easier to admire and like the Jewish people through your broadcast... Your program has helped me to understand the problems of the Jewish race. My husband recently brought home a Jewish soldier and his wife whom he liked and wanted me to also. They are grand people. We have carried on conversations with them about the Jewish religion and their historical background. Many times my only knowledge was what I absorbed from the "Eternal Light." I believe your program will do much to help other Americans understand the Jews, and thus foster a better relationship between them. Our postwar world needs just that. You are doing fine work.

From a Jew in rural Vermont:

> We Jewish people who are scattered in all the small towns throughout the land are very much in need of spiritual guidance, and any little bit we hear through means of radio, is like a bit of manna from heaven.

For both Jews and non-Jews who are too young to have heard *The Eternal Light* on radio or viewed it on television, a great number of the radio programs have survived. Also, a collection of 26 radio scripts written by Morton Wishengrad was published in 1947, and copies of the book may be available from a used book dealer.[81] A documentary movie about the program, *The Eternal Light: A Historical Perspective*, is also available for purchase from the Seminary.

Notes

Abbreviations

AJC   American Jewish Committee Radio Department Archives at Yivo Institute, New York, NY.
MIP   Message of Israel Papers, Central Synagogue Archives, New York, NY.
URJ   Union of Reform Judaism Records (Formally Union of American Hebrew Congregations), American Jewish Archives, Cincinnati, OH.

1. Hal Erickson, *Religious Radio and Television in the United States: 1921-1991* (Jefferson, NC: McFarland & Company, 1992), 1-2.

2. Donna Halper, "Jewish Radio Programs in the United States," in *Encyclopedia of Radio*, Christopher H. Sterling, ed. (Routledge, 2003), 784.

3. Ibid., 784-785. A number of Levi's sermons presented during his six years on radio were collected and published in two volumes. Also, it was not unusual for the rabbi to receive fan mail and friendly visits to his temple from Jew and gentile alike.

4. *Boston Traveler*, March 13, 1925, cited on Temple Israel's web page, www.tisrael.org.

5. Erickson, *Religious Radio*, 3.

6. On the program, couples were introduced to the audience before they took their wedding vows and then interviewed immediately after the ceremony.

7. A December 1, 1931 article in *Variety* notes that the program was broadcast on WABC, "a (CBS) network local station." However, it is not clear if the program was carried on other network stations. The brief article says that the program featured musical stars and tragedians of the Jewish stage and that its time slot had recently been changed to Saturday morning from Sundays at noontime. The series was sponsored by the Jewish newspaper, the "Day." See also Zev Zahavy. "The History and Survey of Jewish Religious Broadcasting," (Ph.D. Thesis, Yeshiva University, 1959), 158.

8. URJ. Manuscript Collection No. 72, Series E: Microfilm Records, Reel #1667. Copies of many of the broadcast schedules are included in the microfilm records. With the exception of four references to a Sunday, 3pm program featuring Rabbi Stephen S. Wise that aired on the "NBC chain" in March-May, 1929, the other broadcasts were all local, were aired on different days and at different times. Although the file does not contain information about the names of the programs, from other sources it appears that one of the New York City programs was most likely called the *Temple Emanuel Hour*. John Dunning, *On the Air: The Encyclopedia of Old-Time-Radio*, (New York: Oxford University Press, 1998), 574, lists a 30-minute *Synagogue Service* broadcast on NBC from 1926-1929 on Wednesdays at 7pm but provides no additional information about the program.

9. "Radio Broadcasting by Synagogues Taken Up in Israelite Survey,"

April 15, 1932, 1. Ibid. The total number of rabbis invited to participate in the survey is not known.

10. Ibid., 4.

11. The three major branches of Judaism differ primarily on how Judaism is practiced.

12. Zahavy, "History and Survey," 46. The dissertation is the most detailed examination of Jewish religious broadcasting through 1959 that the authors are aware of. Much of the information came from records at NBC, CBS and Mutual, as well as other local stations and Jewish organizations. One of the authors also conducted a telephone interview with Zahavy in 2007.

13. Not to be confused with a later program by the same name that was Christian in orientation.

14. Zahavy, "History and Survey," 35-37.

15. Ibid., 39.

16. The authors are indebted to Bryan Cornell, reference librarian at the Recorded Sound Section of the Library of Congress, without whose enormously generous assistance much of this section could not have been properly authenticated. Whereas Dunning, *On the Air*, shows the *Jewish Hour* as starting in 1928, the authors have used the NBC logs to establish the program's correct starting date.

17. Also known as the *CBS Church of the Air* and the *Columbia Church of the Air*.

18. The authors estimate that between 1931-1957, approximately 2,500 programs were broadcast. During the same time period, the Jewish population of the United States ranged between 3-4 percent of the country's total population.

19. Zahavy, "History and Survey," 211-213.

20. Ibid., 215.

21. Ibid., 213-214.

22. Ibid.

23. Ibid., 215.

24. The authors have been able to piece together the history of the program from the following sources: a biography of Rabbi Jonah B. Wise, the program's creator (see footnote 28), Zahavy's "History and Survey," ibid., the archives of the Central Synagogue in New York City and the cooperation and assistance of the Wise family.

25. Dunning, *On The Air*, 572, incorrectly shows the program having begun in 1935.

26. Although the new program was broadcast under the title, *Message of Israel*, NBC viewed it as "formally called *The Jewish Hour*." Rabbi Wise was also a consultant for the Jewish segment of the *Church of the Air* as well as *The Eternal Light*. On September 31, 1931, Wise broadcast a Yom Kippur sermon

on CBS that originated from Central Synagogue.

27. David J. Seligson, "Message of Israel," Sermon, November 1, 1964. MIP, Box 2.

28. Sam Cauman, *Jonah Bondi Wise: A Biography* (New York: Crown Publishers, 1966), 141.

29. "Message of Israel Marks 50th Year," *Reform Judaism*, Summer 1985, 26. The article uses a question and answer format with the answers coming from David Wise recalling events that happened decades earlier. In response to one of the questions, Wise says that he became program director in 1950. However, in the Central Synagogue archives, correspondence shows him as program director in 1946. Also, according to Cauman, in 1949, David Wise became director of the radio and television for the Union of American Hebrew Congregations. In that capacity, he developed several programs, including the *Temple Hour*, "a nationally broadcast religious radio service heard every week since 1950" and also broadcast on the Armed Forces Radio Service. Wise was also responsible for other locally broadcast programs. See Cauman, *Jonah B. Bondi*, 147.

30. Zahavy, "History and Survey," 222.

31. Cauman, *Jonah Bondi Wise*, 142.

32. Zahavy, "History and Survey," 155.

33. Ibid., 218.

34. A complete log of the guest speakers, the dates of their appearances and the title of their sermons is available in MIP, Box 1. Reform rabbis who appeared often included Barnett Brickner, Abraham Feinberg, Roland Gittelsohn. Solomon Freehof, Louis Newman, Irving Reichert and Louis Mann. Orthodox rabbi David de Sola Pool of New York's Spanish-Portuguese Synagogue was a frequent guest.

35. Reverend Sockman had his own radio program, *The National Radio Pulpit*.

36. "Memo from David J. Wise to Sam Cauman," October 13, 1964, MIP, Box 2.

37. Ibid.

38. The sermons were mimeographed on the letterhead of the United Jewish Laymen's Committee that listed both the *Message of Israel* and *Church of the Air* programs. The lower left hand side of the letterhead carried the message: "The United Jewish Laymen's Committee, with whose best wishes this complimentary copy is sent, is supported entirely by voluntary contributions and will be happy to receive your offering." The message in the lower right hand corner of the stationery read: "If you have enjoyed this service, won't you write your local station manager. The good will thus created guarantees the continuation of our broadcasts."

39. In 1943, Lazaron founded the American Council for Judaism, an anti-

Zionist organization. Lazaron's papers, including some material related to his appearances on the *Message of Israel*, are located at the American Jewish Archives. The Archives contain the papers of other rabbis and lay persons associated with the Reform movement who were heard on other religious oriented radio programs.

40. Zahavy does not indicate the methodology he used to categorize the sermons. When one of the authors of this book reviewed a log of the sermons, it was often difficult to determine the exact nature of the sermon from the short sermon title. For example, Zahavy, an Orthodox rabbi, delivered a sermon on the program entitled, "Two Are Better than One." The author would be hard pressed to assign the sermon to any of the categories Zahavy used in his own analysis based on those five words. On page 215 of his dissertation, in the context of another program, Zahavy himself acknowledges that it can be difficult to tell the content of a sermon by its title. Also, in a May 31, 2007 phone interview with Joan Wise Kaufman, Jonah B. Wise's daughter, Ms. Kaufman told the authors that her father avoided political sermons as he believed that religion and politics did not mix.

41. Cauman, *Jonah Bondi Wise*," 130.

42. Zahavy, "History and Survey," 219. Zahavy notes that when the program's time slot was changed to Sunday morning, Orthodox Jews were able to listen to the broadcast.

43. "Message of Israel Marks 50th Year."

44. Cauman, *Jonah B. Bondi*, 143-144.

45. Ibid., 144.

46. AJC, Box 234, Folder 1947.

47. Zahavy, "History and Survey," 223-226.

48. Ibid., 226-229.

49. Erickson, *Religious Radio*, 117-118.

50. The program aired on NBC from March, 1940-June, 1944, then on CBS from June, 1944-August, 1946, and back again to NBC from December, 1946-June, 1950.

51. Jim Cox, *The Great Radio Soap Operas* (Jefferson, NC: McFarland & Company, 1999) 95-96.

52. Ibid., 94-97.

53. Max Wylie, *Best Broadcasts of 1940-41* (New York: Whittesley House, 1942), 331-337.

54. Among those credited with having written scripts for the series are: Don Becker, Margaret Sangster, Noel Gerson and the sisters, Adele and Katherine Seymour.

55. Eli Segal, *The Eternal Light* (Newtown, CT: Yesteryear Press, 2005) and Jeffrey Shandler and Elihu Katz, "Broadcasting American Judaism: The Radio and Television Department of the Jewish Theological Seminary," in

Tradition Renewed, Vol. II, ed. Jack Wertheimer (New York: Jewish Theological Seminary, 1977), 365-401.

56. Shandler, "Broadcasting American Judaism," 366. Finkelstein's interest in radio was particularly noteworthy as those who knew him well doubted that he himself had much experience listening to, or even owning, a radio.

57. Ibid., 394 (n7).

58. Ibid., 366-367. Marjorie Wyler, the Seminary's Director of Public Relations and later producer of *The Eternal Light*, also recalled that the program's advisory committee felt that worship services, sacred music and sermons were "either violations of Jewish tradition or inappropriate for the largely non-Jewish audience." 374, 397 (n58).

59. Ibid., 375-376, 397 (n59).

60. "The Battle of the Warsaw Ghetto" was rebroadcast twice during World War II and was also heard internationally on the Armed Forces Radio Service. A press release marking the 25th anniversary of *The Eternal Light* series claimed that some 10,000 letters had been received in response to the broadcast. Ibid., 395 (n13).

61. Ibid.,371. It cost the Seminary $22,000 to underwrite the pilot series of 13 episodes.

62. Ibid., 387. The new title was also symbolic as in every Jewish synagogue an eternal light hangs over the ark where the sacred Torah scrolls (the first five books of the Old Testament) are kept.

63. Press release announcing the program's debut, August 29, 1944. AJC, Box 235, Folder 1944.

64. Shandler, "Broadcasting American Judaism," 387.

65. Ibid., 395 (n21).

66. Ibid., 387-388. For a more detailed discussion of how different faiths approached the use of radio, see Everett C. Parker, David W. Barry and Dallas W. Smythe, *The Television-Radio Audience and Religion* (New York: Harper & Brothers, Publishers, 1955). Shandler and Katz include a quote from an interview with Moshe Davis, *The Eternal Light's* program editor, in which Davis recalled the time that an NBC executive questioned why the network was airing a "religious" program that to him seemed to have nothing to do with religion.

67. While the start date for the radio version of *The Eternal Light* is known, the records are unclear about the end date. Segal estimates that the radio version ended sometime in 1985-1986 with many of the programs in the later years being rebroadcasts of earlier episodes. The television version started in 1951, initially on a rotating basis with Catholic and Protestant segments as part of the program, *Frontiers of Faith*, and then, beginning in 1953, as *The Eternal Light*. The television version also ended sometime in the 1980s.

68. Cantors Robert Segal and David Putterman alternated opening the

program in 13 and then later 10-week cycles. Original music for the program was composed by Morris Mamorsky.

69. Segal, *The Eternal Light*, 32. Information about specific programs broadcast after 1969 is missing.

70. The speakers were selected by Dr. Finkelstein. "Memo on The Eternal Light from Milton Krents to Abe Feinberg," October 27, 1953. AJC, Box 234, Folder 1952-1953.

71. Segal, *The Eternal Light*, 33.

72. An adaptation of a Stephen Vincent Benét story. Other episodes were also adaptations of other literary works, including some by Sholom Aleichem.

73. See AJC, Box 235, Folder 1946-1945 for the results of a telephone poll conducted in 1945 in New York City and Philadelphia to judge listener reaction to the program.

74. Segal, *The Eternal Light*, 19 and Shandler, "Broadcasting American Judaism," 372-373, 396 (n45). Shandler and Katz also take note of the symbolic overtones of the Seminary's frequent use of the "six million listeners" in its press releases: the number invokes the estimated Jewish population of postwar North America as well as the number of Jewish victims of the Holocaust, 390.

75. *The New York Times*, December 17, 1944, 9.

76. Shandler, "Broadcasting American Judaism," 373.

77. Ibid., 373-374, 397 (n50, 51).

78. In the program's early years, writers received $300 per script. Segal, *The Eternal Light*, 21.

79. Shandler, "Broadcasting American Judaism," 389.

80. Krents, "Memo on The Eternal Light." The memo doesn't explain how the letter writer's religion was ascertained.

81. Morton Wishengrad, *The Eternal Light: 26 Radio Plays From the Famous Eternal Light Program* (New York: Crown, 1947).

9
Jews in the Mainstream

Most of the programs described earlier in this book were aired on a regular basis as part of an ongoing series. In this chapter, the authors examine a sampling of individual episodes of network series that did not typically feature Jewish themes. It also looks at several special broadcasts that were aired on a one-time-only basis for a specific purpose. With few exceptions, news broadcasts are not included.

This portion of the book is organized in four sections. For the most part, within each section, the programs appear in chronological order. Part I includes programs heard from 1930 to 1938; Part II includes programs from 1939 through World War II; Part III includes programs heard after the war; and Part IV includes biographical programs that featured prominent Jews. Some long-running series, such as *The Lux Radio Theatre*, are listed in more than one section.

Part I: The Gathering Storm: 1930-1938

Between 1930 and 1938, with the exception of *The Goldbergs* and the religious program, *Message of Israel*, radio audiences would have been hard pressed to hear an episode with a Jewish theme or Jewish character on programs that were designed to appeal to a broad — or mainstream — audience. (Of course, there was always Father Coughlin.) For the most part, Jews were simply ignored. Why? One explanation is that Jews represented less than 4 percent of the total population. A second reason is that at a time when anti-immigrant sentiments as well as anti-Semitism were increasing, the networks, reacting to those trends, saw little reason to broadcast programs about a group of people who were viewed by many as being different and/or undesirable. And sponsors, concerned about sales, wanted to avoid offending non-Jewish listeners who were potential customers.

Broadcast of the American Jewish Congress Rally

An early exception to this relative silence was the broadcast of the

1933 rally that was organized and led by Rabbi Stephen Wise, president of the American Jewish Congress.

Beginning in 1932, reports reached the United States about the increasing harassment of Jews in Germany. Events became more ominous when in 1933, over a period of three months, Adolf Hitler became Chancellor of Germany (January 30th), the Reichstag building (home of the German Parliament) was set aflame by Nazi agents who placed the blame on communists, socialists and Jews (February 22nd), the Nazi party gained a majority of seats in the new Parliament (March 5th) and the Parliament granted full dictatorial powers to Hitler (March 24th).

On March 12, 1933, a week after the Nazi party won its majority in Parliament, Wise invited concerned individuals and organizations to join together to organize a rally designed to protest the increasing acts of violence against Jews in Germany. Although some of the people attending the meeting urged restraint, arguing that protesting Nazi policies might result in further acts of aggression against Jews, Wise responded by saying, "The time for caution and prudence is past. We must speak up like men. How can we ask our Christian friends to lift their voices in protest against the wrongs suffered by Jews if we keep silent?...What is happening in Germany today may happen tomorrow in any other land on earth unless it is challenged and rebuked. It is not the German Jews who are being attacked. It is the Jews."[1]

The rally was held in New York City's Madison Square Garden on Monday, March 27, 1933 and attracted more than 55,000 people who crammed into the auditorium and the surrounding streets. Similar rallies, sponsored by local affiliates of the American Jewish Congress, were held on the same day in Chicago, Philadelphia Boston, Baltimore, Cleveland and 70 other communities across the country. The rally's goal was to gather national support for a boycott of German goods in the hope that such a boycott would influence the Nazi government to end its anti-Jewish activities.[2]

The rally was broadcast by all three major networks from 10-11pm, and at least two stations in New York City, WMCA and WLTH, a Yiddish station, carried the rally beginning at 9:30pm. Because of the international focus of the event, the rally was also aired via short-wave throughout much of Europe. During the broadcast, listeners heard Senator Robert Wagner, American Federation of Labor president William Green, former New York Governor Al Smith and several Christian clergyman, all calling for an immediate cessation of the brutal treatment being inflicted on German Jewry.

The March 27th broadcast may have raised the consciousness of many American Jews, and even a number of well meaning Christians, about the worsening situation of the Jews in Germany. However, generating sympathy for people living thousands of miles away at a time when Americans were in the midst of a terrible depression proved a hard sell. The boycott turned out to be a failure and the listening audience returned to lighter fare, not giving much thought to the ethnicity or religion of the performers who were entertaining them. Housewives followed the day-to-day adventures of *The Goldbergs*. Entire families listened to Fanny Brice portraying Baby Snooks as well as to the antics of Eddie Cantor and Jack Benny. Music enthusiasts enjoyed the songs of George Gershwin, Irving Berlin and Jerome Kern. Few of the millions of fans who enjoyed the Andrews Sisters singing their hit song, "Bei Mir Bist Du Schoen," gave much thought to its composer, Sholom Secunda.[3]

As the number of radio stations increased during the 1930s and more households owned radios, the networks found themselves under increasing pressure to provide quality entertainment for listeners, regardless of where they lived or the size of their community. It was during this period that radio drama began to compete with the earlier comedy and variety programs that had borrowed much of its talent from the vaudeville stage. In order to attract women who were home during the day and keep them listening to the radio, daytime serials (a.k.a. soap operas because a number of them were sponsored by companies that sold soap such as Procter and Gamble) were developed, often borrowing from popular novels of the day, such as "Stella Dallas" and "David Harum." For the new evening drama programs, scripts were either written especially for the occasion or were adaptations of short stories, novels, plays or films. It is from these adaptations that some Jewish themed episodes were heard in prime time in living rooms throughout America. For the most part, they were few and far between.

The Fleischmann's Yeast Hour

One of the earliest network programs to feature Jewish entertainers performing as Jewish characters was NBC's *The Fleischmann's Yeast Hour* (1929-1936) hosted by the popular crooner Rudy Vallee. In addition to Vallee's singing, the 60-minute variety program featured many well known guest artists from the Broadway stage, the movies and vaudeville. Vallee also invited many talented but lesser known entertainers to appear on the program, regardless of their race or religion and long before African-American and Jewish performers were welcome on other radio programs.[4]

Listening to a few of these surviving programs today, more than 70 years after they were aired,[5] one may be left with mixed feelings. At a time when anti-Semitism was common, Vallee was clearly helping talented Jewish artists advance their careers by introducing them to a nationwide audience. However, as many of the artists used routines that were based on their successful vaudeville acts, what mainstream America often heard on the program were comedy sketches that included unflattering Jewish stereotyped characters. (Readers may recall that when Gertrude Berg created *The Rise of the Goldbergs*, she went out of her way to avoid these stereotypes. See page 22). Some examples.

Jewish Vaudeville Stars

The earliest *Fleischmann's* program known to have survived that showcased a Jewish artist using a Yiddish dialect is a January 12, 1933 broadcast featuring Fanny Brice doing a portion of the "Romeo and Juliet" sketch that she had performed three years earlier on the *Philco Hour* (see page 111).[6]

On the February 16, 1933 broadcast, vaudeville comedienne May Usher, using a heavy Yiddish accent, sang "Sammy Goldberg's Wedding" in which the woman who didn't get to be Sammy's bride mocks the appearance of the bride, her family and the wedding in what can only be described as "a nasty outpouring of jealousy." It may have been funny — but it also re-enforced an unflattering stereotype of a Jewish woman.

The vaudeville comedian Lou Holtz was also a frequent guest on *The Fleischmann's Yeast Hour*, often in routines that used a Yiddish dialect. In a sketch on the March 16, 1933 program, Holtz applies for a job at a shoe factory. When the owner asks him his name and Holtz replies, "Max Shapiro," the owner tells him, "We don't hire Hebrews." Holtz then tells the owner, "I'm Filipino." After some additional dialogue, the factory owner tells Holtz that he has another Filipino working for him and summons the employee, Juan (Vallee), to test Shapiro's knowledge of Spanish. A frustrated Shapiro, who obviously can't understand Juan's few words in Spanish, finally responds with a common Yiddish curse, "Ich hob dir en dred," (drop dead) which generates laughter from the audience. When Vallee repeats the curse to Holtz suggesting that he too may be Jewish, the audience laughs again. The sketch ends when the owner addresses the same curse to both Vallee and Holtz, suggesting the possibility that he also may be Jewish.

Turning the clearly anti-Semitic practice of not hiring Jews into a comedy sketch may have sent a message to listeners about the unfairness of this practice. But, as in the case of the May Usher sketch, did it also send an opposite message? As for the humor in the routine, the New York audience present at the program's live broadcast clearly enjoyed it — and understood its closing Yiddish curse. Did the audience in middle America react in the same way?

"The Baby Carriage"

In a change of pace, the August 10, 1933 *Fleischmann's* program featured a dramatization of the one act play, "The Baby Carriage," written by Crocker Bosworth.[7] and starring Jenny Moskowitz who Vallee had seen on Broadway playing the role of the Jewish mother in "Counselor at Law."[8]

The story was set in the Lezinsky Tailor Shop, circa 1919, and featured four characters in what by today's standards would be considered a maudlin melodrama. Moskowitz (as Mrs. Lezinsky) speaks with a thick Yiddish dialect sprinkled with more than a bit of pathos as though almost every sentence sent a "woe is me" message.

While Mrs. Lezinsky is minding the shop, in walks Mrs. Rooney, a customer who speaks with a thick Irish brogue. Listeners soon learn that Mrs. Lezinsky has two little children with a third on the way. She admires Mrs. Rooney's baby carriage, visible from the shop's window. When told that the carriage is for sale because the Rooneys are moving and can't take it with them, Mrs. Lezinsky becomes obsessed with the desire to have the carriage even though she doesn't have the funds to pay for it. After unexpectedly finding money in the pocket of a pair of trousers left at the shop for mending, she tells Mrs. Rooney that she will buy the carriage. Once the customer returns for his pants, he realizes that not all the money that had been in the pocket is still there. When Mr. Lezinsky arrives at the shop and realizes what has happened, he gives the man the missing $5 (that he had been saving to pay for a needed eye operation) and berates his wife for what she has done. Ashamed of herself, Mrs. Lezinsky gives her husband the money she took from the pants and her husband forgives her.

A heart-wrenching story of a dedicated mother — or a weak immoral

Jewess behaving in a manner hardly in the tradition of Judaic teachings? One can only speculate how audiences reacted to the characterization of Mrs. Lezinsky — or of Mr. Lezinsky who is portrayed as an honest and righteous man with the strength and goodness to forgive his wife for her transgression.

The Lux Radio Theatre

The hour-long *Lux Radio Theatre* was one of the most popular dramatic anthology programs on radio, airing from 1934-1955. Hosted for much of its run by the famed Hollywood producer/director, Cecil B. DeMille, the series specialized in adaptations of stage productions and later of movies.

"Counselor at Law"

On January 13, 1935, the program broadcast an adaptation of the Elmer Rice play "Counselor at Law" that had appeared on Broadway in 1931 and had been made into a movie in 1933.[9] The dramatization featured some of the original Broadway cast, including Paul Muni, Louise Prussing and Jenny Moskowitz. The play was adapted for radio on at least three additional occasions: the first time, four years later, January 6, 1939, on *The Campbell Playhouse* featured Orson Welles in the title role and Gertrude Berg as his mother; the second time, May 16, 1948 on *The Ford Theatre*; and the third time, October 30, 1949, on *The Theatre Guild on the Air* (a.k.a. *The United States Steel Hour)* featuring James Cagney in the title role.[10]

In the play, the counselor has risen far above his immigrant parents' humble background and has become a successful attorney married to a socialite "shiksa" (non-Jewish woman). It is clear, however, from his exchanges with his Italian-American partner that despite their success, there is a chasm between "them" and rival WASP lawyers. As the plot develops, it becomes clear that for all the good deeds the counselor has done helping other people, he is not averse to "bending" or even "twisting" the law to achieve his goal — both for the benefit of his clients and himself. Without the revealing the play's outcome (as readers may someday have an opportunity to listen to one of the broadcasts), the play presents at least two Jewish themes: The "outsider" status of professional Jews, regardless of their ability, and the fact that Jews, like non-Jews, are not perfect, a theme that was heard earlier in "The Baby Carriage." Rice may also have been sending audiences a more universal message found in the Bible (Matthew 16:26): "For what is a man profited, if he shall gain the whole world, and

"The Jazz Singer"

Another Broadway production that circuitously made its way to the *Lux* program was "Day of Atonement" by Samson Raphaelson. Originally a drama, the play was made into a musical, "The Jazz Singer," starring George Jessel. The musical, in turn, was made into the first talking feature film, "The Jazz Singer" starring Al Jolson. The *Lux* adaptation of the film was broadcast on August 10, 1936 and again on June 2, 1947. Al Jolson starred in both broadcasts. The program also adapted Jolson's two biopics, "The Jolson Story," February 16, 1948 and "Jolson Sings Again," May 22, 1950.

The story is about a Jewish boy who breaks with his family's tradition and leaves home to pursue a career on the stage as a "jazz" singer rather than follow in his father's footsteps and become a cantor (a person who sings or chants prayers during a Jewish religious service). Through hard work, the boy becomes a popular entertainer. When the father is dying, the singer returns home to take his father's place in the synagogue on Yom Kippur (the Day of Atonement) and he chants the "Kol Nidre" prayer.

Two additional film versions of the story were made. The 1952 movie starred Danny Thomas and the 1980 version (with an updated story line) starred Neil Diamond.

"The Life of Emile Zola"

On May 8, 1939, *Lux* broadcast an adaptation of the 1937 film, "The Life of Emile Zola." Paul Muni, who portrayed Zola in the film, appeared in the radio version. The program's title notwithstanding, the main focus of both the movie and the radio version was how in 1898, the famous French writer championed the cause of Alfred Dreyfus, a Jewish army captain. In an act of blatant anti-Semitism, Dreyfus was accused of passing military secrets to the Germans, convicted, and sentenced to life imprisonment on Devil's Island, the notorious French prison off the coast of South America.

As the story unfolds, Zola becomes outraged when he learns that the army general staff, even after being shown evidence proving conclusively that Dreyfus is innocent and that another person is responsible for the crime, refuses to acknowledge its error and release the Jewish officer. At that point, he writes his famous "J'Accuse" open letter to the French President that is published in a literary newspaper and which accuses the army of perjury and covering up the entire affair. Zola is then found guilty of libel and sentenced to prison. However, before he is sent to jail, he flees to

England where he continues to write articles on behalf of Dreyfus. Eventually Dreyfus was freed, restored to his military rank and fought for France during World War I.

In a provocative article, "Hollywood, Nazism, and the Jews, 1933-41," writer Felicia Herman examined the history of the film, including how Warner Brothers, the studio that produced the movie, the film industry's censorship office and Jewish organizations approached the issue of how to treat the story's anti-Semitism which was the heart of the movie.[11] The subject was particularly sensitive — and controversial — given what was happening in Europe.

In sharp contrast to the film that deleted the three occurrences of the word "Jew" from the original script under pressure from the Production Code Office, in the radio version, the word "Jew" is mentioned once, in the scene where the army generals were reading through a list of names in search of a person who could be accused of the crime. For listeners unfamiliar with the Dreyfus affair and not knowing where the story was headed, the intermission comments by the movie's director, William Dieterle, delivered between the second and third acts, put the story in clear focus.

> If this play you're so admirably doing tonight has a message to convey, it is that there are millions of people in the world today like Dreyfus. But there is not always a Zola. Yet, there is no reason to despair for any time, for any chance, a Zola might come along. Let's hope so.

The words in the closing scene, taken from the movie script, also drove home the message about what people of good conscience had to do. Following the original movie script, Zola, says:

> To save Dreyfus, we had to challenge the might of those who dominate the world. It's not the swaggering militarists — they are but puppets that dance as the strings are pulled — it is those others, those who would ruthlessly plunge us into the bloody abyss of war to protect their power and their gloom.

> Think of it, Alexandrine (Zola's wife). Thousands of children sleeping peacefully tonight under the roofs of Paris, London, Berlin, all the world, doomed to die horribly on some titanic battlefield unless it can be prevented. And it can be prevented. It must. Not by force, but by ideas. Ideas that liberate.

Jews in the Mainstream 197

The radio drama ends when Anatole France, a fellow writer, tells the crowd at a memorial service for Zola:

> Take to your hearts the words of Zola. Enjoy today's freedom. Do not forget. Do not forget those who fought the battles for you and bought your liberty with their genius and their blood. Do not forget them and applaud the lies of fanatical intolerance. Be human!

For the most part, between the 1933 Stephen Wise rally and November, 1938, mainstream America read or heard little about what was happening to the Jews in Germany.[12] While the press did not completely ignore events occurring in Germany, those stories that did appear were rarely seen on the front page; most were hidden deep within the paper. Radio coverage of events in Germany was even more limited. From the early to mid-1930s, networks focused on providing entertainment programs. Sponsors, who in 1934, accounted for approximately one-third of network time, were either generally less interested in airing anything about current problems or, if they did, wanted veto rights over its content.[13] Radio historian Erik Barnouw notes that in the early 1930s, NBC-Blue had only one daily news program, Lowell Thomas, and NBC-Red had none. Radio was also in a battle with newspaper publishers over the right to air news items that appeared first in a newspaper. This began to change slowly, however, as events unfolded in Europe. Beginning in 1934, the networks started building their news staffs. And newspapers decided that instead of fighting radio, it made more business sense to join the growing trend, either by purchasing existing stations or by applying for new licenses.

Walter Winchell, the columnist for Hearst's *The New York Daily Mirror*, was also known for broadcasting gossip on *The Jergens Journal* (1932-1948).[14] He also happened to be Jewish and was one of the earliest, and certainly the loudest, radio commentator to alert his listeners to the events occurring in Germany. Winchell also spoke out against several neo-Nazi fascist organizations that were growing in strength in the United States and he did not hesitate to name the names of those congressmen whose anti-Semitic views effectively scuttled any hope that significant numbers of refugees fleeing Nazi persecution might find a haven in the United States.

Another outspoken radio personality was the noted raconteur Alexander Woollcott. In 1935, listeners to Woollcott's CBS evening program, *The Town Crier*, heard the critic express his opposition to both Fascism and Nazism.[15] When the program's sponsor, the National Biscuit Company, makers of Cream of Wheat, received letters protesting Woollcott's comments, they asked Woollcott to refrain from such topics. Despite several warnings, the critic refused and the company dropped its sponsorship. Woollcott is reported to have said that anyone with the courage of a diseased mouse would have done what he did.[16] After the show was cancelled, an irate Woollcott sent a letter to the sponsor's advertising agency in which he reminded them that, "These elements (the controversial material) lend the series salt, provoke discussion, whip up attention, and enlarge the audience."[17] The agency, however, was more concerned with selling cereal than Woollcott's opinion. The next fall, Woollcott returned to the CBS line-up, but on a sustaining basis. When the program was picked up by the Liggett & Myers Tobacco Company a few months later, it was renamed *The Granger Program* (Granger is a pipe tobacco) "starring Alexander Woollcott as the Town Crier." The critic got a raise in salary and the program was even more popular than it had been when sponsored by Cream of Wheat. So much for the "alleged" danger of broadcasting controversial material.

Eddie Cantor was another radio celebrity to speak out against Hitler and Father Coughlin and, as noted in Chapter 6, was forced off the air for a year as a result of his outspokenness. He also helped raise money for the Youth Aliyah Movement that relocated Jewish children from Germany to Palestine and the United States. At least two of his appearances on behalf of the organization were broadcast, including one as early as October 20, 1936.[18]

The March of Time

From 1931 to 1945, *The March of Time,* produced by *Time* magazine, offered listeners what then was a highly innovative way to learn about the news of the week. In a newsreel-like style, the program presented the news in a series of dramatizations that gave listeners the sense that they were present while the event was actually taking place. Most of the voices heard on the broadcast, including the reporters as well as the people making the news, were those of actors whose ability to sound much like the people they were portraying caused not a few listeners to think that they were hearing the voice of the "real" person. At one point, it was said that President Roosevelt asked that the program stop having someone impersonate him because the actor was so good it was diminishing the impact of his *Fireside Chats*.[19] The voice most associated with the program was the stentorian sound of the narrator, Westbrook Van Voorhis, who, in addition to the weekly radio program, was also the narrator on the newsreels shown in movie houses across the country.

On the March 24, 1938 broadcast, one of the segments reported on changes that had taken place in Vienna in the two weeks following the Anschluss, the merger of Austria with Nazi Germany. In a dramatization set in a classroom, students are confronted with schoolbooks that had been rewritten and in which Jews were being blamed for anything bad that had happened in history. When students tell their teacher that the new textbooks contradict what the old ones said, the teacher sighs and tells them that they now must use the new books. Isidore, a Jewish student, gets emotional when it is his turn to read a section from the new book out loud and he asks permission to leave the room.

The report that Jewish doctors had been prohibited from practicing medicine was followed by a second dramatization in which soldiers enter the apartment of Dr. Sigmund Freud and, on orders from the government, confiscate all his money and passport and place him in protective custody.

The third and final "Vienna" dramatized segment takes place at a rehearsal of the noted Vienna Philharmonic. There, the orchestra members are told that their noted conductor, Bruno Walter, a Jew, would no longer be able to lead them and that certain members of the orchestra would no longer be employed. When the musicians ask to be led in a farewell piece of music by Franz Schubert, the melody slowly fades away and is overtaken by the Nazi "Horst Wessel" song.

Considering that *The March of Time*, broadcast on NBC-Blue, aired opposite *The Kate Smith Hour* on CBS and *The Rudy Vallee Show* on NBC-Red, one may wonder how many listeners were tuned in to the news program. A fourth choice for network listeners in the 8pm time slot was a classical music program.

Kristallnacht (November 10, 1938)

As events in Europe continued to deteriorate, there were still those who viewed the reports of what was happening as being exaggerated or affecting only a few individuals. However, all that changed after November 10, 1938 as news reports of the pogroms (organized violence, either spontaneous or premeditated against a group of helpless people) against the Jews that had taken place in Germany reached the United States. In what would later become known as Kristallnacht, the night of the broken glass,[20] radio listeners across America were shocked. The pogroms were a reaction to the assassination of a minor German embassy official in Paris by Herschel Grynszpan, a young Polish Jew. In a single evening, some 267 synagogues in Germany were partially or totally destroyed, Jewish owned businesses were attacked, 39 Jews lost their lives, and, in a series of mass arrests, upwards of 20,000 Jews were sent to concentration camps. In many respects, the events of November 10th were a turning point in both the print and radio coverage of what was happening to the Jews in Germany.

At a November 15th press conference, President Roosevelt, who up until that point had made no public comments regarding conditions in Germany, raised the issue of what had just taken place in Germany without being prompted by reporters. In a prepared statement, Roosevelt expressed his own shock and dismay at what had occurred. His comments were, of course, reported in newspapers as well as on radio news broadcasts:

> The news of the past few days from Germany has deeply shocked public opinion in the United States. Such news from any part of the world would inevitably produce a similar profound reaction among American people in every part of the nation. I myself could scarcely believe that such things can occur in a twentieth century civilization. With a view to gaining a first-hand picture of the current situation in Germany I asked the Secretary of State to order our Ambassador in Berlin to return at once for report and consultation.

One of the first non-Jewish print and radio journalists to speak out against the events of November 10th was Dorothy Thompson, the daughter of a Methodist minister who was known for her strong anti-Fascist, anti-Nazi beliefs.[21] In 1939, Thompson was named by *Time* magazine one of the two most influential women in America (the other being Eleanor Roosevelt). Her newspaper column, "On the Record" was syndicated in as many as 170 newspapers and between 1936 and 1945 she was heard on the radio on both the NBC and Mutual networks. In 1938, her program reached a potential audience estimated at six million people.[22]

On November 14th, just four days after Kristallnacht, Thompson spoke to her radio listeners about what had happened in Germany. Although on one level she was concerned about raising money for Grynszpan's legal defense, the focus of her remarks was her outrage at how the Nazis had used the shooting as a justification to persecute the entire Jewish population of Germany.[23]

Who is on trial in this case? I say we are all on trial. I say the Christian world is on trial. I say the men of Munich are on trial, who signed a pact without one word of protection for helpless minorities. Whether Herschel Grynszpan lives or not won't matter much to Herschel. He was prepared to die when he fired those shots.

They say a man is entitled to trial by a jury of his peers, and a man's kinsmen rally around him when he is in trouble. But no kinsman of Herschel's can defend him. The Nazi government has announced that if any Jew, anywhere in the world, protests at anything that is happening, further oppressive measures will be taken. They are holding every Jew in Germany as a hostage.

Therefore, we who are not Jews must speak, speak our sorrow and indignation and disgust in so many voices that they will be heard. This boy has become a symbol, and the responsibility for his deed must be shared by those who caused it.

If you are not Jewish and you feel as I do, I ask you to wire or write me in care of this station.

Thompson's comments were reprinted in the December 10th issue of *Radio Guide*, one of the popular fan oriented radio magazines of the day.[24] In a side bar accompanying her comments, the editor wrote:

A few minutes after Miss Dorothy Thompson made her remarkable plea for the life of Herschel Grynszpan, many thousands of telegrams and letters were on their way to her. Equally remarkable was the fact that such a plea was broadcast at all. It is not policy, ordinarily, for a network to encourage the discussion of (a) controversial matter. Nor is it usually the policy of a sponsor to tread heavily on issues loaded with dynamite. As we grow older in broadcasting experience, we stride ahead, advancing to new frontiers of discussion. The frontier reached by Miss Thompson the other evening is one of which every listener should be proud.

The editor also explained that the magazine was awarding the program the "Radio Guide Medal of Merit" but that the award in effect went to three entities: First to NBC for carrying the message; second to General Electric, the program's sponsor for "its support of a broadcast which had little relation to its responsibility of selling better lighting to the public"; and third to Miss Thompson herself.

Part II: 1939-1945: World War II

In the years prior to America's entry into the war, radio was a powerful tool for awakening the public to the dangers of Fascism and Nazism. While not the sole means of communicating with the public, radio was clearly the instrument of choice as it reached more people than books, magazines or films. Radio's reach into the American home was pervasive. By 1938, an estimated 91 percent of all urban households and 70 percent of rural households had radios, some more than one.[25] A 1939 survey concluded that "70 percent of Americans relied on radio as their prime source of news and 58 percent thought that radio was more accurate than the press."[26] With the country still in a depression, radio continued to be the primary source for entertainment and news for most Americans.

Once America entered the war, radio's mission expanded to include building morale and creating a sense of national identity — and unity. If America was going to win the war, encouraging tolerance of all people, regardless of their race, religion or ethnic background, had to become a national priority. In an article on Jewish identity during World War II, Edward S. Shapiro noted that, "public opinion polls in 1938 and 1940 revealed that nearly two-thirds of Americans believed Jews as a group had 'objectionable traits,' and over 50 percent of Americans thought that German anti-Semitism stemmed either partially or wholly from the actions of the German Jews."[27]

Radio's efforts to forge a sense of wartime national unity were carried out by a variety of government agencies such as the Office of War Information (OWI) and the Treasury Department, the networks and local stations and an array of both Jewish and gentile secular organizations. The programs took many forms. Some, with titles such as *Speaking of Liberty, I am an American, You Can't Do Business With Hitler, This Is War* and *They Call Me Joe,* were series created specifically to bolster the wartime effort. Other programs were individual episodes of recurring series and/or one-time-only broadcasts that delivered messages of tolerance, brotherhood and national unity. Some spoke in very general terms; others were more direct in talking about Jews and the evils of anti-Semitism.

While there is no way to know for sure what effect, if any, these programs had the public's attitude towards Jews, when taken together, like the effect of leaves falling off a tree or the flutter of a butterfly's wings,[28] the programs may well have had some cumulative effect of bringing about a greater sense of tolerance and understanding. For some Americans, that understanding didn't come until the war was over and the full extent of the Nazi persecution of the Jews was exposed for the world to see. By then, of course, it was too late.

News broadcasts

By 1938, NBC, CBS and Mutual had all increased their coverage of foreign affairs, touching not only on the fate of Europe's Jewish population but also on Japan's aggressive actions in the Far East, the Anschluss, Germany's annexation of Czechoslovakia's Sudetenland territory and ultimately the German invasion of Poland in September, 1939. For the very first time, the radio news reports of Edward R. Murrow, Robert Trout, William L. Shirer, Elmer Davis and others brought news of the events of what was happening in Europe and Asia into the homes of millions of Americans.

On October 30, 1939, Edward R. Murrow, broadcasting from London on the CBS news program *Today in Europe*, spoke about a report from the British Consul in Vienna concerning an old Jew who had been kicked by a Nazi storm trooper while the regular police looked on. On his November 10th broadcast, Murrow reported that Jewish elements had been blamed for the failed assassination attempt on Hitler's life. On his November 19th broadcast on the CBS program, *The War This Week,* William L. Shirer reported on an announcement by the Nazis that Polish Jews would be treated no differently than German Jews. And on December 30th, Murrow reported on Hitler's claim that he never wanted the war but had been forced into it by Jewish warmongers who were out to destroy Germany.

Similar news stories of Nazi anti-Jewish activities were broadcast throughout 1940 and 1941. None of the reports, however, ever rose to the point where the issue of what was happening to the Jews became important enough to require extended coverage.[29]

Radio Efforts of Jewish Organizations

Throughout the war, Jewish secular organizations, including the American Jewish Committee, the Anti-Defamation League, the United Jewish Appeal, the American Jewish Congress, B'nai B'rith, the Jewish Labor Committee and the Joint Distribution Committee all used radio to fight anti-Semitism. They did this primarily, but not exclusively, by promoting the message of brotherhood, national unity, the values of American democracy and tolerance for all minorities. In many of these efforts, the word "Jew" was deliberately omitted as part of a strategy designed to foster the idea that Jews were no different than other Americans. These efforts included special series, individual episodes of mainstream programs and one-time-only broadcasts.[30] As described by historian Richard Steele, "the patriotism promoted by the Jewish defense effort had none of the chauvinism and Anglo-conformity traditionally associated with 'Americanism.' It touted 'diversity rather than goose-step uniformity' and argued that the nation's strength lay in 'the variety of its peoples, the richness of its heritage.'"[31] For more insights as to how these groups fought anti-Semitism, as well as the effectiveness of using mass media to fight prejudice, see Stuart Svonkin's *Jews Against Prejudice*, Marc Dollinger's *Quest For Inclusion* and the analysis of listener response to the 1938-1939 series, *Americans All Immigrants All* in Chapter 4."[32]

American Jewish Committee

Of all the Jewish secular organizations, the American Jewish Committee (AJC) was the most aggressive in its use of radio to further its agenda. In 1937, the Committee created a separate Radio Department that initiated its own projects, coordinated the radio efforts of other Jewish organizations and became a clearinghouse for information relating to anything Jewish that was heard on the air.[33] The AJC saw commercial radio as an ideal opportunity to impress the "man in the street" with material that furthered the organization's mission. "For herein lies the opportunity to place material with radio stars who command huge following. Our experience in the past with radio celebrities has been small because we have not engaged in a concentrated drive to reach them. However, we are endeavoring to make this work (as it is) one of our main jobs at the present time."[34]

A key component of the Committee's radio strategy was known as the "salting-in process." The concept utilized existing programs to present Jews in a dignified light and as an integral part of American life and history. The strategy was based on the belief that because the group's own programs would be viewed as being defensive in nature, the organization could be more effective by influencing the content of other programs.[35]

Under the direction of Milton Krents,[36] the Radio Department's activities influenced a broad range of programs, from public affairs forums to women's series, daytime serials, sports broadcasts, news programs, comedy shows and programs for juveniles. A review of the department's monthly reports, several of which are available on the AJC web site, document the broad reach of the Committee's effort to use radio to achieve its overall goals. The department's efforts were both reactive and proactive and fell into four distinct categories.

1) Monitoring both Jewish and non-Jewish programs and suggesting "corrective action" to stations as well as federal authorities in response to programs or material it found objectionable. In October, 1947, for example, the AJC received complaints about a particular episode of Art Linkletter's popular *People Are Funny* program. On the episode in question, a contestant was asked if she would do a particular stunt for $50.00. When she replied, "Yes," she was asked if she would do it for $25.00. She then responded, "Now don't Jew me down." The AJC's concern was not so much what the contestant said, but rather Linkletter's response to the comment. He was reported to have said something to the effect of: "Don't use that type of language on this program," but failed to use the opportunity to make a more positive statement about tolerance.

In a letter to the Committee's Washington office that had initially alerted the New York headquarters to the problem, Krents explained:

> We have been watching this program carefully, and this is the second time in six months that this has happened on the Linkletter program. Several months ago the same thing occurred, but the following week Linkletter apologized to the radio audience. On the more recent occasion, however, Linkletter made no such apology on the broadcast in question or on that of the following week. After the second program, I suggested to Dick Rothschild (Richard Rothschild, the AJC's Public Relations Director) that one of our Chicago friends make representation to the advertising agency who produces the program, Russel M. Seeds of Chicago. Because this program leaves itself wide open to such derogatory comments, I suggested that the agency have Linkletter caution all contestants against making remarks offensive to any race, color, or creed.[37]

In another instance, a letter writer complained to the AJC about what she perceived to be a negative image of a Jew on *Jack Armstrong*, a popular juvenile program. In the February 3, 1950 broadcast cited in the letter, the grocer, a Mr. Klein, was very attentive to a Jewish customer but decidedly less sympathetic to another customer, a Mr. Brown, who did not have enough money to feed his family. As the AJC noted in its response to the person writing the letter: clearly, had the grocer's name been anything but Jewish sounding, the issue would never have surfaced.

(For additional insights into how the AJC dealt with what it perceived to be objectionable representations of Jews, see Chapter 7.)

2) Initiating and/or participating in the creation of new programs. In 1939, the organization was in discussions with network officials regarding a number of programs, including *Totalitarian Tennis*, a sports program; developing a program in conjunction with the World's Fair that would have called attention to the contributions of various immigrant groups to the building of America; and interesting Fred Allen in a program that included Allen interviewing the caretaker of the Statue of Liberty.

3) Furnishing ideas and material for existing programs and for one-time-only broadcasts and participating in virtually all aspects of these programs, from securing time and participation to the preparation of scripts and publicizing the programs. The AJC was particularly active in suggesting questions for radio's many quiz programs. For example:

For the *Take It Or Leave It* program, a suggested question was: The Pilgrims are said to have gotten the idea for Thanksgiving from a similar holiday found in the Old Testament. What is the biblical holiday? The answer was the harvest festival of Succoth or the Feast of the Tabernacles. (This question was "shopped around" to more than one quiz program.)

For *Dr. I.Q.,*, which used a true or false format, the challenged statement was: The Jews are not a race. The answer was: True. Jews are any people who follow the religion of Judaism. There are Jews of all races and nationalities.

4) Advising local Jewish communities on how they could use radio for their own purposes. On a periodic basis, the AJC sent multi-page bulletins to its constituent groups identifying specific "pro-democracy" programs for which transcription discs and/or scripts were available for re-broadcast by local radio stations and for re-enactments by educational and interfaith groups. The bulletins listed special broadcasts produced by the AJC and other Jewish organizations as well as commercially produced programs such as *The Columbia Workshop, Mr. District Attorney* and *The Lux Radio Theatre*.[38] When local stations aired these and other programs of note, the Committee reminded local groups to send thank you notes to the

stations for having aired the programs.

During the postwar years, the Radio Department, appropriately renamed the Radio and Television Department, continued to monitor radio's treatment of Jews as well as influence program content. A 1947 report, "Radio Has A Job To Do," was a reminder that even though Hitler had been defeated, Americans still had to fight to "win the peace" and that radio had a big job in that "battle."[39] The new postwar proactive strategy called for:

1) Introducing minority characters in leading roles without "tagging" them with the usual clichés. "Present them as individuals involved in common human situations, people who simply 'happen' to be Jewish, Catholic, Italian or Negro."

2) Giving sympathetic characters names like Malinowsky and Epstein and Schrieber as well as Jones and Smith. "One name is as American as another."

3) Having Italian, Irish, Jewish, Negro and other minority characters speak as fluently as anybody else.

4) Attributing warm, admirable traits to minority characters, such as Papa David on *Life Can Be Beautiful.*

5) When showing a person offering a helping hand, make him a rabbi or pastor instead of the more usual Catholic priest.

6) Showing members of minority groups as having the same interests, tastes and way of life as other Americans.

7) Showing that minorities are an asset to community life.

8) Weaving the problems of minorities into plots, such as a "native" boy helping a "refugee" boy.

9) Making it a point to show that minorities fought in the war.

The report also listed five specific pitfalls to avoid so as not to inadvertently foster any negative Jewish stereotype.

1) Jokes that show Jews as money-graspers, pawnbrokers, sharp traders, etc.

2) Depicting Jews as clownish, foreign or involved mainly in their own problems.

3) Depicting Jews as pathetic, stepped-on underdogs, asking for sympathy.

4) Tagging characters with stereotyped names like "Abie."

5) Getting laughs by using broken English.

In addition to the above activities, the American Jewish Committee also initiated its own special broadcasts. Examples of two such broadcasts follow.

"Behold the Jew"

On Sunday, September 17, 1944, between 2:00-2:30pm, NBC-Red's flagship station in New York, WEAF, broadcast "Behold the Jew," a poem by the British poet Ada Jackson, adapted for radio by Milton Geiger. The text was narrated by the noted stage actress Florence Eldridge, the wife of actor Fredric March. In strong, rich tones, Eldridge is heard expressing admiration for the Jewish heroes of the Bible. She wonders why, for so many generations, and after so many cultural contributions, people continue to find reason to cry out against the Jews. Making it quite clear that she is not Jewish, the poet/narrator speaks tenderly of some Jews she has known over the years, among them a tailor who was kind to her as well as a child she knew when she was growing up and whose life ended sadly.

The program elicited more than 3,000 letters in what the AJC considered to be "an emotionally deep-dyed response from Jews and Christians throughout the country. The letters from gentiles were phenomenal in content."[40] One person wrote: "I am not Jewish, but I too, would be proud to be a Jew with that record and history." Another non-Jew wrote that she would be like a copy of the script for four reasons:

1) To show it to her younger brother who is being pressured not to make friends with Jews.

2) To show to a Jewish boy she recently met who was denying his Jewishness. "I could not help but hate him, for if he is ashamed of what he is, then he surely would be afraid of what he believes, and what good is a man who will not stand up for what he believes?"

3) To show to her best friend who cannot conceive of anyone being of any other faith but her own and will not believe that people of so opposite a faith can be good.

4) For herself, so that she can reread it whenever she is tempted to say that a person is lacking in intelligence or virtue because he believes something that is different from her beliefs.

Other letters from gentiles requested copies of the script for use in their own church work and discussions groups. Letters from Jews praised the AJC for its effective use of radio to foster religious amity.

"Jewish Religious Service From Germany"

On Sunday, October 29, 1944, at 9:30am, listeners tuning in to NBC stations on the east coast heard the following announcement: "The National Broadcasting Company, in cooperation with the American Jewish Committee, brings you now a special broadcast of historic significance...We turn you over now to James Cassidy, NBC war correspondent in the Aachen area."

The announcement was followed by a voice heard over what was clearly a short-wave signal[41] saying: "This is James Cassidy with the American First Army speaking from Germany. Today the National Broadcasting Company brings its listeners a program of historic moment, the first direct broadcast of a Jewish religious service on German soil since Adolf Hitler and his Nazis began the destruction not only of the Jewish religion but of all religions here more than a decade ago."[42]

Three months earlier, on July 23rd, also with the cooperation of the American Jewish Committee, listeners heard a special 15-minute broadcast from the Synagogue of Rome celebrating the first religious service from an Axis nation that had been liberated by the Allies. Anton Zolli, the Synagogue's chief rabbi, officiated at the service. During the war, the 73 year old rabbi had been hidden by friends.[43]

Anti-Defamation League (*Lest We Forget*)

Like the AJC, the Anti-Defamation League (ADL) preferred to take a low key, subtle approach in its fight against anti-Semitism. It did this through generalized programs that promoted the virtues of tolerance towards all races, ethnic and religious groups. During the 1940s and 1950s, the ADL's efforts to reach a national audience via mainstream radio were carried out under the auspices of the Institute for Democratic Education (IDE) and the Institute for American Democracy (IAD), both nominally independent agencies. The rational for using the intermediary organizations was the belief that the programs would appear to be more objective and therefore carry more weight if they were presented by non-Jewish groups. Through the IDE, the ADL developed the *Lest We Forget* series, 15-minute programs made available on transcription discs to stations throughout the country as well as to school systems and non-sectarian clubs and business organizations.[44] In addition to the recordings, stations and organizations also received spot announcements, promotional ideas, photographs of the programs' stars, posters and press releases.

Lest We Forget was actually the umbrella name for at least 16 sub-series, each focusing on a different aspect of American life, culture and government: "Great Americans," "A Better World For Youth," "Democracy Is Our Way of Life," "Eternal Vigilance Is the Price of Liberty," "One Nation Indivisible," etc. Taken together, the programs carried the same basic message of patriotism, American values and ideals — and the contributions made by Americans of different ethnic, racial and religious backgrounds. "The Great Americans" sub-series, for example, included sketches of prominent Jews such as Judah Benjamin, a major figure in the Confederacy, the labor leader Samuel Gompers and Haym Solomon, the financier who raised money for George Washington during the Revolutionary War.

Although the ADL (or possibly the IDE) used spot announcements to alert listeners to the program, the actual size of the listening audience was small and varied over the number of years that the series was broadcast. In 1943, for example, a study of the program's effectiveness concluded that the stations that carried the program were disproportionately small and that while station owners liked the program, the audience was limited. A Hooper report based on a survey of five stations rated the program as having been heard by less than 1 percent of the potential audience. The results did not, however, discourage the ADL and the group continued to produce the series.[45] In 1946, an article in *Variety* reported that according to the IDE, the program was being aired 52 percent of the time during prime time evening hours.[46] A year later, *Variety* reported that the programs were being "grabbed up" by as many as 750 stations and also went to 1,900 schools.[47] By 1950, an ADL newsletter noted that the program was carried by approximately 1,000 stations with "an audience numbering in the tens of millions."[48] What the bulletin did not say, however, was how many of the stations that received the discs actually used them, and if they were used, at what time of the day were they aired and how many people actually listened to them. As 15-minute "freebies," the stations mostly likely used the program as "fillers" dictated by the needs of their schedules.

Commenting on the program, an AJC report stated that, "The audience's response to these broadcasts has been excellent, and a number of school systems in various cities have incorporated the playing of *Lest We Forget* records into the regular public school curriculum. Important nonsectarian clubs and business organizations similarly are using the recordings or the scripts. This program has received the endorsement of outstanding leaders and educators..."[49] Over the many years it was broadcast, the program received numerous awards for excellence in the field of public service from both *Variety* and the Institute for Education by Radio.

Joint Distribution Committee (*Cable From Lisbon*)

On May 7, 1941, the Joint Distribution Committee presented a special half hour fund raiser that was carried by WOR, Mutual's New York flagship station. The agency, which had been helping Jewish refugees since 1919, was in dire need of funds to assist what was clearly becoming a flood of Jewish refugees fleeing Germany and other European countries that had been occupied. The program featured the writers Edna Ferber and George S. Kaufman and news commentator Raymond Gram Swing. The format was part dramatization and part a straightforward appeal for funds. The dramatizations told of the difficulties families were facing as they tried to escape and how the local offices of the JDC in several continents was providing them with the necessary funds.

What follows are selected examples of individual episodes of mainstream programs as well as special broadcasts where Jews were a central focus of the story. In some cases, the Jewish theme was treated head-on; in others it was subtler.[50]

The Columbia Workshop

The Columbia Workshop was created by CBS in July, 1936 for the express purpose of encouraging creativity in radio production. Considered an experimental program, its format varied and might feature an original drama written especially for the series one week, followed by an opera, an adaptation of a Shakespearean play, a murder mystery or a comedy in subsequent weeks.

"Mr. Cohen Takes a Walk"

On December 21, 1939, the *Workshop*, presented what must have seemed to listeners a most unusual Christmas program: a story about a Jew. With hard times still very much a reality, and the war in Europe having begun only three months earlier, the series presented "Mr. Cohen Takes a

Walk," a dramatization of a short story by Mary Roberts Rinehart, better known as a writer of mystery stories.[51] The program featured Judah Black, an actor from the Yiddish Theater, whose milder Yiddish accent had more in common with "Papa David" on *Life Can Be Beautiful* than the squeaky voiced "Uncle David" played by Menasha Skulnik on *The Goldbergs.*

The dramatization begins with a father and son scene. Mr. Cohen, the owner of an apparently successful clothing store, tells his first generation son that he's planning to take a walk. The listener soon discovers that, unlike those walks generally taken for exercise, Mr. Cohen's outing will be an extended walk retracing his early experiences as a peddler before he was able to save enough money to settle down and open his own store.

In a series of Frank Capra-like scenes that follow, the kind and generous old man runs into several people in need (a reflection of the depression economy), and in ways that might almost warm the heart of the staunchest bigot, he reaches out by both deed and dollar to help them. In the process, he restores their faith and hope for the future. If the plot seemed a bit sugarcoated, one may well wonder had the "good Samaritan" not been clearly identified as a Jew but more as an "all-American" type, would the issue even be raised.

26 by Corwin

In 1941, CBS gave writer/director Norman Corwin complete control over 26 *Workshop* programs that became known as *26 by Corwin*. The assignment followed on the heels of Corwin's two earlier successful series for the network: *Words Without Music* (that included the famous "The Plot to Overthrow Christmas" program) aired during the 1938-1939 season and *The Pursuit of Happiness* broadcasts from 1939-1940. Three of the programs in the new series dramatized stories from the Old Testament. Of the many possible biblical stories that Corwin could have selected, the ones he chose appear to have been selected because of their relevance to what was happening to Jews in Europe.

The first two episodes, "Samson," broadcast on August 10th and the story of "Esther"[52] presented in the form of an opera on August 17th, dealt with historic threats to the Jewish people and the efforts of heroic Jews to save their people from an almost certain death. In the third episode, "Job," broadcast on August 24th, an individual's faith in God remained steadfast despite continued trials and suffering.

In 1941, with Europe's Jews again facing the danger of extinction, would a new savior appear, either in the form of a political or religious leader? Or, like Job, would Jews have to accept their latest ordeal? More than 60 years later, historians and theologians are still arguing over whether more might have been done — but wasn't to avert what became known after the war as the Holocaust.

A Passport for Adams

On May 23, 1944, as part of *Columbia Presents Corwin*, the *Workshop* rebroadcast a Corwin script, "Tel Aviv" that had been part of the special 1943 wartime series, *A Passport for Adams*. Written in response to a request from the Office of War Information, the *Passport* programs were designed to address the objections some Americans had to providing aid to Russia. Although an ally in the fight against Germany, some believed that the United States should not be helping a communist country, no matter which side it was on in the war. The government was equally concerned about the continuing anti-Semitic charge that it was "the Jews" who got America into the war.

A Passport for Adams was about Douglas Adams, a fictional newspaper editor, and his cameraman, Perry Quisinberry. Together, the pair visited foreign cities populated by some of the same people who were being criticized at home. The idea was for this typical small-town newspaperman from middle America to report back to the nation on what he learned on his fact-finding tour. Robert Young (later to portray the father in *Father Knows Best* on both radio and television) played the part of Douglas Adams and Dane Clark was his cameraman.

The sixth program in the series, originally broadcast on September 21, 1943, featured a stop in Tel Aviv, in what was then the British mandate of Palestine. In a 1944 rebroadcast, Adams was played by Myron McCormick and Quisinberry by Paul Mann. The story begins with Adams and Quisinberry flying to Tel Aviv from Cairo. During the flight they meet a Jewish woman in an army uniform who is returning to her home in Palestine. Once in Tel Aviv, they arrange to visit the woman and her family on a nearby Kibbutz (collective farm). As the story progresses, the newspapermen learn that there are over 20,000 Jews serving the Allied cause as members of the British Army; that Jews built the city of Tel Aviv in what had been a barren desert; and that Jews are a warm, friendly, cultured people who are concerned for the well being of others. Four years before the State of Israel came into being, Americans heard of the idealism that motivated Israel's early Jewish pioneers.

The University of Chicago Round Table

Responding to the growing problems Jews were experiencing in Europe and continuing anti-Semitism in the United States, the prestigious NBC-Red network's public affairs program, *The University of Chicago Round Table*, aired "The Jews" on January 28, 1940. The program was broadcast only after Sherman H. Dryer, head of the University's Radio Department, overcame the objections of NBC executives who initially viewed the program as being too controversial.[53]

Participating in the 30-minute discussion were two gentiles, John A. Wilson, Director of the Oriental Institute at the University of Chicago and Malcom Willey, Professor of Sociology at the University of Minnesota, and a Jew, Louis Wirth, an Associate Professor of Sociology at the University of Chicago.[54] The program was carried by 85 stations with an estimated potential audience of five million listeners.

The discussion started out by asking the question: What is a Jew? The answer from the three panelists was a combination of history, anthropology and sociology with the word "religion" used only once in the program. One of the non-Jewish panelists defined Jews as having "a common tradition and a common emotion, and that is part of their history and that is what makes them Jews."[55] Wirth stated, "(the) one thing that accounts for the character of the Jews and their cohesion — if they do have any unity at all — is that they are held together by persecution. In periods of persecution the Jews identify themselves as Jews and when persecution ceases they disintegrate as a group." After adding, "we cannot really define a Jew except to say that a Jew is a person who thinks of himself as a Jew and who is treated by others as if he were a Jew," another panelist concluded: "That seems to me a reasonable definition."[56]

The panelists then dealt with the litany of standard anti-Semitic stereotypes and myths, from that of Jews dominating certain professions to being criminals and radicals and being too aggressive in business practices. In each case, Wirth provided facts discrediting the myths and finally asked his co-panelists, "To what would we attribute this survival of anti-Semitic feeling in view of the fact that most of the alleged sins of the Jews are not borne out by experience?"⁵⁷

Wirth then took a more proactive stance and asked his colleagues if they thought that the quota system was consistent with American principles and why people were afraid of more Jews going into certain professional fields or businesses. "Do they believe that Jews are not interested in the same things that other people who are not Jews are interested in?" The program then went on to discuss the evils of the quota system ("After all, if Jews are subject to quotas today may not some other minority group be quotaed [sic] at another time?")⁵⁸

The last part of the program raised the question of assimilation, which all agreed was part of the solution to the problem and which would involve the efforts of both Jews and gentiles. But the panelists disagreed over whether assimilation meant biological assimilation (as in intermarriage and inbreeding, the approach favored by Wirth, the Jew) or more simply cultural assimilation, which accepted the fact that Jews were no different from other Americans and had the same values as the rest of society.

Anti-Semitism, all three panelists agreed, was wrong and contrary to America's democratic spirit. Speaking at a time when totalitarianism was on the rise in Europe, Wirth ended the program by telling listeners, "We cannot really afford to allow organized anti-Semitic movements to be used as tools by propagandists to distract attention from our real problem and to undermine the values we cherish in our social order. It is not a question of Jews versus gentiles. It is really a question of democracy versus totalitarianism."⁵⁹

After the program aired, Dryer wrote to the University's vice president that the program "was one of our most successful. We received 500 letters on it Monday, and 1,400 letters on it Tuesday."⁶⁰ When the American Jewish Committee tried to get more information about the mail response, including what percentage of the letters were from non-Jews, the organization was blocked by NBC. Representatives of the Committee even made their case directly to David Sarnoff, head of the network — and a Jew — but to no avail. Sarnoff explained that it was the network's policy not to help an organization with a one-religion point of view. He intimated that the "Jew versus non-Jew tabulation" might be available to a third party organization such as the National Conference of Christians and Jews whose purpose was to strengthen the American principle of freedom for all religious.⁶¹

Several weeks after the program had been broadcast, and after having the opportunity to read a printed copy of the text, Frank N. Trager, the AJC's

Program Director, sent a three-page letter to Wirth detailing his comments about the program in what he said was a "constructive spirit."[62] While in general, he thought that the program did a "good job in presenting many of the facts concerning Jews," his overriding critique of the program was that it did not go far enough to "crystallize public opinion along healthy, pro-democratic lines. As was pointed out in the broadcast, the entire Jewish question is a smokescreen behind which demagogues seek to achieve their totalitarian ends — a smokescreen which is strengthened by any apologetic information, no matter how well-intentioned, which accepts the issue of anti-Semitism as the true issue."

Specifically, Trager criticized the way Wirth answered the questions about Jewish "control" over certain industries such as banking and the media and suggested (as if Wirth would be in a position to speak on the subject again at a future date), a better, more positive way, to address the issue. "If Mr. Sarnoff is president of R.C.A.," he wrote, "it is not because he is a Jew nor is it an indication of 'Jewish control'; it is rather an indication of the fact that the board of directors of the R.C.A. considers him to be the best president available. The same applies to any industry, no matter under whose alleged control."

Trager was also critical of Wirth's downplaying the role of Jews in certain professions and not doing enough to bring attention to the achievements of "eminent" Jews such as Albert Einstein, Franz Boas (a pioneer in modern anthropology) and Felix Frankfurter (Associate Justice of the United States Supreme Court), as well as his response to a question about Jewish business ethics and the very definition of what a Jew was.

Treasury Star Parade ("Address Unknown")

Imagine if you can two childhood friends, one a Jew (Max) and one a gentile (Martin), both growing up in Germany. Both were in the art business and both eventually emigrated to America and went into business together. Each remembers Germany fondly, and in 1932 Martin decides to return to Germany and conduct his business from there. The two friends communicate with each other in a series of letters. It is these letters that became the script for "Address Unknown," a 1942 episode on the wartime series *Treasury Star Parade*.[63] The script, based on the 1938 short story "Address Unknown" by Kathrine Kressmann Taylor, featured Fredric March. In 1939, the story was reprinted in *Readers' Digest*.

In a brief 15-minute program, the letters expose the horrors of Nazism and the poisonous effect it is having on ordinary people. In the initial exchange of letters, Martin tells his old friend how wonderful things are in Germany and how things are looking better all the time. There's this "new fellow" called Hitler who is going to "straighten things out," although he does have some strange ideas regarding Jews. But not to worry. As the exchange of letters continues, Martin begins to heap more and more praise on the new German government and comments that even though some of its policies might be extreme, they appear to be necessary. When a letter Max mailed to his sister in Berlin is returned marked "Address Unknown," he writes Martin asking him to check on her. Martin writes back that when the sister sought refuge in his home, he was unable to grant her sanctuary because by doing so he would have endangered himself. When he turned the sister away and she tried to escape from her pursuers, she was shot.

As the letters continue, Martin pleads with Max to stop writing him as the Nazis are censoring his mail. Max, however, continues to send long friendly letters saying "thank you" for all he's done for "our people" and also containing many phrases involving the business which make no sense but which clearly could be interpreted as a code that could incriminate the letter's recipient. In what can only be called poetic justice, it becomes obvious that Max is seeking revenge for Martin's failure to save his sister. When Max's final letter to Martin is returned, stamped "Address Unknown," it is clear that Martin has been arrested and must face the kind of justice that he had been praising earlier.

In 1944, Columbia Pictures turned the story, although with some plot changes, into a movie by the same name staring Paul Lukas as Martin.

Arch Oboler Scripts

Although radio writer/director Arch Oboler is best known for his skill as a writer of the classic radio horror show *Light's Out*, he did, however, write numerous scripts for other series. And, not unlike other writers, on more than one occasion, he recycled a script to be used on a different program. On January 20, 1940, the script "Sensitive Mr. Ginsberg" became the 44th episode on an NBC anthology series known as *Arch Oboler's Plays*. The very same script, with the title changed to simply "Mr. Ginsberg" was heard a year later, on February 21, 1941, on another NBC anthology program, *Everyman's Theater*. The second broadcast featured Benny Rubin in the title role.

At least three factors identify the program as having something to do with Jews: Ginsberg is generally recognized as a Jewish name; in the event that the listener had any doubts about Ginsberg's religion, the character is heard referring to himself more than once as a "schlemiel" (an inept person, a bungler); and when Ginsberg's father urges him over and over again to "get a job," the elder Ginsberg's speech pattern has the unmistakable Yiddish sing-song intonation.

The theme of this simple non-horrific plot is Ginsberg's struggle with his conscience. Having discovered a boxer with promise, rather than bring his boxer along slowly, Ginsberg allows greed to influence his decision and he pits his fighter against an opponent who far outclasses him. His boxer loses both the fight and his sight. Haunted by the blind fighter's words, repeated over and over again, "Why is it so dark? Why is it so dark?" Ginsberg's conscience leads him to give his proceeds from the fight to a church as a way of repenting for his sin. As was the case of the lawyer in the Elmer Rice play, "Counselor at Law," the Jewish protagonist is faced with the ethical dilemma that comes with losing one's moral compass by surrendering to the desire to achieve financial success.

One may wonder why Oboler chose to purposely have his Jewish character give his money to a church rather than to a synagogue. Also, why did Oboler portray the conscious-stricken manager as a Jew when the program aired in 1940 and again in 1941 – but changed the name of the protagonist from Ginsberg to Miller when the script was broadcast a third time on October 4, 1945, a scant six months following the surrender of Nazi Germany and only two months after Japan's surrender. Also, in the 1945 broadcast, Eddie Cantor was featured in the title role and the Yiddish word "schlemiel" was replaced by "fool." The father's voice, urging his son to "get a job" no longer had any traces of a Yiddish accent. Was it Mr. Oboler's conscience that led him to the remove the Jewish elements from the script — or was there another explanation? A print copy of "Mr. Ginsberg" is available in two collections of radio dramas.[64]

"Suffer Little Children"

In 1939, in the wake of Kristallnacht and in the midst of a controversial Congressional debate over the Wagner-Rogers bill that would have permitted 20,000 German refugee children to emigrate to America, supporters of the measure asked Oboler to write a radio drama that would create public support for the legislation. The result was "Suffer Little Children," the story of four children on a boat who had been refused admittance to America. By the time the play was broadcast, however, on September 16, 1939, as part of a trilogy of plays on *Arch Oboler Plays*, the legislation had effectively been defeated in Congress. Although the word "Jewish" is not mentioned in the text (two German words, "Herr" [mister] and "Bitte" [thank you] are used), given the political climate at the time, there can be little doubt that the script meant Jewish children. When the radio drama was rebroadcast on November 21, 1946, the United States was still grappling with the refugee (a.k.a. displaced persons) issue. A copy of the play, as well as Oboler's reaction to reading a transcript of the Congressional hearings is included in the book, *This Freedom; Thirteen New Radio Plays*.[65]

Another Oboler wartime script, "Chicago, Germany" broadcast on *Treasury Star Parade* was strikingly similar to the week-long soap opera *Life Can Be Beautiful* segments aired on *Victory Front* (discussed in Chapter 6) in which the Nazis occupied America and Papa David's bookshop was visited by a Nazi officer.

(See *Free World Theater* below for an additional Oboler script.)

The Orson Welles Theater

After the Campbell Soup Company discontinued its sponsorship of Orson Welles' *The Mercury Theater* (a.k.a. *The Campbell Playhouse*) in June, 1941, three months later, the actor/director returned to the air with a new CBS series, *The Orson Welles Theater*. The program's 30-minute format varied from week to week and ranged from comedy and music to drama. The first broadcast, aired on September 15, 1941, featured three short dramatic sketches: "Sredni Vashtar," by Saki about a young boy who rebels against his guardian, "Hidalgo," a Mexican tale featuring Dolores Del Rio and "An Irishman and a Jew."[66]

Ordinarily mentioning an Irishman and a Jew in the same sentence would lead one to expect a joke that might be told on *Can You Top This*? However, this brief sketch told the poignant story of a young Irish veterinarian named Donno who was bound for Brazil on an old steamer during the early days of the war. Wandering below deck in the midst of a storm, Donno runs into a family of Jewish refugees recently escaped from Germany. The daughter, Bertha, is suspicious when Donno offers to buy her a drink. Without commenting further on the plot, considering the fate of so many Jews who were unable to escape from Germany, or who sailed on ships from which they could not disembark, this story, aired three months before Pearl Harbor, could well have been considered prophetic. The sketch ends on a note of a potential romance between the two young people of vastly different backgrounds and a possibly updated version of *Abie's Irish Rose*.

The Free World Theater

The Free World Theater was a wartime series that was a joint presentation of the Office of War Information, the Hollywood Victory Committee and the Hollywood Writers Mobilization. The series was produced and directed by Arch Oboler and carried by NBC-Blue. The scripts were based on suggestions and statements by a diverse group of well known individuals that included President Franklin D. Roosevelt, Secretary of State Cordell Hull, the conductor Arturo Toscanini and Adolf Hitler.

In the Introduction to a collection of the plays that was published in 1944, the noted German author Thomas Mann acknowledged that the plays were propaganda—but went on to explain that propaganda can be used for good as well as evil. "It is good propaganda insofar as it is effective, absorbing and entertaining. And it is good propaganda insofar as it awakes our hearts which are so much inclined to drowse in indifference, and summon them to hate evil and to believe in a better world as the fruit of victory."[67]

"I Have No Prayer"

This 15-minute radio drama was written by Arch Oboler and broadcast on March 14, 1943. The script is based on a statement by Arthur H. Compton.[68] The drama featured Lloyd Nolan as a tough army sergeant from New York who is assigned to train a diverse group of G.I.s to work together as members of a tank crew. The group includes a Boston brahman, a laborer from Detroit, a country boy from the south and Jake, a middle-class "Hebe" from Chicago. Different as their backgrounds are, the team begins to coalesce. As the script unfolds, the sergeant recounts a battle against Field Marshal Rommel's tank corps on the sands of North Africa. During the action, the crew destroyed several enemy tanks before being hit by return fire. The only crew member to perish was Jake who, having performed with valor in combat, earned the respect of his comrades. At Jake's graveside, the sergeant expresses regret in that he "had no prayer" for his fallen comrade who fought bravely and gave his life for his country. Clearly, the script was designed to counter those home-front hate mongers who whispered that Jews were avoiding military service to remain at home and profit while others fought and died. This was despite statistics that showed that the number of Jews serving in the military in both world wars far exceeded the percentage of Jews in the total population.

"The Second Battle of the Warsaw Ghetto"

In June, 1943, just one month following the actual event, *The Free World Theater* aired Irving D. Raveth's radio play, "The Second Battle of the Warsaw Ghetto." Based on a statement by playwright Lillian Hellman, the broadcast starred John Garfield and Anne Baxter.[69]

The play explores the moral choices facing a family on the eve of the uprising: should they take advantage of the opportunity given to them to escape, commit suicide (as did the ancient Jews at Masada), or join the other ghetto residents and fight to the end, knowing that they would most likely die. When the family rejects the escape option, listeners are reminded of the other Jews who earlier had tried to escape only to be turned away by the Allies.

> Dovid: And if we slip through the forests, and make hazardous flight across the border, what then? The sea? And then? And then an old, leaking vessel, and the journey — the endless journey, from shore to shore, from land to land, touching at all of them — and turned back, each time — back into the sea.
>
> Chaim: No Father! They will have us, they must have us!...We are the first, the first to fight the beast!... How can they close their doors to us?
>
> Dovid: So soon you have forgotten. It is too soon, Chaim. To forget the word 'quota:—to forget that we are only the unwanted, refuse, scum. The others, Chaim, the others who got out—did they win freedom and honor? Who helped them — who were their friends? Nowhere, nothing. They will not have us. Such a prospect you offer, Chaim — one hell into another... The freedom of starvation and hopeless on a ship that never stops...I am too old and too tired for such a journey.

The family then rejects the suicide option as the father, Dovid, courageously tells his children:

No, not that. We are Polish citizens, and this is our home. And here we shall stay – and here we shall die. But there is only one way for free men to die. And that is in defense of their freedom...Children, what is freedom? Only a word? No! If we want it, we must struggle every day of our lives to win it anew, only so we can be worthy of it.... We are men and women, with wills, with hands—we are two—spirit and body, The spirit fights for the body, the body for the spirit. Such we must do.

Seeing his three family members lying lifeless, Zelbel calls out to his dead grandfather, intoning the names of the great Jewish heroes of the past, Bar Kochba, Maccabeus and Gideon. And over the sounds of thunder, he asks:

Oh, Zaida (grandfather), will the world know of us? Will the world know...? Or are we alone here?

"The Battle of the Warsaw Ghetto" (Morton Wishengrad)

Although this radio play is generally associated with *The Eternal Light* (see Chapter 8), its impact on the listening audience was such that it warrants inclusion in this overview of special mainstream broadcasts.

In the summer of 1943, Milton Krents of the American Jewish Committee asked Morton Wishengrad to consider writing a special Yom Kippur program for NBC. The writer agreed to take on the assignment, suggesting the recent events that had taken place in Poland as a likely subject. Working from a file of newspaper clippings that Krents provided him with, Wishengrad recounted the bravery of the 37-day struggle of Warsaw's Jews.[70] In addition to being rebroadcast several times in the United States, the play was also performed in Yiddish by inhabitants of DP (Displaced Persons) camps in Europe and in Hebrew over the Palestine radio. It has also been re-enacted in more recent times by several amateur radio groups.[71]

Using a combination of dramatization and narration, the play begins with the narrator describing the dignity and self respect of the Jews as they are forced into the ghetto and must endure intolerable living conditions. As the Nazis methodically reduce the population of the ghetto, ("they sent the black trucks because the hunger and pestilence were too slow and too merciful") the remaining residents resolve to take action and reach out to the Allies for help – which does not come.

Through the Polish underground which carried our appeals we asked England, Russia and the Untied States for weapons. And there was

Jews in the Mainstream

silence. You did not answer. And then through the Polish underground there came your answer: resolutions of sympathy, phrased with felicity. It was a greater injury than silence...We waited for weapons that did not come. Five hundred thousand waited. (*Pause*) Three hundred thousand waited. (*Pause*) One hundred thousand waited. And finally thirty-five thousand who did not know where to look...but the answer came from under their feet — the sewer under the Warsaw Ghetto...

April 19, 1943. Thirty-five thousand men, women, children stood ready. It was the day. Trenches were dug during the night. Every house, every room, every cellar, every roof was prepared. At 4am a detachment of Storm Troopers in light tanks escorted the black trucks to the walls of the Ghetto. They came as usual on their daily errand. (*Music up higher*) We waited until the vehicles were within range...Fire!

On March 30, 1950, the radio audience heard a third version of the uprising when the Mutual network, with the cooperation of the American Jewish Committee, broadcast a special Passover season presentation of John Hershey's novel about the uprising, "The Wall," adapted for radio by Morton Wishengrad.

Words at War

This NBC wartime series debuted on June 24, 1943. The program was special for two reasons: its concept and its production values. Produced in cooperation with The Council on Books in Wartime, it was based on the idea of dramatizing the most recent influential books dealing with the war. In producing the series, NBC spared little expense and made its best production staff available for each 30-minute episode. The program's musical score, under the direction Frank Black and performed by members of the NBC Symphony Orchestra, played a significant role in keeping audiences tuned to the program on a weekly basis.[72]

Programs About Anti-Semitism

In his book on wartime radio programs, also entitled *Words at War,* Howard Blue noted that when the series' editor, Erik Barnouw, wanted to air an episode about anti-Semitism, the idea was vetoed by NBC executives concerned that such a program would "open us to the charge that we are 'Jew dominated.' And this would be embarrassing to Mr. Sarnoff." To get around the problem, Blue wrote, "the staff became adept at presenting programs that avoided the obvious but subtly got a message across."[73] Three episodes, did, in fact, deal with anti-Semitism.

The February 22, 1944 episode, "Assignment USA," rebroadcast on April 4, 1944, was based on a national tour taken by the author Selden Menefee. The program focused on the many problems facing wartime America, including anti-Semitism in Boston, racial bigotry and economic discrimination, and how these problems were related to the war effort.

The March 21, 1944, "Der Furhrer," program exposed *"The Protocols of the Elders of Zion,"*[74] the long discredited book that became a potent weapon used by many to justify anti-Semitism. In documenting why the book was a hoax as well as being historically inaccurate, the program traced the publication's history from its origin as a minor German fictitious ghost story to Russia where agents of the czar intentionally added the anti-Semitic elements that became the excuse for a series of pogroms. From Russia, the book went back to Germany where it was used to justify the anti-Jewish measures initiated by the Nazi government. Although the program focused only on anti-Semitism in Europe, the *Protocols* had been used in the United States by Henry Ford, Father Coughlin and others to stir up anti-Jewish sentiments in America.

The December 26, 1944 episode, "Scapegoats in History: History of Bigotry in the United States," as its title implies, was based on two books, each dealing with the subject of bigotry. After detailing numerous examples of bigotry against Christians during the early years of the church, the program went on to talk about what happened when Christianity became the majority religion in many nations and people sought out new victims of bigotry, including the Jews.

"The Bid Was Four Hearts"

A fourth *Words at War* program was an inspirational one based on a real incident. The February 27, 1945 episode, "The Bid Was Four Hearts," dramatized one of the most stirring acts of ecumenical bravery to be recorded in United States history. When the troop ship, the U.S.S. Dorchester was hit by an enemy torpedo and sank on February 3, 1943, the four army chaplains on board, a priest, two Protestant ministers and a rabbi (Alexander D. Goode) gave their life jackets to soldiers, sacrificing their own lives. In 1948, postage stamps with the caption "These Immortal Chaplains" honored the four clergymen.

The story of the four chaplains was also dramatized as part of the Anti-Defamation League's *Lest We Forget* series"[75]

Mr. District Attorney

Phillips H. Lord of *Gang Busters* fame devoted at least two broadcasts to the subject of bigotry in 1944 on another long-running series he created, *Mr. District Attorney.*[76] The first episode, "The Case of the Misguided Mothers," aired on April 26th and dealt with the efforts of a secret organization of Nazi sympathizers (read the Fifth Column) to organize a group of naïve mothers, all wishing the war would end soon so that their sons could return home unharmed. Once organized, the plan was to encourage the mothers to lobby for an early peace and to conduct racial boycotts. (If today's readers think it strange to consider organizing a peace protest to be an act of betrayal of one's country, they are reminded that the concept of national unity and the threat to America's security was very real for those who lived through World War II.)

The second program, "The Case of the Peddlers of Prejudice," aired on December 20th. In this episode, a school janitor is called into the assistant principal's office and encouraged to read a book about racial tolerance because he called some students "names reflecting their racial background." Not interested in heeding the school official's warning to change his way of thinking, the janitor proceeds to enlist the aid of a gang of boys to rough-up students with foreign names. Matters go from bad to worse when the assistant principal is beaten up. By the end of the 30-minute broadcast, the district attorney "gets his man" and today's reader is left to wonder how effective such a highly sanitized approach to discouraging bigotry actually was. Here's how Harrington, the district attorney's private investigator, tries to set Rick, one of the trouble makers, on the right path:

Harr:	Just listen a minute, son. What's the difference between you and one of those kids on Tenth Street?
Rick:	They're foreigners.
Harr:	What's a foreigner?
Rick:	Somebody who don't belong here.
Harr:	Why?
Rick:	'Cause this is America.
Har:	Are you an American? A blood line American I mean?

Rick:	Sure.
Harr:	Pure Indian blood?
Rick:	What do you mean?
Harr:	Those are the only real Americans I know of…the rest of us all came here from Europe or Africa or Asia.
Rick:	Look, I was born here, see!
Harr:	So were most of those kids on Tenth Street…and as far as bein' Americans are concerned…they work at it a lot better than you do. If you listened in school son, you must know that this country is a democracy …a democracy…says that everybody gets an even break…whether he's white or colored…Catholic, Protestant or Jew…Your little party the other night went against all that.

They Call Me Joe

In 1944, as part of its contribution to the war effort and the need to promote unity among all Americans, *The NBC University of the Air* broadcast a series of 11 episodes entitled, *They Call Me Joe*. The series was also carried by the Armed Forces Radio Service. Each episode told the story of fictitious servicemen representing different ethnic, racial and religious backgrounds. The program's theme song was the "Ballad for Americans" with music by Earl Robinson and lyrics by John LaTouche. The song had been made famous by Paul Robeson who sang it on the November 5, 1939 broadcast of the CBS series, *The Pursuit of Happiness*. The opening dialog for each episode also borrowed heavily from the song, especially the famous line: "I'm just an Irish, Negro, Jewish…"

Narrator:	Say, what's your name?
Soldier:	Hey, call me Joe. (Or José, or Giuseppe, depending on the ethnicity of the serviceman.)
Narrator:	But well, who are you anyhow? What's your racket? Who are you? Are you an American?
Solider:	I'm just an Irish, Negro, Jewish, Italian, French and English, Spanish, Russian, Chinese Polish, Scotch, Hungarian, Litvak, Swedish, Finnish, Canadian, Greek and Turk, and Czech and double Czech American.
Chorus:	Holy Mackerel! You sure are something.

(Music interlude)

Narrator: This is a series entitled They Call Me Joe. It's about G.I. Joe and the generations behind it. Its about the men and women who came from many lands to make America a free way of life. What they saw. What they stood for. All help to explain G.I. Joe. So NBC's University of the Air brings you a series about Joe's heritage.

The August 19, 1944 episode, "The Jew," featured a pilot on his way to a bombing raid recounting the story of how his family emigrated from Russia. The script, written by Morton Wishengrad, was rebroadcast three months later on *The Eternal Light* as "Candelabra of the Steppes."

The Theatre Guild on the Air (a.k.a. *The United States Steel Hour*)

On September 16, 1945, listeners to ABC's *The Theatre Guild on the Air* heard a one hour adaptation of the stage play, "Jacobowsky and the Colonel," that had appeared on Broadway from May 14, 1944 to March 10, 1945. The radio cast featured three of the actors who had appeared in the stage production.[77]

The play tells the story of an autocratic and probably anti-Semitic Polish colonel played by Louis Calhern who is anxious to leave Paris before the arrival of German troops. The colonel finds himself in the company of a quite clever and resourceful Polish Jew, played by Oscar Karlweiss[78] who also, for rather obvious reasons, is most eager to "get out of town." The two men reach a reluctant agreement to work together as Jacobowsky is clever enough to bargain for a car that he can't drive and the colonel needs a way to escape.

The radio adaptation, directed by Elia Kazan, had both its light moments and some rather tense ones as the relationship between the two men changes (much like the dilemma faced by Tony Curtis and Sidney Poitier who were chained together when they escaped from a southern chain gang in the 1958 movie "The Defiant Ones").

Columbia Pictures released a film version of the play entitled "Me And The Colonel" in 1958 starring Danny Kaye and Kurt Jurgens in the title roles. The play was also revived as a musical with songs and lyrics by Jerry Herman in a production entitled The Grand Tour. The musical opened at New York's Palace Theatre on January 11, 1979 and ran for only 61 performances. Joel Grey of Cabaret fame played the Polish Jew and Ron Holgate was the colonel.

"The Liberation of Buchenwald Concentration Camp"

On April 15, 1945, listeners who tuned in to a CBS news broadcast heard the familiar voice of Edward R. Murrow reporting what he had witnessed a few days earlier when he entered the liberated Buchenwald concentration camp. In an example of broadcast journalism at its finest, Murrow's voice, as much as his words, painted a picture of conditions at the camp that were as telling as any newsreel coverage could possibly be. On a day when many Americans would learn for the first time that the rumors regarding the plight of Europe's Jews were hardly exaggerated, Murrow reported the following:

> As I walked down to the end of the barracks, there was applause from the men too weak to get out of bed. It sounded like the hand clapping of babies; they were so weak. We went to the hospital; it was full. The doctor told me that two hundred had died the day before. I asked the cause of death; he shrugged and said, 'Tuberculosis, starvation, fatigue, and there are many who have no desire to live.' It appeared that most of the men and boys had died of starvation; they had not been executed. But the manner of death seemed unimportant. Murder had been done at Buchenwald. God alone knows how many men and boys have died there during the last twelve years. I pray you to believe what I have said about Buchenwald. I have reported what I saw and heard, but only part of it. For most of it I have no words. If I've offended you by this rather mild account of Buchenwald, I'm not in the least sorry.[79]

Another Concentration Camp Liberation

New York City's colorful mayor Fiorello La Guardia was one of many people tuned to WOR, Mutual's flagship radio station in the City at 4pm on July 10, 1945. In a broadcast originating from Europe, he heard Kathryn Cravens, a veteran radio commentator and reporter interviewing several people who had previously been held by the Nazis in concentration camps. One of Cravens' guests was Gemma Gluck, the mayor's sister, who a year earlier had been arrested in Hungary along with her Jewish husband Herman Gluck. The two had been sent to Mauthausen concentration camp on orders from Adolph Eichmann. Although not generally known, Gemma, like her mother and brother was also Jewish. Her survival was attributed to the expectation that she might be a worthwhile hostage or trading pawn, should the need arise, because of her relationship with the New York City mayor who had for years been speaking out against Hitler and the Nazis.

Archivists continue to search for a transcription of that broadcast which clearly had an impact beyond the personal lives of those directly involved. It took another two years before arrangements could be made for Gemma's return to America.

Part III: The Postwar Years

The postwar period was a watershed for radio in more ways than one. Radio historian Fred MacDonald observed that one of the key postwar issues was the "intense argument" that took place over what direction radio should take and whether it should "rediscover its social importance by developing 'socially responsible' programs."[80] In a continuation of the trend that had begun before the war, Jewish humor no longer poked fun at the Jewish immigrant with the heavy Yiddish accent.[81] First and second generation children of Jewish immigrants saw themselves as being fully assimilated into mainstream American life. In a provocative 1952 article, "The Vanishing Jew," drama critic Henry Popkin argued that Jewish characters had virtually disappeared from all forms of popular culture.[82] Anti-Semitism, however, did not disappear, although it manifested itself in more subtle ways then had been the case during the 1930s and early 1940s. And of course, postwar radio began to grapple with a new competitor for the attention of the American audience — television.

Many of these trends were reflected in the changing nature of radio programming. With the exception of two religious programs, *The Eternal Light* and the *Message of Israel*, recurring Jewish themed programs vanished from the network schedules.[83] The Jewish presence did not, however, disappear from radio entirely as several popular mainstream programs broadcast episodes that focused on the issue of intolerance. Several of these programs dealt with a generic form of bigotry that could be applied to any minority. The scripts typically employed euphemisms such as "foreigners," "people who speak different languages," or "people who look different" in place of the more emotionally charged words, "Jew" or "Negro." Underlying this generic approach was the premise that anti-Semitism could best be fought as part of a broader struggle against all forms of prejudice.[84] From the perspective of sponsors, this "softer" approach also had the advantage of being less likely to offend too large a segment of their audience. Other programs, however, possibly the product of more socially committed or less risk-adverse producers, writers and sponsors, tackled anti-Semitism head-on and treated the controversial issue in a more open manner.

What follows selected examples of both types of programs arranged in chronological order.

1946
The Adventures of Superman
There is a wonderful story in Jewish folklore about Rabbi Lowe of Prague, Czechoslovakia who, many years ago, when the local Jewish population was threatened with danger, employed the mystical powers of the Kabbalah to create a powerful figure out of clay that was called the Golem. Unlike Samson, the Golem had no hair which, if cut, would drain him of his strength. Nor was he likely to be tempted by a woman. But, like Samson, the Golem was endowed with enormous strength that could protect the Jews from pogroms.

Whether Jerry Siegel and Joe Shuster, two friends from Cleveland, had ever heard of the legend of the Golem is unknown. What is known, though, is that both teenagers were blessed with fertile imaginations (fans will never know if their imagination led them to a hidden Nietze-like "über [super] mensch" concept or simply a Walter Mitty-like fantasy). Both were science fiction fans. Both were ambitious. And both were Jewish.

The concept of Superman was developed in 1933, the year Hitler was named German Chancellor. Siegel wrote the text and Shuster did the artwork. It took another five years, to June, 1938, however, before the friends were able to convince a publisher that their hero had commercial value.[85] Two years later, in 1940, *Superman* made his radio debut. In later years, the "Man of Steel" would appear in movie serials, on television and in major motion pictures. Of all of his media appearances, perhaps the most remembered part of the *Superman* mystique are the opening lines of the radio program: "Faster than a speeding bullet, more powerful than a locomotive, able to leap tall buildings at a single bound. Look up in the sky. It's a bird, it's a plane, it's SUPERMAN."

Anyone doubting Superman's antecedents as a Jew (aside from his two creators being Jewish) is invited to consider his earlier life. Like the biblical Moses, Superman also had to be saved from certain destruction while still a baby. When Egypt's Pharaoh decreed that all first born Hebrew male babies were to be killed, Moses' mother saved him by placing him in a floating basket. When Krypton, Superman's birth-planet, was endangered, his parents placed him in a rocket ship bound for earth. Indeed, German propaganda minister Joseph Goebbels took note of Superman and his connection to Jews as early as April, 1940, a year-and-a-half prior to America's entry into the war when *Das Schwartze Korps,* the weekly newspaper of the Nazi SS attacked both Superman and its Jewish creators by name.

Once war was declared on Germany and Japan, and throughout the war years, both the comic book Superman and his radio counterpart clearly demonstrated their effectiveness as morale boosters, both for the nation's G.I.s as well as for the civilians back home. When the war ended, it didn't take Superman long to find a new evil to combat: the vestiges of hatred against Jews, Negroes, and in some quarters Catholics, which was still pervasive in American society. Like the lyrics to Oscar Hammerstein's provocative song, "You've Got to Be Carefully Taught," in 1946, the writers of radio's *Superman* took on the challenge of developing a plot line that would convey to their young listeners the message that bigotry, intolerance and anti-Semitism were evils and were wrong.

The multi-episode plot, commonly referred to among old time radio collectors as "The Hate Mongers Organization," (a.k.a. Unity House) began on April 16, 1946 and ran for 25 consecutive broadcasts through May 20th. The series started with an episode in which Hoffman's drugstore was set on fire. When Danny, the young Irish boy who saw the people set the fire tells the police, Superman (Clark Kent) and Jimmy Olsen (*The Daily Planet* cub reporter) have the following exchange:

Jimmy: He knew they'd do something to him for squealing.
Kent: Don't use that word, Jim. Danny didn't squeal. He reported an act of violence against the public. Not only against Dave Hoffman and his drugstore but against all of us. The fire was only the beginning. There's a lot more to come — unless we nip it in the bud. This sort of thing — hating people and trying to destroy them because they don't go to the same church you do — is like poison ivy. If you don't kill the roots, it spreads.

Over the next several episodes, listeners learned that the "Guardians of America" organization was trying to disrupt the efforts of the clergy, several businessmen and some leading citizens to develop positive relationships between religious and ethnic groups in the community. Unlike some prime time programs that were to approach the issue of bigotry and anti-Semitism more timidly by simply using phrases like "people who were different," *Superman*, aimed at a juvenile audience, did not hesitate to specifically include a rabbi and a local Jewish temple as targets of the fictional evildoers. In the final installment of the series, Superman tells the gang members:

> Remember this as long as you live: Whenever you meet up with anyone who is trying to cause trouble between people — anyone who tries to tell you that a man can't be a good citizen because of his religious beliefs — you can be sure that the troublemaker is a rotten citizen himself and an inhuman being. Don't ever forget that.

Shortly after the new story line appeared, Jack Gould, the radio critic for *The New York Times*, commented on the possible long term significance of Superman's new focus on combating the more mundane evils of racial and religious intolerance:

> The significance of the new radio Superman is not only that he is a reflection of these times but that now he is to be a constructive participant in them. If Superman holds an iota of the influence attributed to him by his critics, then his adoption of a new way of life must be regarded as an encouraging augury transcending radio itself. Certainly, everyone will wish him well on what by all odds could be his most important adventure.[86]

To their credit, neither the program's sponsor, the Kellogg company, or the network, NBC, were intimidated by protests from certain segments of the country — and ratings for the program actually increased, shooting up to a #1 Hooper rating. The series earned its producers endorsements from a wide array of organizations, including the National Conference of Christian and Jews, the American Newspaper Guild, the American Veteran's Committee, the United Parents Association, the Associated Negro Press and the Boys Clubs of America.

Less than a month after the end of the "Hate Mongers" series, Superman took aim against bigotry a second time — at the anti-Negro, anti-Jewish anti-Catholic Ku Klux Klan. The very first episode of that series, commonly referred to as the "Clan of the Fiery Cross," was aired on June 10, 1946 and continued for 16 consecutive programs through July 1st.[87]

1947
Exploring the Unknown

Anti-Semitism might seem an unlikely topic for a radio series devoted to science, but Sherman H. Dryer, the producer of *Exploring the Unknown*, clearly defined the word "science" broadly to include sociology and psychology as well as nuclear physics and medicine. The program's April 6, 1947 broadcast, "Fury of Man," is significant on two accounts. First, it presented a no-holds-barred treatment of bigotry. Second, it called attention to the fact that not all Jewish organizations approached the problem of fighting anti-Semitism in the same way.

The story line is simple. A university is situated near a slum neighborhood and students must traverse the unsafe streets on their way to and from the trolley line. All too often, youth gangs attack Negroes, Jews and other students who appear to be "different" as they make their way through the neighborhood.[88] Peter Keller, the story's protagonist, is a sociology professor at the university who happens to be a refugee from Germany — but is not Jewish. When he discusses the problem with one of his colleagues, Professor Grant plays down the seriousness of the problem — and also blames the victims, accusing them of inviting trouble.

Grant: Oh, you know Peter...These boys wouldn't be here except for the G.I. Bill.[89]

Peter: Why do you blame the victim and not the tormentor? Why shouldn't these boys be able to walk on any street they choose without the fear of being beaten up?

Grant: You exaggerate! You make it sound as if the streets were littered with beaten people!

Peter: Exaggerating? I wish it were so. But just come to my office and see the facts and figures. City after city — Look! Washington Heights, our neighborhood — New York University made a study. Twenty-eight percent of the children have been beaten in fights over race and religion.

Grant: Maybe so. But I still believe, Peter, that the victim begs for trouble. After all, the people around here have a perfect right to hate whomever they want. We're not going to change that. Let's be practical.

Peter: I'm practical too, Grant. But is the answer to murderers avoiding them? Sure a person has the *right*

	to hate, but he doesn't have the right to go out and beat up people.
Grant:	Poppycock! Leave it alone! That's something these minority groups better learn!

Later, at meetings with the university president and board, Keller's plan to actually go into the neighborhood to gather facts so that he can learn *why* the people act the way they do is criticized. A Negro minister and a rabbi on the board assure Keller that they too oppose the violence and that they're working to combat the problem by holding interfaith meetings. The minister tells Keller: "We Negroes have suffered much. But one thing we've learned — to let well enough alone — let sleeping dogs lie." To which Keller replies: "But why — why, gentlemen?"

The story ends on a positive note when Keller's plan is eventually put into action and produces results. In his final didactic monologue, Keller sends out a call for communities to "recruit an army" to begin the battle against intolerance. The program closes with the announcer, Andre Baruch, telling listeners that the sponsor, Revere Copper and Brass, would be pleased to send them a special pamphlet that explains the psychology of hate and provides concrete things that they can do to fight intolerance.

Shortly after the program aired, Arnold Harris, the executive secretary of the Jewish Community Relations Council of Essex County (New Jersey), wrote to the American Jewish Committee explaining that he had been told about a "splendid radio story" in which a professor wanted to do something to fight prejudice. He asked the AJC if, by chance, it had either a copy of the script or a transcription of the program.[90] In its response to Harris, the Committee wrote that another Jewish secular group, the American Jewish Congress, "had a finger in developing materials for this show" and that he should contact them for a copy of the script. The Committee also told Harris that, "from our point of view, that is, from the standpoint of combating anti-Semitism — we consider this a bad broadcast" and that the Committee was in the processes of preparing a critical analysis of the program. Unfortunately, the American Jewish Committee's radio archives do not contain the analysis so one can only speculate as to what the organization's objections were. However, if one compares "The Fury of Man" and the earlier *Mr. District Attorney* scripts that the Committee was involved with, the differences are striking. In the "Fury" broadcast, the fight against anti-Semitism becomes much more aggressive and hard-hitting.

Jews in the Mainstream 235

The call for action takes on a preaching, moralistic tone. It also makes a strong case that the factors that drive prejudice, such as the lack of jobs, poor housing, etc., need to be addressed as a way to solve the problem. In contrast, the message in the *Mr. District Attorney* scripts is far subtler. Was one approach better than the other? The authors leave that for the reader to judge.

Treasury Agent

Phillips H. Lord, the producer of several series mentioned earlier, also created *Treasury Agent*. The April 14, 1947 episode, "The Case of the Hate Racket," was a reminder that even two years after the war, bigotry remained a serious problem. The episode features a rather convoluted plot in which a Washington bigwig is profiting from the monies raised by "traveling emissaries of hate" who rouse local populations. A new recruit, who sounds like he really believes the trash he has been preaching, is brought to Washington to meet the "head man." In the process, the listener hears snatches of one of the hate messages and of the most unlikely lyrics of the organization's theme song which presumably rallies mobs against "those people." The plot thickens…and by the end of the program, the good guys come out ahead. Could it have been any different?

The Adventures of Ellery Queen

Anti-Semitism was also the clue that lead the opera singer Patrice Munsel, the "Guest Armchair Detective" on the August 17, 1947 episode of *The Adventures of Ellery Queen* to solve the mystery. As the episode, "Murder for Americans," unfolds, the city is being flooded with hate pamphlets and there has been a series of racist activities. Ellery is asked by his friend Sylvia, who happens to be Jewish, to help find her friend Madeleine who has disappeared. Listeners are also told that Madeleine's father is a policeman who dislikes Jews.

"The Right To Live"

In this United Jewish Appeal program broadcast on NBC on May 18, 1947, a young Jewish girl who escaped from a European ghetto to America feels guilty that she lives while so many others died. The program featured movie mogul Samuel Goldwyn speaking on behalf of the UJA and several stars of both Hollywood and radio including Katharine Hepburn, Dana Andrews, Elliott Lewis, Lurene Tuttle, Norma Jean Nilsson, Veola Vonn, Hanley Stafford and Frank Lovejoy. The program was directed by the noted radio director/producer Himan Brown.

Studio One

Studio One, the prestigious CBS drama anthology program, broadcast two stories dealing with anti-Semitism over a four month period in 1947. The first program, "An Act of Faith," aired on September 16th and was an adaptation of a short story by Irwin Shaw that had appeared in the February 2, 1946 issue of *The New Yorker* magazine. The story, set in France in October, 1945, is about a Jewish solider about to go on leave to visit Paris with two of his buddies who happen to be gentiles. Before leaving the base, the solider receives a letter from his father who shares with him — for the first time — his unease and concern over growing anti-Semitism back home. The soldier begins to recall the anti-Semitic slights he experienced before the war as well as the surprise of some of the Holocaust survivors he met who couldn't believe that an American Jew was allowed to fight alongside non-Jews. As he begins to worry about what he might find once he gets home, he decides to ask his army buddies if they know what a Jew is…and the story continues.

The second program, "Earth and High Heaven," broadcast on December 1st, was based on a 1944 award winning Canadian novel of the same name written by a gentile, Gwethalyn Graham. Originally published as a serial in *Collier's* magazine, the novel was slated to be made into a movie by MGM, but the project was cancelled after Darryl Zanuck's film "Gentleman's Agreement," also about anti-Semitism, was released first.[91] Set in Montreal in 1942, the story focuses on a wealthy gentile young lady who falls in love with a Jewish lawyer, much to the chagrin of her family who clearly want to limit its contacts with Jews to only necessary business dealings.

Al Jolson Appearances
"Operation Nightmare"

One week after Al Jolson had appeared on *The Lux Radio Theatre* in the second radio adaptation of the 1927 film "The Jazz Singer," he returned to radio, but this time, as the master of ceremonies on a special broadcast, "Operation Nightmare." Produced by the United Jewish Appeal and carried on the CBS network on June 9, 1947, the program focused on the problems of the displaced persons still in European refugee camps and the need for funds to help resettle them. The cast included John Garfield, Hanley Stafford and Lurene Tuttle. It is likely that Jolson's chanting of the Hebrew song "Eli Eli" at the close of the program brought tears to the eyes of many a listener.[92]

Almost a year later, on April 10, 1948, with conditions in the displaced persons' camps still critical, Jolson took to the airwaves a second time to narrate chapter two of "Operation Nightmare," broadcast this time on the ABC network. Joining him were George Jessel, Richard Widmark and Alan Reed. Once more, the call went out for funds.

"Leo Forbstein Memorial Program"

On April 28, 1948, two weeks after his appearance on the second "Operation Nightmare" program, Jolson was heard again by radio listeners. This time he was part of an all star cast honoring the life of the late Leo Forbstein, a prominent Jewish musician. The broadcast featured Jolson singing "Kol Nidre," the same prayer he sang in the final scene of "The Jazz Singer" when he honored the wishes of his late father by taking his place as cantor on Yom Kippur.

1948
Suspense

From June, 1942 to September, 1962, a remarkable 20 year run, listeners with a taste for mystery, intrigue and, on occasion, the macabre, tuned their radios to CBS to listen to *Suspense*. The weekly anthology series included adaptations of stories as varied as H. P. Lovecraft's, "The Dunwich Horror" and Marie Belloc Lowndes' "The Lodger," as well as the works of John Dickson Carr and Edgar Allen Poe. The casts featured such diverse luminaries as Boris Karloff, Bela Lugosi, Jack Benny, Milton Berle and Agnes Moorehead.

On April 10, 1948, listeners heard a different kind of suspense story. For a short period of time, the series had been expanded from 30 to 60 minutes, and on that evening the drama focused on the murder of a Jewish war veteran whose killer was most likely one of three returning G.I.s. The script was adapted from the controversial 1947 RKO film, "Crossfire," which in turn was an adaptation of Richard Brooks' 1945 novel, "The Brick

Foxhole." While the subject of anti-Semitism was not a typical theme for Hollywood, and an even more unlikely one for a *Suspense* program, it was certainly far more acceptable than the subject of Brooks' original novel that dealt with the murder of a homosexual. Indeed, RKO's willingness to make the film, and CBS' decision to give it more prominence by bringing the movie version to radio, may be seen as a step forward in the struggle to end bigotry and intolerance.

The *Suspense* adaptation of "Crossfire" featured the same outstanding performers who had appeared in the film. Robert Young played the police detective, Sam Levine portrayed the murder victim, and the three Army buddies who were the suspects were portrayed by Robert Mitchum, Robert Ryan and George Cooper.[93]

The Lux Radio Theatre

Whereas "Crossfire" dealt with the violent aspect of anti-Semitism, "Gentleman's Agreement" took aim at a more genteel form of religious discrimination. The story, broadcast on *The Lux Radio Theatre* on September 20, 1948, and again on March 15, 1955, was an adaptation of the 1947 20th Century Fox Oscar winning movie, "Gentleman's Agreement," which was based on the best selling book of the same name by Laura Hobson. In the story, a gentile magazine writer pretends to be Jewish so that he can experience anti-Semitism first hand before writing about it. His "charade" creates tensions with his gentile girlfriend as well as problems for his school-aged son. Gregory Peck, who played the lead in the movie, and Anne Baxter starred in the first broadcast; Ray Milland and Dorothy McGuire played the leads in the 1955 rebroadcast.

1950

Broadway Is My Beat

Broadway Is My Beat was a weekly New York City based police investigation series similar in style to programs like 21st Precinct and Dragnet that aired between 1949-1954. Most of the cases, solved by Detective Danny Clover, dealt with the typical crimes of burglary, armed robbery, larceny, arson and kidnapping. Most often, the plots were fairly straightforward. In an episode broadcast on June 16, 1950, the murder victim turns out to be Morris Bernstein, a truck driver who works for a Jewish bakery. Clover senses something a bit peculiar about the motive for

Jews in the Mainstream   239

the crime and becomes even more suspicious when a woman who witnessed the murder is assaulted. The woman, it turns out, is a Holocaust survivor and she tells the detective about a person who has been calling her names similar to the invectives she had experienced in Europe. The message for listeners: five years after the concentration camps had been liberated, anti-Semitism remained an ever-present danger.

1954
Dr. Six-Gun

Westerns attracted large audiences during radio's Golden Age with programs such as *The Lone Ranger, The Tom Mix Ralston Straightshooters, Death Valley Days, The Roy Rogers Show* and *Gene Autry's Melody Ranch*. Most followed the concept of describing life in what one might call, "the old west."

In the 1950s, network radio executives, perhaps worried about the growing competition from television, decided to try a more modern approach to the popular western genre as a way of retaining its audience. This led to a series of "adult westerns" including *Gunsmoke* (1952-1961), *Tales of the Texas Rangers* (1950-1952), *The Six Shooter* (1953-1954) and one short-lived series that aired on NBC from 1954-1955, *Dr. Six-Gun*. The program was about the continuing tale of a medical doctor who traveled the West treating frontiersmen and Indians alike.

In the September 23, 1954 episode, the doctor meets a cattle rancher, new to the town, who turns out to be Jewish. As the two men converse, the radio audience is treated to what is truly a rare opportunity to learn about some of the customs and traditions of Judaism. Although the rancher does not claim to be excessively religious, in a sign of respect for his father and for the traditions of his people, he makes every effort to follow the practices called for by his faith.

When he celebrates Rosh Hashanah (the Jewish New Year), he invites the doctor into his home to share the traditional holiday dessert of apples and honey that symbolize the ushering in of a sweet New Year. He also explains to the doctor that he doesn't travel on the Sabbath, which for him means from sundown Friday to sundown Saturday. When he prays, he wears a fringed prayer shawl (the term "tallith" is not used) that has been handed down for generations (but which is also sometimes used as a burial shroud) and he reads from a book intoning words in a "strange language."

Invited to join some townsfolk for breakfast in a local saloon, he passes up the traditional menu of steak and eggs and asks simply for a boiled egg (The program does not explain the Jewish dietary laws that forbid the man from eating non-kosher meat.)

The tension in the program is brought about by a drunken cowboy who challenges the new comer to a gunfight. Although the cowboy calls the rancher a coward, listeners have already been told that the new comer served as a colonel in the Confederate army and is skilled with a gun. The challenge does, however, create a moral dilemma for the rancher because it is scheduled to take place the following day which is Yom Kippur, the most sacred day in the Jewish year and the day when Jews atone for their sins.[94]

For readers wishing to learn the outcome of this story, the good news is that audio copies of this episode have survived.

1955
No Brass Bands

A February 22, 1955 episode of a sustaining (non-sponsored) CBS program, *No Brass Bands,* told the heart warming story of the spirit of fellowship that grew between two religious congregations, one Lutheran and the other Jewish. Like *Dr. Six-Gun,* the program demonstrated that there was more than one way to deal with the issue of intolerance.

Part IV: Biographies of Prominent Jews

In programs that featured the lives of prominent individuals, the person's religion was typically not identified. In part, this reflected the decision of the scriptwriter and/or producer that the person's religion was irrelevant. Also, as noted earlier, sponsors generally wanted to avoid mentioning anything that could possibly have a negative impact on sales.[95] For Jewish secular organizations trying to promote a more positive image of Jews, the "identity" issue often brought two goals into conflict. The American Jewish Committee, for example, was eager to publicize the contributions that Jews had made to American society and its Radio Department, in its contacts with network executives, was always suggesting the names of people who could be featured on biography-style programs. At the same time, however, the AJC did not want to call attention to the "Jewishness" of the people whose lifestory was being suggested, believing that religion was a private matter. (See pages 77-78 about the AJC objections to including a separate program about Jews in the *Americans All, Immigrants All* series.) Which leads one to wonder: Would a listener know that the subject was a Jew if he wasn't identified as such?

Of course, an argument could be made that listeners would *assume* that individuals with names like Straus or Goldberger had to be Jewish — although the composer Richard Strauss was not Jewish. But what about less common Jewish names such as Gershwin, Romberg, Gerber or Ochs?

With this in mind, it is worth recalling the experiences of two popular radio personalities who featured black performers on their programs — long before radio was generally open to blacks in non-stereotypical roles. In 1935, when Josephine Baker appeared on Rudy Vallee's *The Fleischmann's Yeast Hour*, the host introduced her as a "colored singer." Ten years later, however, when Eddie Cantor hired Thelma Carpenter as the regular solo vocalist on his *Time to Smile* program and *Time* magazine asked him if he was going to introduce Carpenter as a "colored singer," Cantor replied: "I don't remember having introduced Dinah Shore as a white singer."[96]

The issue over how to identify a person continues to this day.

The Cavalcade of America

DuPont's weekly anthology series, *The Cavalcade of America*, broadcast on NBC from 1935-1953, celebrated American patriotism, history and scientific progress by highlighting the lives of noted Americans. In 1937, as part of a special sub-series, "The Cavalcade of Music," devoted to twelve American composers, the program featured the music and lives of eight Jewish composers: Irving Berlin (July 7th), George Gershwin (July 14th), Richard Rodgers (July 21st), Vincent Youmans (July 28th), Rudolph Friml (August 4th), Jerome Kern (August 11th), Sigmund Romberg (August 18th) and Arthur Schwartz (August 25th). However, as these programs were devoted to music rather than drama, it was unlikely that listeners associated any of the composers with their Jewish heritage.

At least five additional *Cavalcade* broadcasts focused on people of the Jewish faith.

October 30, 1940, "The Red Death," featured the story of Dr. Joseph Goldberger and his work discovering the cause of pellagra. The episode made no mention of the fact that Goldberger was Jewish.[97]

November 4, 1946, "An Honorable Titan," celebrated the life Adolph Ochs, the newspaperman who transformed *The New York Times* into one of the country's leading newspapers. The only possible indication in the script that Ochs might have been Jewish was when he asked a Dr. Weiss (who speaks with a mild European accent), for permission to marry his daughter.

April 19, 1948, "Winner Takes Life," told the story of Dr. Selman A. Waksman who, in 1945, discovered the life-saving antibiotic streptomycin. There was no indication in the script as to Waksman's immigrant background, other than the fact that he was played by Paul Lukas who spoke with a European accent. (The press release describing the program referred to Waksman as an immigrant.)

February 28, 1950, "Young Man in a Hurry" dramatized the story of Joseph Gerber, a refugee who escaped from Nazi-controlled Austria in 1940 and arrived in the United States with the help of the Hebrew Immigrant Aid Society. Gerber became an engineer and invented the variable scale, an instrument used in engineering to measure things. The script never explicitly identified Gerber as being Jewish.

April 11, 1950, "Citizen Straus," related the story of financier and department store owner Nathan Straus who implemented Louis Pasteur's theory of pasteurization, thereby saving the lives of thousands of children. The only indication in the program that Straus was Jewish was a passing reference to his father having read to him from the Talmud (the first five books of the Torah or Bible) when he was a young boy growing up in the South.

Three Hallmark Programs
The Radio Reader's Digest

"Disraeli," the June 2, 1946 episode of this CBS drama anthology program, told the love story of how Benjamin Disraeli cast aside the chance to become Prime Minister in order to be with his wife. (He later did become Prime Minister.) Although born a Jew, Disraeli converted to Christianity at the age of 13.

The Hallmark Playhouse

A later incarnation of *The Radio Reader's Digest*, this program featured adaptations of well-known literary works. The October 12, 1952 episode, "Mr. Young Disraeli" offered listeners a second look at the English statesman.

The Hallmark Hall of Fame

An outgrowth of the earlier *The Hallmark Playhouse, The Hall of Fame* celebrated historic events and noteworthy individuals from all walks of life. Four episodes highlighted the lives of Jews, although no mention was made of their religious background.

George Gershwin, September 20, 1953
Sigmund Freud, February 6, 1955
Bernard Baruch, February 28, 1954
Lew Kowarski,[98] March 20, 1955

The CBS Radio Workshop

As late as January 13, 1957, *The CBS Radio Workshop* (formerly *The Columbia Workshop*) aired "No Time for Heartaches," a biography of the Jewish singer Sophie Tucker. The former vaudeville star narrated the program, singing her own songs, but was portrayed in the dramatic sketches by Margaret Whiting. While there was no mention of her religion in the narrative, Tucker didn't hesitate to speak about her physical appearance (as the last of the "Red Hot Mamas," her figure was closer to that of Kate Smith's than the more typical image of a slender vocalist). She explained that in the early days of her career, she used blackface as a way to detract from what might be viewed as her lack of sex appeal.

The 50+ mainstream programs discussed in this chapter were broadcast over a span of 24 years; ranged from a political rally to a religious service; from a public affairs forum to adaptations of novels and movies; from programs listened to by children to those for adults; and from presentations lasting a brief 15 minutes to an hour. Different though they were in content and format, they all had two things in common. Each in its own way, was about Jews, and each presented Jews in a positive light, or at least as a minority group that should be respected and accepted as an integral part of American society.

Did any of the programs influence how listeners perceived Jews? Did they make intolerant individuals any less intolerant? The answers to those questions may never be known. But it is worth reflecting on comments made previously about the *Americans All, Immigrants All* series. In analyzing listener response to that program, researcher Dorothea Seeyle noted that the key to radio becoming an effective tool in promoting tolerance was getting intolerant people to listen to the program in question. In that regard, raising the issue of anti-Semitism on series such as *Suspense, The Lux Radio Theatre* and *Mr. District Attorney* may indeed have broadened the audience that was, at a minimum, exposed to messages of tolerance. And possibly, the generation that grew up listening to Superman fight intolerance, carried their hero's message with them into adulthood.

Notes

Abbreviations

AJC   American Jewish Committee Radio Department Archives at Yivo Institute, New York, NY.

1. *The New York Times*, March 21, 1933, 1.
2. To this very day, apologists for the Nazis suggest that had American Jewish voices not sounded a call for a boycott on German goods in 1933, all might have gone well for Germany's Jewish population. The German government, they argue, was merely acting in self defense in response to the economic war declared against it by the international Jewish "powerbrokers."
3. The song also became popular in Europe and was played in Germany until it was revealed that the composer was Jewish.
4. Over the years, Vallee hosted a number of Jewish personalities. In addition to those mentioned in this chapter, Walter Winchell, Benny Fields, Eddie Cantor, Stella Adler and Morris Carnofsky also appeared on his program.
5. Some of the recordings are not complete broadcasts.
6. Program logs prepared by old time radio fans based on a variety of print sources indicate that in 1930, comedienne Fanny Brice, vocalist Belle Baker and actress Molly Picon were Vallee's guests. All three performers were Jewish. Sadly, as recordings of these broadcasts are not known to have survived, it is not known if they performed using a Yiddish accent.
7. Bosworth was the pen name of Mary Arnold Crocker-Smith, a.k.a. Mary Arnold Lewisohn. "The Baby Carriage" was originally performed in 1919 by the Provincetown Players.
8. Little is known about Moskowitz beyond a brief obituary that appeared in *The New York Times* on July 27, 1953 indicating that she had been a Jewish actress known for playing "mother roles." Born in Rumania, Moskowitz

Jews in the Mainstream   245

also appeared in a 1929 motion picture, "Mother's Boy" starring Morton Downey. Her papers are located in the New York Public Library for the Performing Arts, Billy Rose Theater Collection.

9. Like scores of other Jews who changed their names for "professional" reasons, Rice's original name was Reizenstein. "Counselor at Law" ran on Broadway for 397 performances.

10. A recording of *The Campbell Playhouse* version is extant.

11. Felicia Herman, "Hollywood, Nazism, and the Jews, 1933-1941," *American Jewish History*, Vol. 89, #1, 2001, 61-90.

12. Many articles and books have been written, and documentaries produced, raising the issue of why the media, including the prestigious *The New York Times*, owned and operated by a Jewish family, failed to inform readers of the ever increasing German persecution of its non-Aryan population. Other publications have raised the issue of why the United States government did so little to intervene earlier on behalf of Europe's Jews. See Laurel Leff, *Buried by the Times: The Holocaust and America's Most Important Newspaper* (Cambridge, MA: Cambridge University Press, 2006).

13. For a discussion of the beginning of radio news broadcasting, see Erik Barnouw, *The Golden Web: A History of Broadcasting in the United States 1933-1953* (New York: Oxford University Press, 1968), 16-22.

14. From 1949-1955, Winchell was on the air with different sponsorship.

15. One source, Barnouw, *The Golden Web,* 35, refers to a controversial broadcast in 1935. A second, Howard Teichman, *Smart Aleck: The Wit, World and Life of Alexander Woollcott* (New York: William Morrow and Company, 1976), 200, says the controversial broadcast was in 1936. And a third source, Samuel Hopkins Adams, *A. Woollcott: His Life and His World* (New York: Reynal & Hitchcock, 1945), 245-247, implies that there was more than one controversial broadcast.

16. Barnouw, *The Golden Web,* 35. According Hopkins, *A. Woollcott,* 246, in later years, Woollcott had a change of heart and acknowledged that his earlier controversial material was out of place on a commercial radio program. And although Cream of Wheat offered Woollcott a new contract, the deal was never consummated.

17. Teichman, *Smart Aleck*, 200.

18. James Fisher, *Eddie Cantor: A Bio-Bibliography* (Westport, CT: Greenwood Press, 1997), 130, 133.

19. John Dunning, *On the Air: The Encyclopedia of Old Time Radio* (New York: Oxford University Press. 1988), 436.

20. The name Kristallnacht comes from Kristallglas (beveled plate glass) and refers to the broken shop windows of Jewish stores. The full story of Kristallnacht is available online and in numerous books.

21. In a 1961 television documentary about the Holocaust, news com-

mentator Lowell Thomas reminded viewers that he was one of the few reporters who spoke out about Kristallnacht on his radio program at the time. While William L. Shirer, one of Edward R. Murrow's "boys," wrote about the events in his book, "Berlin Diary," he failed to speak about them on his CBS radio report back home.

22. Irving E. Fang, *Those Radio Commentators!* (Ames, IA: Iowa State University Press, 1977), 142.

23. The full text of Thompson's broadcast can be found in Fang, ibid., 142-145.

24. The last line of Thompson's broadcast in the above paragraph appears in the December 10, 1938 *Radio Guide* article but not in the text as reprinted in Fang.

25. Christopher Sterling and John M. Kittross. *Stay Tuned: A Concise History of American Broadcasting* (Belmont, CA: Wadsworth, 1978), 183.

26. Cited in Marc Dollinger, *Quest For Inclusion; Jews and Liberalism In Modern America* (Princeton, NJ: Princeton University Press, 2000), 67.

27. Edward S. Shapiro, "World War II and American Jewish Identity," *Modern Judaism*, Vol. 10, No. 1, February, 1990, 68-69.

28. The phrase refers to how a seemingly insignificant event can affect other events, creating a ripple effect that results in an unanticipated outcome.

29. For more information about radio coverage of European Jews during World War II, see Joyce Fine, "American Radio Coverage of the Holocaust" *Annual 5*, (Simon Wiesenthal Center, 1988). The report is available online at the Simon Wiesenthal Multimedia Learning Center, http://motlc.wiesenthal.com. See also Howard Blue, *Words at War: World War II Era Radio Drama and the Postwar Broadcasting Industry Blacklist* (Lanham, MD: Scarecrow Press, 2002), 309-318.

30. Only a few one-time-only broadcasts are discussed in this chapter. For additional examples, see the web page of the American Jewish Committee, www.ajcarchives.org, as well as Zev Zahavy's Ph.D. dissertation, "The History and Survey of Jewish Religious Broadcasting," (New York: Yeshiva University, 1959).

31. Richard W. Steele, "The War On Intolerance: The Reformulation of American Nationalism, 1939-1941," *Journal of Ethnic History*, Vol. 9, 1989, 3-35 as cited in Michele Hilmes, *Radio Voices: American Broadcasting, 1922-1952* (Minneapolis: University of Minnesota Press, 1997), 239.

32. Stuart Svonkin, *Jews Against Prejudice: American Jews and the Fight For Civil Liberties* (New York: Columbia University Press, 1997); Marc Dollinger, *Quest For Inclusion*. See also Felicia Herman, "Hollywood, Nazism, and the Jews."

33. See "A Report on the Radio Work of Four Jewish Agencies," n.d., AJC web site, www.ajcarchives.org.

34. "A Report on the Goals of the AJC's Radio Department," January 1, 1939. AJC web site, ibid.

35. Ibid. Recounting the Committee's experience with the "salting-in process" in a 1950 report, "The American Jewish Committee's Fight Against Anti-Semitism 1938-1950," Richard C. Rothschild, the AJC's Director of Public Relations wrote: "I believe that it (the salting-in process) was the first time in American propaganda that such a method was used – at least on such an extensive scale." The full text of the report is available on the AJC web site. A second AJC report, also available on the Committee's web site, "The Use of Mass Media in Combating Anti-Semitism," 1949 (no author) concluded that: "It is said that radio speeches are not as effective as radio dramatizations, and that as much harm can be done by a *Can You Top This?* joke as can be overcome by a dozen other radio programs. Granted. And that is why we try for dramatizations wherever possible, and why it is our constant effort to eliminate harmful jokes on the air. (It is interesting to note that this very objection implies that at least some radio programs *are* effective, for good or ill.)", 7.

36. Working as a freelance consultant for the Jewish Theological Seminary, Krents was also the producer for *The Eternal Light* program.

37. Letter of October 14, 1947 from Milton Krents to Marcus Cohn. The letter refers to articles that appeared in the *New York Post* on September 25, 1947 and an unspecified article that appeared in *Variety*. AJC, Box 234, Folder 1947.

38. For commercially produced programs such as those on *The Columbia Workshop,* the organization's Community Service Department sought the appropriate releases.

39. "Radio Has A Job To Do," 1947, AJC, Box 235, Folder 1947.

40. "Reactions to the Broadcast *Behold the Jew*," October 17, 1944. AJC, Box 235, Folder 1940-44.

41. At the time, the reception from short-wave often included scratchy sounds and the voices were subject to fading in and out.

42. An audio recording of the broadcast can be heard on the AJC web site. An excerpt of the broadcast is included in the CD that is part of this book.

43. The Synagogue was closed by the Nazis on September 9, 1943 and reopened on June 16, 1944 when the Allies liberated Rome. An audio recording of the broadcast can be heard on the AJC web site.

44. At least some of the programs were also made available in German and Italian versions. See "A Report on the Radio Work," 2.

45. Assorted papers, AJC, Box 238, Folder Lest We Forget.

46. *Variety*, October 16, 1946, cited in ibid.

47. *Variety*, March 12, 1947, cited in ibid.

48. "ADL Bulletin," 7, 2, March, 1950, 4, cited in Svorkin, *Jews Against Prejudice*, 46.

49. "A Report on the Radio Work," 2-3.

50. For more information about other wartime programs that dealt more generally with the issue of intolerance, national unity and the Nazi menace see Barnouw, *The Golden Web*; J. Fred MacDonald, *Don't Touch That Dial! Radio Programming in American Life, 1920 to 1960* (Chicago: Nelson-Hall, 1980); Michele Hilmes and Jason Loviglio, eds. *Radio Reader: Essays in the Cultural History of Radio* (New York: Routledge, 2002); Hilmes, *Radio Voices;* and Blue, *Words at War.*

51. The story was made into a movie in 1935 by Warner Brothers First National studio in Great Britain. While both the film and radio plots dealt with a former peddler, that may have been the only similarity between the two versions of the same story.

52. The story of Esther is the basis of the Jewish holiday of Purim. For a modern look at the story, see Rafael Medoff, "A Purim Lesson: Lobbying Against Genocide, Then and Now," May 9, 2007, on the David S. Wyman Institute For Holocaust Studies web site, www.wymaninstitute.org/articles.

53. In May, 1939, NBC executives cancelled a planned program entitled, "Is the Negro Oppressed?" telling University officials that the danger of broadcasting controversial programs dealing with race or religion was "not worth it." See Hugh Richard Slotten, "Commercial Radio, Public Affairs Discourse and the Manipulation of Sound Scholarship: Isolationism, Wartime Civil Rights and the Collapse of the Attractiveness of Communism in America, 1933-1945," *Historical Journal of Film, Radio and Television*, Vol. 25, No. 3, August 2005, 382-384.

54. Wirth was the author of *The Ghetto*, a look at the effect of isolation on Jewish life, character and institutions, with a special reference to Chicago. The book was published by the University of Chicago Press in 1928.

55. "A Discussion of The Jews," Program #98, 4. A transcript of the broadcast is available from the University of Chicago Library Archives.

56. Ibid., 5.

57. Ibid., 13. Records of the American Jewish Committee indicate that the organization provided background information to the *Round Table* for this broadcast.

58. Ibid., 14.

59. Ibid., 21.

60. Slotten, "Commercial Radio," 384. The University of Chicago Archives does not have the transcript of the following week's program that would have included comments about "The Jews" program.

61. "Report on Interview with David Sarnoff," January 18, 1940. AJC, Box 235, 1944.

62. "Letter from Frank N. Trager to Dr. Louis Wirth," March 4, 1940. AJC, Box 238, Folder Radio-TV Programs, 1940-44. In a short follow-up letter

on March 6th, Trager suggested to Wirth that the two meet, either in Chicago or New York as it was difficult to communicate all that he felt could be said on the subject by mail.

63. The series was created by the government as a way to sell war bonds. Individual episodes was prepared on transcription discs and distributed to the more than 800 stations that aired the individual episodes on different dates and times. The "Address Unknown" episode is #21 in the series.

64. Arch Oboler, *Fourteen Radio Plays* (New York: Random House, 1940) and Norman S. Weiser, ed. *The Writer's Radio Theater, 1941: Outstanding Plays of the Year* (New York: Harper & Brothers, 1941).

65. Arch Oboler, *This Freedom: Thirteen New Radio Plays* (New York: Random House, 1942), 2-12.

66. The author of "The Irishman and the Jew" is not identified on the script.

67. Arch Oboler and Stephen Longstreet, eds., *Free World Theatre: Nineteen New Radio Plays* (New York: Random House, 1944), ix-xi.

68. Ibid., 56-60. Most likely the Arthur H. Compton referred to as providing the inspiration for the script was a scientist and head of the government's Office of Scientific Research and Development during World War II.

69. Ibid., 221-235.

70. For some insights into how Wishengrad approached writing the script, as well as a copy of the script, see Erik Barnouw, ed. *Radio Drama in Action: Twenty-Five Plays of a Changing World* (New York: Farrar & Rinehard, 1945), 32-45. The drama is also included in a collection of Wishengrad scripts written for *The Eternal Light*.

71. A 2004 re-enactment by the Gotham Radio Players is available on DVD from www.SatelliteMediaProductions.com.

72. Radio historian John Dunning describes the musical score in these words: "The sound patterns came rumbling like Japanese dive bombers, the growl of heavy machinery, the sudden ripping chatter of machine guns..." Dunning, *On the Air*, 727.

73. Blue, *Words at War*, 152-153.

74. See Chapter 3 for more background about *The Protocols of the Elders of Zion*.

75. The episode is listed as Program #2 of the sub-series "One Nation Indivisible." As a syndicated program, the episodes were broadcast on different dates. The Radiogoldindex.com database shows this episode as possibly having been broadcast in 1944.

76. See MacDonald, *Don't Touch That Dial*, 78, 374 (n71). Referring to an article that appeared in the January 9, 1946 issue of *Variety,* MacDonald writes about the broadcast philosophy of two of the people involved in producing and writing *Mr. District Attorney*, Edward Bryon and Bob (Robert) Shaw, both of whom argued that "there was a 'noblesse oblige' inherent in the radio

business and that it was the obligation of broadcasting to battle the evils that menaced Americans. Specifically, they maintained that the 'multitude of anti-democratic whispers and rackets perpetrated on the people' must be exposed in programming." The American Jewish Committee's Radio Department also "fed" ideas to the program's producers. Copies of the scripts and sound recordings are available on the AJC web site.

77. The play had a rather unusual history. The story is based on the real life experience of playwright Franz Werfel, an Austrian Jew, who met a Polish Jew in Paris in 1940 when both men were desperately seeking to escape from France before the Nazis occupied the country. Once safely in the United States, Werfel told the story of the wily Polish Jew at a party in Hollywood at which playwright S. N. Behrman was present. The two men discussed the possibility of turning the idea into a play but when it turned out that each man wanted to approach the story differently (Werfel felt that any telling of the story should be done in a serious manner while Behrman believed a humorous touch would be more effective). Rather than working together, the two agreed to disagree and each wrote a separate treatment. Both plays were eventually produced but Behrman's lighter version, "Jacobowsky and the Colonel," was the more successful production.

78. In real life, Karlweiss actually lived the life of a Jacobowsky, escaping from Paris by car in 1940, the time in which the play was set. *Time* magazine, March 27, 1944.

79. www.jewishvirtuallibrary.org/jsource/Holocaust/murrow.html. Excerpts from the program are included in the book's CD.

80. MacDonald, *Don't Touch That Dial*, 76-81.

81. See Sam Levenson, "*The Dialect Comedian Should Vanish*," *Commentary*, August, 1952, 168-170. The article was written in response to Popkin's "Vanishing Jew," article. See footnote 82. See also Josh Kun, "The Yiddish Are Coming: Mickey Katz, Anti-Semitism, and the Sound of Jewish Difference," *American Jewish History*, Vol. 87, #4, December, 1999, 343-374.

82. Henry Popkin, "The Vanishing Jew of Our Popular Culture: The Little Man Who Is No Longer There," *Commentary*, Vol. 14, No. 1 (July, 1952) 46-55. Screenwriter and novelist Ben Hecht expressed a similar concern, writing: "The greatest single Jewish phenomenon in our country in the last twenty years has been the almost complete disappearance of the Jew from America fiction, stage, radio and movies. Ben Hecht, *A Guide for the Bedeviled* (New York, 1944).

83. *The Goldbergs* ended its long radio run in 1945, although it returned briefly for the 1949-1950 season when it also appeared on television. The TV program ended in 1954. Berg's *House of Glass* returned to radio in 1953 but lasted only six months. For more insights into the "disappearance" of Jews from mainstream network radio see Popkin, "The Vanishing Jew," as well as Edward S. Shapiro, "World War II and American Jewish Identity," in *Modern Judaism*,

Vol. 10, #1, February, 1990, 65-84, and Hilene Flanzbaum, ed. *The Americanization of the Holocaust* (Baltimore: Johns Hopkins University Press, 1999). One of the challenges facing media historians interested in examining this aspect of radio history is identifying and then locating sufficient material to study.

84. For more insights into the role of the American Jewish Committee, the Anti-Defamation League and the American Jewish Congress in fighting anti-Semitism after the war, see Svonkin, "Jews Against Prejudice."

85. If there is a stereotype suggesting that Jews are clever at making business deals, somehow it did not rub off on the teenagers who sold the rights to *Superman* to a comic book company for the grand sum of $130.00. Another Jew who was better as a song writer than a businessman was Sholom Secunda who sold the rights to his "Bei Mir Bist Du Schoen" song for a mere $30.00.

86. *The New York Times*, April 28, 1946, 7.

87. Between 1948-1950, the AJC produced spot opening and closing announcements that were aired on the *Superman* program.

88. Today's reader (and possibly yesterday's listener) may wonder how the gang members knew that the student passing through their neighborhood was a Jew. In fact, in the very beginning of the story when the gang stops a student, accusing him of being a Jew, the student answers back: "I'm not a Jew. My name is Aldo Ferrenzi. I'm Italian...Catholic." A gang member then proceeds to make an anti-Catholic remark.

89. The G.I. Bill was a federal program enacted into law in 1944 that provided benefits to soldiers. One of the most popular benefits gave veterans money to attend college.

90. April 15, 1947 letter from Harris to AJC and AJC's April 24, 1947 response. AJC, Box 235, Folder 1947.

91. Ring Lardner, a non-Jew, was originally hired by MGM's Samuel Goldwyn to write the screenplay for the movie adaptation of "Earth and High Heaven." In an interview, Lardner recalled that when he delivered the script to Goldwyn, the studio head wasn't pleased with the job and accused the writer of having betrayed him because he was "writing like a Jew." By the time Goldwyn had gone through a series of other writers, Zanuck had already released "Gentleman's Agreement" and Goldwyn is reported to have said, "He (Zanuck) stole my idea." See Pat McGilligan, *Backstory 3 Interviews with Screenwriters of the 1960s* (Berkeley, CA: University of California Press, 1977).

92. The song is a plaintive cry to God (Eli, Eli) about the suffering of the Jews and their resolve to keep their faith in the Lord.

93. Although the movie version of "Crossfire" has been written about extensively in books and articles dealing with anti-Semitism, the authors are not aware of any discussion of the radio version of the film. The same is true for the *Lux* broadcast of "Gentleman's Agreement."

94. In real life, the Jewish baseball player Hank Greenberg of the Detroit

Tigers confronted a somewhat similar moral dilemma in 1934 when he had to decide if he could, in good conscience, play ball on Yom Kippur. He chose not to play and the public's reaction was, as might be expected, mixed.

95. See Barnouw, *The Golden Web*, 89-91 for a discussion of the *Cavalcade's* selectivity of both topics and words. Barnouw notes that a Negro was not featured on the program until 1948. Also Blue, *Words at War*, 315-316, states that *Cavalcade* never mentioned the Holocaust and that the series either rarely or never mentioned the existence of Jews. "Possibly, the only *Cavalcade* show that even acknowledged their existence, let alone their persecution by the Nazis, was...the April (19th), 1943 Arthur Miller play about Pastor Martin Niemoller. Blink, however, and you can miss the allusion to the Jews...'Out over the American land...under the sign of the cross and under the six pointed star of Israel...' ")

96. Gregory Koseluk, *Eddie Cantor: A Life in Show Business* (Jefferson, NC: McFarland & Company, 1995), 370.

97. Goldberger's story was also told on the *Blue Playhouse* on January 29, 1944 from 12-12:25pm on WJZ, the flagship station of NBC's Blue network. No additional details about this program are known. His contribution was also included in the Jewish episode of *Americans All, Immigrants All* and was the subject of an episode on *The Eternal Light*.

98. Kowarski was a nuclear physicist.

Appendix 1
Availability of programs discussed in the book

Series	Program Title	Date	Script[1]	Audio[1,2]
Abie's Irish Rose		4/25/42-6/26/43	DSS	*
		3/20/43-2/19/44	TOL	*
Adventures of Ellery Queen		2/26/44-9/2/44	DSS	*
Adventures of Superman	Murder for Americans	8/17/47		*
	Hate Mongers, The	4/16/46-5/20/46		*
Americans All, Immigrants All		1938-1939	UMN, NARA	*
Arch Oboler's Plays	Sensitive Mr. Ginsburg (Pgm #44)	1/20/40	Biblio	*
	Suffer Little Children	9/16/41	Biblio	*
Broadway Is My Beat		6/16/50		
Bronx Marriage Bureau		1932-33/34		
Burbig's Rhythm Boys		1931 ?		
Burbig's Syncopated History		1930-1931		
Campbell Playhouse	Counselor at Law	1/6/39		*
Can You Top This?		1940-1954		*

[1] See explanation of abbreviations at end of Appendix. Some scripts may also be available on the Internet.
[2] The * denotes that audio versions of the program are known to have survived. In the case of long-running series, only some episodes may be available. Copies of these programs may be obtained by contacting dealers who sell old time radio programs, many of whom can be found on the Internet. One such dealer is Jerry Haendiges Productions, the producer of the CD in this book. Some programs are also available for listening only at The Jewish Museum/National Jewish Archive of Broadcasting and the Paley Center for Media (formerly the Museum of Television and Radio) in New York City and the Museum of Broadcast Communications in Chicago (closed until 2008).

Series	Program Title	Date	Script	Audio[1,2]
Cavalcade of America	An Honorable Titan	11/4/46		*
	Citizen Straus	4/11/50		*
	Red Death, The	10/30/40		*
	Winner Take Life	4/19/48		*
	Young Man in a Hurry	2/28/50		
CeCo Couriers		1931		
Church of the Air		1931-1957		
Cohen the Detective		*1943*		
Columbia Workshop	Esther	8/17/41		*
	Job	8/24/41		*
	Mr. Cohen Takes a Walk	12/21/39		*
	Samson	8/10/41	Biblio	*
Columbia Workshop/CBS Radio Workshop	No Time For Heartaches	1/13/57		*
Columbia Workshop/A Passport for Adams	Tel Aviv	9/21/43	Biblio	*
Dr. Six-Gun		9/23/54		*
Eternal Light		1944-1986	Biblio	*
	Battle of the Warsaw Ghetto	Varied	Biblio, AJC-W	*
Everyman's Theater	Mr. Ginsburg	2/21/41	Biblio	*
Exploring the Unknown	Fury of Man	4/6/47	AJC-Y	*
Faith In Our Time		1940s		
(Father Coughlin: See Golden Hour of the...)				
Fleischmann's Yeast Hour	Baby Carriage, The	8/10/33		*
	Fanny Brice/Romeo & Juliet	1/12/33		*
	Lou Holtz	3/16/33		*
	May Usher -Sammy Goldberg's Wedding	2/16/33		*

Series	Program Title	Date	Script[1]	Audio[1,2]
Fred Allen Show	Allen's Alley (Mrs. Nussbaum)	Varied	Biblio	*
Free World Theater	I Have No Prayer	3/14/43	Biblio	*
	Second Battle of the Warsaw Ghetto	6/1943		[3]
The Goldbergs (Rise of the Goldbergs, The)		1929-1934	GBC	*
		1936-1945	GBC	*
		1949-1950	GBC	
Golden Hour of the Little Shrine (Father Coughlin)		1932-1939	UB	*
Hallmark Hall of Fame	Bernard Baruch	2/28/54		*
	George Gershwin	9/20/53		*
	Lew Kowarski	3/20/55		*
	Sigmund Freud	2/6/55		*
Hallmark Playhouse	Mr. Young Disraeli	10/12/52	GBC	
House of Glass		4/17/34-12/25/35	GBC	*
		1954-1955	GBC	*
Houseboat Hannah		1936-1941		*
Jack Benny Program	Mr. Kitzel	Varied		
	Shlepperman	Varied		
Jewish Hour		1929-1930		
Jewish Poker Game		1926 ?		
Kaltenmeyer's Kindergarten		1932-1940	LAB	*
Krausemeyer & Cohen		1935 ?		*
Lamplighter, The		Varied	AC	
Lest We Forget		1940s		*

---

[3] April 13, 1934 (Passover Begins) is only program known to have survived

Series	Program Title	Date	Script[1]	Audio[1,2]
Life Can Be Beautiful		1938-1954		*
Life Can Be Beautiful/Victory Front		1944		*
Life With Luigi		1948-1953		*
Light of the World		3/18/40-6/2/50	Biblio	*
Lux Radio Theatre				*
	Counselor at Law	1/13/35		*
	Gentlemen's Agreement	9/20/48		*
	Jazz Singer, The	4/23/45		*
	Life of Emile Zola, The	5/8/39		*
Mama Bloom's Brood		1934 ?		*
March of Time		3/24/38		*
Meet Millie		1951-1954		*
Message of Israel		1934-1986		[4]
Meyer the Buyer		1932		
Mr. District Attorney	Case of the Misguided Mothers	4/26/44	AJC-W	AJC-W
	Case of the Peddlers of Prejudice	12/20/44	AJC-W	AJC-W
NBC University of the Air	Jew, The (They Call Me Joe)	8/19/44		*
No Brass Bands		2/22/55		*
Orson Welles Theater	Irishman and a Jew, The	9/15/41	Welles	
Potash and Perlmutter		1933		LC
Radio Reader's Digest	Disraeli	6/2/46		*
Rise of the Goldbergs (See Goldbergs, The)				
Studio One	An Act of Faith	9/16/47		*
	Earth and High Heaven	12/1/47		*

[4] Only broadcasts generally after ca. 1960 are available through AJA and CS.

257

Series	Program Title	Date	Script[1]	Audio[1,2]
Sunday Radio Chapel		1940s		*
Suspense	Crossfire	4/10/48		*
Theatre Guild on the Air	Jacobowsky and the Colonel	9/16/45		*
Treasury Agent	Case of the Hate Racket, The	4/14/47		*
Treasury Star Parade	Rumor, The (#82/162)	3/1/43	Prince	*
	Address Unknown (Pgm #21)	1942		
University of Chicago Round Table	Jews, The	1/28/40	Chi, NYPL	*
Words at War	Assignment USA	2/22/44		*
	Bid Was Four Hearts, The	2/27/45		*
	Der Furher	3/21/44		
	Scapegoats in History	12/26/44		*
SPECIAL BROADCASTS				
	American Jewish Congress Rally	3/27/33		
	Behold the Jew	9/17/44	AJC-W	AJC-W
	Cable From Lisbon	5/7/41		
	Charles Lindbergh	9/11/41	CL	*
	Cohen on the Telephone	Varied	Biblio	RD
	Gerald L. K. Smith	1936-70	GLKS	GLKS
	Jewish Religious Service/Germany	10/29/44	AJC-W	AJC-W
	Jewish Religious Service/Rome	7/23/44		
	Leo Forbstein Memorial Program	4/28/48		*
	Liberation of Buchenwald	4/15/45	[5]	[6]

[5] www.jewishvirtuallibrary.org/jsource/Holocaust/murrow.html   [6] http://www.buchenwald.de/index_en.html

Series	Program Title	Date	Script[1]	Audio[1,2]
(Special Broadcasts/con't.)	Operation Nightmare I & II	6/9/47; 4/10/48		*
	Right to Live, The	5/18/47		*
	Sam Lapidus (Lou Holtz)	Varied		*
	Wall, The	3/30/50	AJC-W	

Explanation of Abbreviations

- AJC-W: www.ajcarchives.org (American Jewish Committee Archives)
- AJC-Y: American Jewish Archives at Yivo Institute for Jewish Research
- AJA: American Jewish Archives
- Biblio: Refers to a book listed in the bibliography. See text in chapter for the exact title of the book.
- Chi: University of Chicago
- CL: www.charleslindbergh.com
- CS: Central Synagogue Archives, New York, NY.
- DSS: David S. Siegel Radio Archives
- GBC: Gertrude Berg Collection, Syracuse University
- GLKS: Gerald L. K. Smith Collection, Bentley Library, University of Michigan, Ann Arbor
- LAB: Library of American Broadcasting, University of Maryland, College Park, MD
- LC: Library of Congress
- NARA: National Archives, Washington, D.C.
- NYPL: New York Public Library for the Performing Arts
- Prince: Princeton University
- RD: Record dealers
- TOL: Thousand Oaks Public Library, Thousand Oaks, CA
- UB: Used book dealers
- UMN: Immigration History Research Center, University of Minnesota
- Welles: Orson Welles Collection, Lilly Library, University of Indiana, Bloomington, IN

Appendix 2
Abie's Irish Rose Controversy

The following objections to *Abie's Irish Rose* are taken from selected letters and memos written by staff members of the American Jewish Committee. The authors, having access to the actual scripts, believe that the objections do not reflect a full understanding of the many ongoing story lines and are therefore taken out of context.

February 20, 1943 Script
AJC Objection

"The Jews are pictured as sharp in their way of getting around things. When Mr. Levy wishes to be looked upon with favor by someone who lost her pocketbook in his store, he uses conniving and cunning schemes to regain her favor. He, not Murphy, usually does the scheming. Murphy sort of follows along on Levy's ideas. This fans the flames of basic anti-Semitism."

Plot Recap

In the previous week's episode, Mamale was shopping for a pocketbook in the Levy department store when she accidentally picked up the pocketbook of another customer by mistake. When the customer tried to retrieve it, Mamale created a fuss and accused the woman of trying to steal the pocketbook. Patrick grabbed the woman while Mamale yelled, "stop thief." The customer then proved that the pocketbook in question did indeed belong to her. During the February 20th episode, the Cohens, Levys and Patrick are trying to figure out how to make amends to the customer (Ms. Stonehill). To make matters worse, Ms. Stonehill owns the land underneath Patrick's store — which relates to another ongoing story line.

Actual Script

Mr. C: You two (Pat and Solomon) are getting nowhere fighting! — Why don't you sit down calmly and think of something to do?

Pat: How can I sit down calmly when the very ground under my store is slipping through my hands!!

February 20, 1943 Script (con't.)

Mr. C: Why don't you use some psychology on Emma Stonehill?
Sol: All right, all right — Where can you buy it!
Mr. C: You can't buy it!
Sol: Then how can we use it?
Mr. C: This way!! Find out what she likes — and take it to her. Find out what appeals to her!

....

Mr. C: ...Every woman likes something! With Mamale, she likes five pound boxes of candy! ...Now, maybe Emma Stonehill likes candy, too!
Sol: So Pat'll take her ten pounds!! — Won't you, Pat?
Pat: (NOT SOLD) I don't know!
Mr. C: And most everyone is won over by flowers!
Pat: Flowers!? Now, that appeals to me! — I used to court Rosemary's mother with flowers!
Rose: Well, Dad — you're not exactly going to court Emma Clatchie Stonehill, are you?
Pat: I should say not!
Sol: Rosele, if he wants to save his store — he has got to start pitching in too!!

February 20, 1943 Script AJC Objection	Authors' Comments
"Anybody listening to the program would think that the Jews do not know the English language, are vulgar, cheap, uneducated, and without taste or sensitivity. The heavy, guttural accents of the Levys are most distasteful and unpleasant to the ear, as are the many Jewish expressions that are used, such as: "oy vey is mere" (oh woe is me), "oy, yoi yoi" (exclamatory bitter sigh), "sloog the kup in vont" (beat your head on the wall), "oy gevalt (oh horror)," "voos hock ze a chinick" (what is she 'gabbing about), etc. Mrs. Levy (Cohen), he noted was "constantly arguing with Mr. Levy (Cohen) and saying, 'shut up, Solomon,' and is certainly not a refined or dignified character."	The excessive use of Jewish phrases is subjective and a separate and distinct issue from the voices used to say them. Patrick Murphy used two of the expressions objected to by the AJC — and in the right context — in an earlier episode. Some expressions are "defined" for the audience. It is debatable whether others, such as "oi vey is mere" when said with the proper intonation and in the right circumstances really needed an explanation.

April 17, 1943 Script	Authors' Comments
AJC objection	Patrick Murphy, not Mr. Levy (neither the two Mr. Levys or Mr. Cohen, frequently mistaken for "Levy") uses the word "shrimp" in a derogatory sense to Mr. Flannagan — who in earlier episodes "put one over" on Patrick in a business deal. His Irish sounding name notwithstanding, Flannagan is Jewish. The AJC documents do not make any reference to these earlier dealings.
"Obnoxious is the discussion between Mr. Levy and another when Mr. Levy says that he does not want to be called anything but Kosher: 'I don't like to be called anything but Kosher', when he is called 'a little shrimp.' Shrimp is not Kosher," says he, and he did not want to have anything to do with anything that was not Kosher. 'How can you look at my face and say that I am not Kosher?', said Mr. Levy. Then told his face was "shmootsig" (dirty).	
	Actual Script
	Pat: Help me! HELP ME! Why if it weren't for that little shrimp I wouldn't be in the mess I am.
	Flan: Mr. Murphy — calling me any names but shrimps. I don't like to be called anything that ain't strictly kosher — And shrimps ain't kosher!
	Pat: Well, you're not kosher — you know that don't you!
	Flan: How can you look on my face and tell me I'm not kosher!
	Pat: Because Kosher means clean — and you're not clean!
	Sol: (LAUGHS) that's a good one, Pat! — You're right — he ain't clean! He's a just plain smootzik.

April 24, 1943 Script	Authors' comments
AJC Objections	The bickering between Solomon and Patrick is part of their persona and the show's humor. The arguing and the "name calling" is devoid of any true nastiness.
(Note: the following objections are paraphrases from an internal memo.)	
Same arguing, calling of names and Yiddish expressions continue.	**Actual script** (Recap: In the previous episode Patrick gave Flannagan $500 to "buy off" Ms. Stonehill. The other characters agree that this was a stupid thing to do. So Solomon says that if Patrick keeps us this kind of behavior, "you will be mehullah.")
	Pat: I'll be what?
This once, there's a short scene in which a Jew makes fun of an Irishman.	Sol: Mehullah! That's what you'll be.
	Pat: I will?
	Sol: You can't escape it.
	Pat: Sol — what's mehullah?
There's a great deal of discussion about the word "machoola" which the audience is told means "busted."	Sol: Busted — ruined — wrecked.
	Pat: Busted? — Ruined? — Wrecked??
	Sol: Busted — Ruined — Wrecked.
	Pat: SOL, you're right. If I don't watch my step, I WILL be mehullah.
	After more bickering between Solomon and Patrick...
	Mr. C: Stop it — stop it — stop it!!! You're getting me all upset. I can't stand arguments.
	Rose: Yes, that's right — Instead of fighting all the time, you two should do all you can to be companionable.
	Pat: We are companionable — I'm the best friends he's got — Ain't I, Sol?
	Sol: You betchalife you are — and I'm the best friend you've got, ain't I Patrickle.
	Pat: That you are.
	Sol: Good. Check hands.

263

April 24, 1943 (Con't.) AJC Objections	Authors' comments
When Mrs. Levy returned from the beauty parlor having "glamorized" herself, Mr. Levy says he does not recognize his "zoftik Mamila" (Juicy, flabby, buxom wife).	The word "zoftik" does not appear in the printed script. While there would be general agreement that "zoftik" means fat or buxom, many would disagree with the negative overtones of the words "juicy" and "flabby." The word could easily be defined as "pleasantly plump."

Also, when Patrick says that Mamale looks like "Frankenstein," Mr. Cohen comes to his wife's defense and tells Patrick: "Mr. Murphy — Be careful what you say to my wife." In a later scene, Papale reminds Mamale that she does not need make-up and he sings the opening refrain of the well-known Yiddish song, "Bie Mir Bist Du Chayn."

    Bie Mir Bist Du Chayn.
    Please let me explain.
    Bie Mir Bist Du Chayn.
    Means that you're grand.
    Mine little darling honya.
    Bie Mir Bist Du Chayn. |

Selected Bibliography

Archival Collections

American Jewish Committee, Radio Department Archives, Gen-10 Folder. Yivo Institute For Jewish Research, New York, NY.

Anne Nichols Papers. New York Public Library for the Performing Arts, Billy Rose Theater Collection, New York, NY.

David S. Siegel Radio Archives. Yorktown Heights, NY.

Gertrude Berg Papers. Bird Library. Syracuse University, Syracuse, NY.

Gerald L. K. Smith Papers. Bentley Historical Library, University of Michigan, Ann Arbor, MI.

Message of Israel Collection. American Jewish Archives, Cincinnati, OH.

Message of Israel Papers. Central Synagogue Archives. Central Synagogue, New York, NY.

Radio and Television Department Files and related files. Jewish Theological Seminary, New York, NY.

Union of Reform Judaism Records, (Formally Union of American Hebrew Congregations). American Jewish Archives, Cincinnati, OH.

Books

Allen, Fred. *Treadmill to Oblivion*. Boston: Little, Brown and Company, 1954.

Baldwin, Neil. *Henry Ford and the Jews: The Mass Production of Hate*. New York: Public Affairs, 2001.

Barnouw, Erik. *A Tower in Babel: A History of Broadcasting in the United States to 1933*. New York: Oxford University Press, 1966.

_____. *The Golden Web: A History of Broadcasting in the United States 1933-1953*. New York: Oxford University Press, 1968.

Barnouw, Erik, ed. *Radio Drama in Action: Twenty-Five Plays of a Changing World*. New York: Farrar & Rinehard, 1945.

Berg, Gertrude. *The Rise of the Goldbergs*. New York: Barse & Co., 1931.

Berg, Gertrude and Cherney Berg. *Molly and Me*. New York: McGraw-Hill, 1961.

Bilby, Kenneth. *The General: David Sarnoff and the Rise of the Communications Industry*. New York: Harper & Row, 1986.

Blue, Howard. *Words at War: World War II Era Radio Drama and the Postwar Broadcasting Industry Blacklist*. Lanham, MD: Scarecrow Press, 2002.

Brinkley, Alan. *Voices of Protest: Huey Long, Father Coughlin, and the Great Depression*. New York: Knopf, 1982.
Brown, Robert J. *Manipulating the Ether: The Power of Broadcast Radio in Thirties America*. Jefferson, NC: McFarland, 1998.
Buhle, Paul. *From the Lower East Side to Hollywood: Jews in American Popular Culture*. New York: Verso, 2004.
Cauman, Sam. *Jonah Bondi Wise: A Biography*. New York: Crown Publishers, 1966.
Corenthal, Michael. *Cohen on the Telephone: A History of Jewish Recorded Humor & Popular Music, 1892-1942*. Milwaukee, WI: Yesterday's Memories, 1984.
Cox, Jim. *The Great Radio Soap Operas*. Jefferson, NC: McFarland & Company, 1999.
Dollinger, Marc. *Quest For Inclusion; Jews and Liberalism in Modern America*. Princeton, NJ: Princeton University Press, 2000.
Douglas, Susan J. *Listening In: Radio and the American Imagination from Amos 'n' Andy to Edward R. Murrow to Wolfman Jack and Howard Stern*. New York: Times Books, 1999.
Dreher, Carl. *Sarnoff: An American Success*. New York: Quadrangle, 1977.
Dunning, John. *On the Air: The Encyclopedia of Old-Time Radio*. New York: Oxford University Press. 1998.
Erickson, Hal. *Religious Radio and Television in the United States: 1921-1991*. Jefferson, NC: McFarland & Company, 1992.
Fang, Irving E. *Those Radio Commentators!* Ames, IA: Iowa State University Press, 1977.
Fisher, James. *Eddie Cantor: A Bio-Bibliography*. Westport, CT: Greenwood Press, 1997.
Flanzbaum, Hilene, ed. *The Americanization of the Holocaust*. Baltimore: Johns Hopkins University Press, 1999.
Freeman, James A. and Gilbert A. Williams. "Stereotypes on Radio," in *Encyclopedia of Radio*, Christopher H. Sterling, ed. Routledge, 2003, 1337-1341.
Goldman, Herbert G. *Banjo Eyes: Eddie Cantor and the Birth of Modern Stardom*. New York: Oxford University Press, 1997.
Gutterman, Leon, ed. *The Wisdom of Sarnoff and the World of RCA*. Wisdom Society, 1968.
Halper, Donna. "Jewish Radio Programs in the United States," in *Encyclopedia of Radio*, Christopher H. Sterling, ed. Routledge, 2003, 784-787.
Havig, Allen. *Fred Allen's Radio Comedy*. Philadelphia: Temple University Press, 1990.
Hayman, Joe. *Cohen on the Wireless*. London: Austin Rogers, 1920s.
_____. *Twenty Different Adventures of Cohen on the Telephone and Other Samples of Hebrew Humor*. New York: George Sully & Co., 1927.

Herman, Lewis and Marguerite Shalett Herman. *Foreign Dialects: A Manual for Actors, Directors and Writers*. Chicago: Ziff-Davis Publishing Company, 1943.

Hershfield, Harry and "Senator" Ed Ford and Joe Laurie, Jr. *Can You Top This?* Garden City, NY: Blue Ribbon Books, 1945.

_____. *Cream of the Crop*. New York: Didier, 1947.

Hilmes, Michele. *Radio Voices: American Broadcasting, 1922-1952*. Minneapolis, University of Minnesota Press, 1997.

Hilmes, Michele, ed. NBC: America's Network. Berkeley, CA: University of California Press, 2007.

Hilmes, Michele and Jason Loviglio, eds. *Radio Reader: Essays in the Cultural History of Radio*. New York: Routledge, 2002.

Jeansonne, Glen J. *Gerald L. K. Smith: Minister of Hate*. New Haven, CT: Yale University Press, 1988.

Jessel, George. *Hello Momma*. Cleveland: World Publishing Company, 1946.

Josefsberg, Milt. *The Jack Benny Show*. New Rochelle, NY: Arlington House, 1977.

Koseluk, Gregory. *Eddie Cantor: A Life in Show Business*. Jefferson, NC: McFarland & Company, 1995.

Lazarsfeld, Paul F. and Frank N. Stanton. *Radio Research 1942-1943*. New York: Essential Books, 1944.

Lee, Albert. *Henry Ford and the Jews*. New York: Stein and Day, 1980.

Leff, Laura. *39 Forever*, 2 vols. Piedmont, CA: The International Jack Benny Fan Club, 2004.

Leff, Laurel. *Buried by the Times: The Holocaust and America's Most Important Newspaper*. Cambridge, MA: Cambridge University Press, 2006.

Livingston, Mary, Hilliard Marks and Marcia Borie. *Jack Benny: A Biography*. Garden City, NY: Doubleday, 1978.

Lyons, Eugene. *David Sarnoff: A Biography*. New York: Harper & Row, 1966.

MacDonald, J. Fred. *Don't Touch That Dial! Radio Programming in American Life, 1920 to 1960*. Chicago: Nelson-Hall, 1980.

Marcus, Sheldon. *Father Coughlin: The Tumultuous Life of the Priest of the Little Flower*. Boston: Little, Brown and Company, 1973.

Myers, Gustavus. *History of Bigotry in the United States*. New York: Random House, 1943.

Oboler, Arch. *Fourteen Radio Plays*. New York: Random House, 1940.

_____. *This Freedom: Thirteen New Radio Plays*. New York: Random House, 1942.

Oboler, Arch and Stephen Longstreet, eds. *Free World Theatre: Nineteen New Radio Plays*. New York: Random House, 1944.

Paper, Lewis J. *Empire: William S. Paley and the Making of CBS*. New York: St. Martin's Press, 1987.

Parker, Everett C., David W. Barry and Dallas W. Smythe, *The Television-Radio Audience and Religion*. New York: Harper & Brothers, Publishers, 1955.
Paulson, Roger C. *Archives of the Airwaves*. 7 vols. Boalsburg, PA: Bear Manor Media. 2003-2007.
Ribtiffo, Leo. *The Old Christian Right*. Philadelphia: Temple University Press, 1983.
Savage, Barbara Dianne. *Broadcasting Freedom: Radio, War and the Politics of Race, 1938-1948*. Chapel Hill, NC: University of North Carolina Press, 1999.
Segal, Eli. *The Eternal Light*. Newtown, CT: Yesteryear Press, 2005.
Shandler, Jeffrey and Elihu Katz, "Broadcasting American Judaism: The Radio and Television Department of the Jewish Theological Seminary," in *Tradition Renewed*, Vol II, ed. Jack Wertheimer, New York: Jewish Theological Seminary, 1977, 365-401.
Sies, Luther E. *Encyclopedia of American Radio 1920-1960*. Jefferson, NC: McFarland & Company, 2000.
Silver, Monroe. *Monroe Silver's Famous Cohen on the Telephone: Over 100 Original Jokes, Stories, Monologues and Parodies as Recorded by the Author in His Popular Series of Phonograph Records*. New York: Irving Berlin Standard Music Corporation, 1927.
Smith, Glenn D. Jr. *Something on My Own: Gertrude Berg and American Broadcasting, 1929–1956*. Syracuse, NY: Syracuse University Press, 2007.
Smith, Sally Bedell. *In All His Glory: The Life & Times of William S. Paley and the Birth of Modern Broadcasting*. New York: Touchstone/Simon & Schuster, 1990.
Smulyan, Susan. *Selling Radio: The Commercialization of American Broadcasting 1920-1934*. Washington, DC: Smithsonian Institution Press, 1994.
Sobel, Robert. *RCA*. New York: Stein and Day, 1986.
Stegner, Wallace. "The Radio Priest and His Flock," in *The Aspirin Age: 1919-1941*. Isabel Leighton, ed. New York: Simon and Schuster, 1949.
Sterling, Christopher and John M. Kittross. *Stay Tuned: A Concise History of American Broadcasting*. Belmont, CA: Wadsworth, 1978.
Svonkin, Stuart. *Jews Against Prejudice: American Jews and the Fight For Civil Liberties*. New York: Columbia University Press, 1997.
Taylor, Robert. *Fred Allen: His Life and Wit*. Boston: Little, Brown and Company, 1989.
Trav, S.D. *No Applause, Just Throw Money*. Faber and Faber, 2005.
Tull, Charles J. *Father Coughlin & the New Deal*. Syracuse, NY: Syracuse University Press, 1965.
Ward, L.B. *Father Charles E. Coughlin*. Detroit: Tower Publications, 1933.
Warren, Donald. *Radio Priest, Charles Coughlin the Father of Hate Radio*.

New York: The Free Press, 1996.

Weber, David. "Goldberg Variations: The Achievements of Gertrude Berg," in *Entertaining America: Jews, Movies, and Broadcasting*. J. Hoberman and Jeffrey Shandler, eds. Princeton, NJ: Princeton University Press, 1994.

Weinstein, David. "Why Sarnoff Slept: NBC and the Holocaust," in *NBC: America's Network*. Michele Hilmes, ed. Berkeley, CA: University of California Press, 2007.

Weiser, Norman S. ed, *The Writer's Radio Theater, 1941: Outstanding Plays of the Year* New York: Harper & Brothers, 1941.

Wishengrad, Morton. *The Eternal Light: 26 Radio Plays From the Famous Eternal Light Program.* New York: Crown, 1947.

Wylie, Max. *Best Broadcasts of 1940-41*. New York: Whittesley House, 1942.

Periodicals, Papers, Dissertations and Internet Sites

Athans, Mary Christine. "A New Perspective on Father Charles E. Coughlin," *Church History*, Vol. 56, #2, June, 1987, 224-235.

Birnie, William. "Molly Goes Marching On."*American Magazine*, November, 1941.

Cypkin, Diane. "A Rhetorical Critical Analysis of Father Coughlin's November 20, 1938 Radio Broadcast." *Journal of Radio Studies*, Vol. 4, #1, 1997, 134-150.

Fine, Joyce. "American Radio Coverage of the Holocaust" *Annual 5*, Simon Wiesenthal Center, 1988, 145-165.

Fishwick, Marshall W. "Father Coughlin Time: The Radio and Redemption," *Journal of Popular Culture*, Vol. 22, Fall, 1988, 33-47.

Freedman, Morris. "The Real Molly Goldberg: Baalebosteh of the Air Waves." *Commentary*, Vol. 21, # 4, April, 1956, 359-364.

Gordon, David. "America First: The Anti-War Movement, Charles Lindbergh and the Second World War, 1940-1941." Paper delivered by a joint meeting of the Historical Society and the New York Military Affairs Symposium, September 26, 2003.

Havig, Alan R. "Critic From Within: Fred Allen Views Radio," *Journal of Popular Culture*, Vol. 12, #2, Fall, 1978, 328-340.

Herman, Felicia. "Hollywood, Nazism, and the Jews, 1933-1941," *American Jewish History*, Vol. 89, #1, 2001, 61-90.

Janowitz, Morris. "The Technique of Propaganda for Reaction: Gerald L.K. Smith's Radio Speeches,"*The Public Opinion Quarterly*, Vol. 8, #1, Spring, 1944, 84-93.

Jeansonne, Glen J. "Gerald L.K. Smith: From Wisconsin Roots to National Notoriety" *Wisconsin Magazine of History*, Winter 2002-2003, 18-29.

Kun, Josh. "The Yiddish Are Coming: Mickey Katz, Antic-Semitism, and the

Sound of Jewish Difference," *American Jewish History*, Vol. 87, #4, December, 1999, 343-374.

Levenson, Sam. "The Dialect Comedian Should Vanish," *Commentary*, August, 1952.

Logsdon, Jonathan R. "Power, Ignorance, and Anti-Semitism: Henry Ford and His War on Jews." *The Hanover Historical Review*, Vol. 7, Spring, 1999. Also available online at http://history.hanover.edu/hhr/99/hhr99_2.html.

Maroun, Alexander B. "Pushing Technology: David Sarnoff and Wireless Communications, 1911-1921." Paper presented at the IEEE 2001 Conference on the History of Telecommunications, July 26, 2001.

Merwin, Ted. "The Performance of Jewish Ethnicity in Anne Nichols' Abie's Irish Rose." *Journal of American Ethnic History*, 2001, Vol. 20, #2.

Popkin, Henry. "The Vanishing Jew of Our Popular Culture: The Little Man Who Is No Longer There," *Commentary*, Vol. 14, #1, July, 1952.

Radiogoldindex.com. Database of 90,000+ radio programs. Continally updated.

Sapoznik, Henry. "Broadcast Ghetto: The Image of Jews on Mainstream American Radio," *Jewish Folklore and Ethnology*, Vol. 16, #1, 1994, 37-39.

Seldes, Gilbert. "The Great Gertrude." *Saturday Review*, June 2, 1956.

Shapiro, Edward S. "World War II and American Jewish Identity," *Modern Judaism*, Vol. 10, #1, February, 1990, 65-84.

Slotten, Hugh Richard. "Commercial Radio, Public Affairs Discourse and the Manipulation of Sound Scholarship: Isolationism, Wartime Civil Rights and the Collapse of the Attractiveness of Communism in America, 1933-1945," *Historical Journal of Film, Radio and Television*, Vol. 25, #3, August 2005, 382-384.

Steele, Richard W. "The War On Intolerance: The Reformulation of American Nationalism, 1939-1941," *Journal of Ethnic History*, Vol. 9, 1989, 3-35.

University of Chicago. "A Discussion of The Jews," University of Chicago Round Table, Program #98. January 28, 1940.

Zahavy, Zev. *The History and Survey of Jewish Religious Broadcasting*, Ph.D. Thesis, Yeshiva University, 1959.

Index

(Names of radio programs are italicized. Other titles are in quotation marks.)

A

Aachen (Germany), 209, 257
Abbott and Costello Program, 116
ABC network progams, 123, 160, 164, 174, 227, 237
Abie the Agent (comic strip), 88, 102n3
Abie's Irish Rose (radio): 103, 110, 138-153, 220, 253; controversy over, 140, 147-153, 253, 259-264
"Abie's Irish Rose" (play), 135-138, 152, 154, 156n27
"Abie's Irish Rose" (movie), 138, 153
"Act of Faith," 236, 256
Adams, Bill, 141
Adams, Nick 89
"Address Unknown," 217, 257
Adler, Cyrus, 174, 178
Adler, Stella, 244n4
Adventures of Ellery Queen, 235, 253
Adventures of Superman, 230–232, 251n87, 253
African-Americans, 106, 141, 192, 232, 241, 248n53
Al Pearce and His Gang, 116
Alfred Prinzmetal (character) 127
Allen, Charme, 101
Allen, Fred, 106, 112, 206. *See also* Allen's Alley
Allen's Alley, 103, 112–113, 124, 255
Alsop, Carlton, 139
America First Movement, 45, 66n10, 110
American Jewish Committee, 77, 125, 147-151, 153, 155n24, 170, 174, 203, 204–209, 210, 215-216, 222, 223, 240, 241, 259-264, programs, 208, 209; radio strategy (salting-in) 204, 247n35. *See also Krents, Milton and Rothschild, Richard C.*
American Jewish Congress 189–190, 203, 234
American Jewish Congress Rally, 189-191, 244n2, 257
Americans All, Immigrants All, 73–84, 84n7, 126, 133n36, 178, 204, 241, 243, 253; Jewish episode 78–83
Amos 'n' Andy 26, 27, 88, 94, 108, 141, 147
"Anne Frank's Diary," 178
Anti-Defamation League, 71n57, 152, 203, 209-210, 225. *See also Lest We Forget*
Anti-Semitism, 30, 34, 41-43, 63-64, 74, 115, 147, 153, 155n24, 165, 192-193, 194, 229, 259; programs about, 195-197, 208, 209-210, 214-216, 223-224, 225-226, 230–232, 233-234, 235, 236, 237-238, 240, 248n50, radio's effectiveness as a change agent, 83–84, 202, 243-244, 249n76; strategies for fighting,203, 204-208, 229, 234, 247n35. *See also* American Jewish Committee, Anti-Defamation League, Father Coughlin, Charles Lindbergh and *University of Chicago Round Table*
Antoine, Tex, 181
Appel, Anna,140, 149; photograph 146. *See also Abie's Irish Rose* and Mrs. Cohen/Mamale (character)

A

Applebaum, Rabbi Saul, 165
Arch Oboler's Plays, 217, 219, 253
Armed Forces Radio Service, 165, 187n60, 226
Artzt, Billy 100
"Assignment USA," 224, 257
Auerbach, Arthur (Artie), *See* Mr. Kitzel (character)
Avery, Ira, 181

B

Babcock, Celia, 100
"Baby Carriage," 193, 194, 254
Baker, Belle, 244n6
"Ballad for Americans," 226
Bar Mitzvah 24, 25
Barnouw, Erik, 181, 223
Baron Munchausen. *See* Pearl, Jack
Baruch, Bernard, 243, 255
"Battle of the Warsaw Ghetto," 175, 178, 187n60, 222–223, 254. See also "Second Battle of the Warsaw Ghetto" and "Wall"
Baxter, Anne, 221, 238
Becker, Dan, 186n54
Becker, Don, 120
"Behold the Jew," 208, 257
"Bei Mir Bist Du Schoen," 191, 244n3, 251n85, 264
Bell, Ralph, 181
Benjamin, Judah, 79, 210
Benny, Jack, 106, 107, 110. See also *Jack Benny Program*
Berg, Gertrude 95, 100, 192, 194; as producer and director, 25, 29–30; other projects 29, 30, 35–36, 39n30; overall assessment of, 36; personal life, 19–21, 39n34, 40n45; photographs, 23, 32; use of other writers and freelancers, 37n7, 38n14. *See also House of Glass*
Berger, Sylvia, 181
Bergman, Teddy. *See* Reed, Alan
Berle, Milton, 107
Berlin, Irving, 241
Berns, Julie. *See* Bernstein, Julie
Bernstein, Julie, 101
"Bid Was Four Hearts," 224, 257
Bible. *See* Old Testament
Bigotry. *See* Anti-Semitism
Bildersee, Adele, 162
Bixby, Carl, 120
Black, Frank, 223
Black, Judah, 212
"Black Death, The," 178
Blackburn, Arlene, 100
Blanc, Mel, 114
Blue Playhouse, 252n97
B'nai B'rith, 203
Boas, Franz, 80, 216
Bond, Richard, 140
Bosworth, Crocker, 193
Brad and Al Program, 111
Brandeis, Louis, 80, 178
Brandt, Mel, 181
Brice, Fanny, 108, 111, 131n21, 192, 244n6, 254
"Brick Foxhole," *See* "Crossfire"
Broadway Is My Beat, 238, 253
Bronx Marriage Bureau, 101, 253
Brown, Himan, 21, 25, 37n4, 101
Brown, John, 101, 112
Bryant, Geoffery, 89
Buchenwald, 228
Bulloff, Joseph, 100
Burbig, Henry, 108, 110–111
Burbig's Rhythm Boys, 111, 253
Burbig's Syncopated History, 111, 253
Burns, George, 100, 107

C

"Cable From Lisbon," 211, 257
Cagney, James, 194
Calhern, Louis, 227
Cameron, William J., 43–44
Campbell Playhouse, 194, 219, 253
Can You Top This? 88, 123–125,

247n35, 253
"Candelabra of the Steppes," 227
Cantor, Eddie,107, 108–109, 131n18–19, 198, 218, 241, 244n6
Cantor, Natalie, 101
Cardozo, Benjamin, 80
Carnofsky, Morris, 244n6
"Case of the Hate Racket," 235, 257
"Case of the Misguided Mothers," 225, 256
"Case of the Peddlers of Prejudice," 225, 256
Catskill Mountains, 19, 99, 142
Cavalcade of America, 241–242, 252n95, 254
CBS: controlled by Jews, 78; Father Coughlin, 51–52; programs, 20, 30, 39n32, 76, 81, 82, 83, 88, 110, 111, 120, 125, 127, 160, 163, 164, 203, 211, 219, 228, 236, 237, 240, 243. *See also* Paley, William S.
CBS Church of the Air. See Church of the Air
CBS Radio Workshop, 243, 254
CeCo Couriers, 110, 254
Censorship, 42, 52, 53, 63, 64-65, 65n2, 68n28, 72n69, 109. *See also* National Association of Broadcasters and Sponsors: censorship
Central Synagogue (New York), 164–165, 170
Cheer Up America, 111
Chesterfield Show, 129
"Chicago, Germany," 219
Church of the Air, 163–164, 168, 170, 185n38, 254
"Citizen Straus," 242, 254
Civoru, Sophia, 37n7
"Clan of the Fiery Cross," 232, 253
Clark, Philip, 172
Cohen, Myron, 129, 130n11
Cohen on the Telephone, 107, 125, 130n13, 137, 257

Cohen, Rabbi Samuel, 161
Cohen, the Detective, 101, 254
Collins, Ray, 86n14
Collyer, Clayton, 32, 140
Columbia Church of the Air. See Church of the Air
Columbia Presents Corwin. See Passport for Adams
Columbia Workshop, 206, 211–213, 254. *See also CBS Radio Workshop*
Committee on Jewish Religious Radio Programs, 162
Communism, *See* Coughlin, Father Charles E. and Smith, Gerald L. K.
Concentration camp liberations, 228
Conried, Hans, 126
Coogan, Richard, 140; photograph, 146
Cooper, Geroge, 238
Corn, Alfred. *See* Ryder, Alfred
Corwin, Norman, 212
Coughlin, Father Charles E., 48–62, 69n32-34, 72n62, 74, 82–83, 109, 163, 198, 224, 255
Council on Books in Wartime, 223
"Counselor at Law," 193, 194, 218, 253, 256
Cowan, Cantor Maurice, 157
Cravens, Kathryn, 228
"Cross and the Flag," *See* Smith, Gerlad L. K.
"Crossfire," 5, 237–238, 257

D

Damon, Lester, 121
Davis, Moshe, 175
Daytime serials. *See* Soap operas
"Dearborn Independent," 42, 43, 53, 83
DeKoven, Roger, 179, 181
Delmore, Irwin, 112
"Der Furhrer," 224, 257
Dewey, John, 167

Dialect (Jewish). *See* Yiddish
Dialects (non-Jewish), 108, 112, 114, 121, 122, 124, 126, 140, 193
Dieterle, William, 196
Displaced persons. *See* Refugees
"Disraeli," 242, 256. *See also* "Mr. Young Disraeli"
Donald, Peter, 112, 124
Double or Nothing, 31
Douglas, Nancy, 121
Douglas, Paul, 89, 141
Dr. I.Q, 206
Dr. Six-Gun, 239–240, 254
Dreyfus, Alfred, 195–197
Dryer, Sherman H., 214, 215, 233
Dubois, Rachel Dubois, 74–75, 76–77, 78
Dumas, Helene, 100
Dwyer, Virginia, 121

E

"Earth and High Heaven," 236, 251n91, 256
Eastman, Carl, 141, 153
Effie and Laura, 20, 37n3
Einstein, Albert, 216
Einstein, Harry, 108, 109
Eisenstein, Rabbi Ira, 164
Eldridge, Florence, 208
"Eli, Eli," 237
Ellery Queen. *See Adventures of Ellery Queen*
Erickson, Thor, 122; photograph, 118
"Esther," 212–213, 254
Eternal Light, 173–182, 187n58, n61-62 and n67, 227, 188n70, n74, 229, 254; cast photograph, 179
Ethnic groups, 6, 27, 41 76–77, 85n8, 106, 113, 121. *See also Abie's Irish Rose, Kaltenmeyer's Kindergarten*, Immigrants and Immigrant themes and *Life With Luigi*
Everyman's Theater, 217, 254

Exploring the Unknown, 233-235, 254

F

Faith in Our Time, 171, 254
Family themes, 22, 24, 30-31, 96–97
Feinberg, Rabbi Abraham, 162
Ferber, Edna, 211
Fields, Benny, 244n6
Finkelsein, Abe (character), 121
Finkelstein, Rabbi Louis, 174, 177, 188n70
Fitzpatrick, Leo. *See* WJR
Fleischer, Max, 91
Fleischmann's Yeast Hour, 107, 108, 128-129, 191–193, 241, 254
Flick, Pat C. (Patsy), 101, 112
Forbstein, Leo, 237, 257
Ford, Henry 42–44, 66n4 -5, 72n67, 74, 224
Ford, "Senator" Ed, 124
Ford Sunday Evening Hour, 43-44
Ford Theatre, 194
Forte, Joe, 126
Foster, Rabbi Solomon, 157
Frankfurter, Felix, 80, 216
Fred Allen Show. 255. *See* Allen's Alley
Free World Theater, 220–222, 255
Freehof, Rabbi Solomon, 163
Freeman, Florence, 141
Freud, Sigmund, 199, 243, 255
Friedman, Morton, 139
Friml, Rudolph, 241
Frome, Anthony. *See* Feinberg. Rabbi Abraham
"Fury of Man," 233–235, 254

G

Gallagher, Don, 121
Garfield, John, 221
Gary, Arthur, 181
Geiger, Milton, 208
Geller, Isidor, 179

"Gentleman's Agreement," 5, 236, 238, 251n91, 256
Gerber, Joseph, 242
German American Bund, 109
Gershwin, George, 80, 241, 243, 255
Gerson, Noel, 186n54
"Gertrude Berg Show," 36
Gillen, Dorothy, 141
Ginnes, Abram, 38n14
Glamour Manor, 115
Glass, Montague, 92-93, 135
"Glorifying the American Girl," (movie), 108
Gluck, Gemma, 228
Goldberger, Dr. Joseph, 80, 241, 252n97
Goldbergs, 30-35, 74, 87, 100, 103, 108, 110, 119, 140, 148, 189, 191, 212, 255; comic strip, 32; television, 35-36. *See also Rise of the Goldbergs*
Golden Hour of the Little Flower. See Coughlin, Father Charles E.
Goldenson, Rabbi Samuel, 163
Goldfort, Dr. David, 162
Goldstein, Rabbi Herbert S., 163
Goldstein, Rabbi Israel, 162, 163
Gompers, Samuel, 80, 210
Gonshak, Irwin, 181
Good News, 129
Goode, Rabbi Alexander D., 224
Gordon, Bert, 109, 131n18
Gottschalk, Norman, 121
Graham, Gwethalyn, 236
Gratz, Rebecca, 178
Great Gildersleeve, 115
Greenberg, Hank, 80, 251n94
Greenwald, Joseph, 94, 100
Gross, Milt, 91, 111
Gruenberg, Axel, 139

H
Hadassah, 81
Hallmark Hall of Fame, 243, 255

Hallmark Playhouse, 242, 255
Halop, Florence, 127
Hammerstein, Oscar, 80
Hammerstein Music Hall, 111
Harrington, Dot, 89
Hart, Madame Bertha, 162
"Hate Mongers," 231-232, 253
"Hatikvah," 80
Haupt, James, 139
Hayman, Joe, 107
Hearn, Sam: photograph, 118. *See* Shlepperman (character)
"Hello, Momma." *See* Jessel, George
Henry Street Settlement, 79
Hernandez, Juano, 181
Hershey, John, 223
Hershfield, Harry, 88–89, 90, 91, 123-125, 135
Hoffman, Rabbi Josef, 158
Hollywood and Jews, 97, 196, 236, 237, 238, 251n91
Hollywood Victory Committee, 220
Hollywood Writers Mobilization, 220
Holt, Ethel, 89
Holtz, Lou, 110, 128-129, 134n44, 192, 254, 258
"Honorable Titan," 242, 254
Hour of Smiles, 112
House of Glass, 30, 99–100, 255
Houseboat Hannah, 121, 255
Howard, Willie, 108, 110
Hummert, Frank and Anne, 121, 171

I
"I Have No Prayer," 220, 255
Immigrant themes, 6, 22, 23, 28, 126, 229
Immigrants, 73–76, 104–105. *See also* Ethnic groups and Refugees
Institute for American Democracy, 209
Institute for Democratic Education, 209, 210
Intercultural education. *See* Ameri-

cans All, Immigrants All
Intermarriage. See Abie's Irish Rose
"International Jew," 42, 43, 66n4
Intolerance. See Anti-Semitism
"Irishman and a Jew," 219, 256
Izzy Finkelstein (character), 104, 122-123, 255

J
Jack Armstrong, 205
Jack Benny Program, 114-117, 255. See also Mr. Kitzel and Shlepperman
Jackson, Ada, 208
"Jacob and the Indians," 178
"Jacobowsky and the Colonel," 227, 250n77, 257
Janney, Leon, 181
"Jazz Singer," 195, 236, 237, 256
Jessel, George, 107, 108, 125, 195, 237; photograph, 118
Jewish (Jews): contributions of, 79-80, 208, 210, 213, 216, 241-243; disappearance from popular culture, 229, 250n82,n83; dialect. see Yiddish; during Revolutionary War. 79, 80, 177, 210; hereos, 208, 222, 224. See also Warsaw Ghetto; holidays, 163. See also Bar Mitzvah, Passover, Rosh Hashanah and Yom Kippur; identified as Jews, 240-241, 252n95; in military, 79, 213, 220, 224, 226-227, 240; music, 163, 168; stereotype of, 22, 51, 53, 88, 97, 98, 103, 104, 110, 112, 113, 117, 119-120, 124, 137, 147, 148, 152, 153, 192, 193, 205, 207, 214-216, 247n35, 251n85, 259; themes in programs, 4-5, 24, 31, 110, 189, 212-213, 239-240
Jewish Art Program, 158, 183n7
Jewish Community Relations Council of Essex County (NJ), 125, 234
Jewish Hour, 161-162, 184n26, 255
Jewish Labor Committee, 203
Jewish Poker Game, 91, 255
"Jewish Religious Service From Aachen, Germany," 209, 257
"Jewish Religious Service From Rome," 209, 257
Jewish Theological Seminary, 160, 174, 175
"Jew," 226, 256
"Jews," 227, 257
"Job," 212–213, 254
Johnson, Raymond Edward, 181
Joint Distribution Committee, 203, 211, 257
Jolson, Al, 107, 134n44, 195, 236–237, 258
Jordan, Jim and Marian, 122; photograph, 118
Judaism explained, 163, 166, 176, 239-240, 254. See also Religious programs and specific religious programs
Jung, Dr. Leo, 162

K
Kahn, Otto, 80
Kaltenmeyer's Kindergarten, 122-123, 125, 255; cast photograph, 118. See also Izzy Finkelstein (character)
Kamman, Bruce, 122; photograph, 118
Kaplan, Marvin, 127
Karlweiss, Oscar, 227
Kate Hopkins, Angel of Mercy, 39, 30
Kate Smith Hour, 116
Katims, Milton, 100, 181
Kaufman, George S., 211
Kazan, Elia, 227
KDKA, 157, 158
Kern, Jerome, 241
KHJ, 89
Kilpatrick, Dr. William H., 167

Kindergarten Kapers. See
  Kaltenmeyer's Kindergarten
King, Ed, 181
Kinoy, Ernest, 181
Kinsella, Walter, 140; photograph, 146
KMOS, 89
Knickerbocker Playhouse, 138
"Kol Nidre," 24, 195, 237. See also Yom Kippur
Kowarski, Lew, 243, 255
Kraft Music Hall, 129
Krass, Rabbi Nathan, 161
Krausemeyer and Cohen, 97–99, 255
Krents, Milton, 148, 174–175, 204, 205, 222. See also American Jewish Committee and *Eternal Light*
Kristallnacht, 31, 55-60, 86n.21, 199–201, 218, 245n20
Kroeger, Berry, 181
KSD, 161
KSL, 161
Ku Klux Klan, 74, 232
Kuhn, Fritz, 74

L

La Guardia, Mayor Fiorello, 177, 228
Lamplighter, 160–161, 255
Larkin, John, 121
Laurie, Joe, Jr., 124
Lazaron, Rabbi Morris S., 167, 185n39
Lazarsfeld, Paul F. 33–34, 83
Lazarus, Emma, 178
Leader, Anton M., 181
Lechner, Frederick, 168
"Leffing Ges." *See* Burbig, Henry
Lenrow, Bernard, 179
"Leo Forbstein Memorial Program," 237, 257
Lest We Forget, 209–210, 225, 255
Levenson, Sam, 129
Levi, Rabbi Harry, 157–158, 167

Levine, Sam, 238
Levy, Uriah P., 79
Lewisohn, Adolph, 79
"Liberation of Buchenwald Concentration Camp," 228, 257.
Liebman, Rabbi Joshua Loth, 167
Life Can Be Beautiful, 34, 103, 117–120, 207, 212, 219, 256; cast photograph, 118; *Victory Front*, 120, 219, 256
"Life of Emile Zola," 195–196, 256
Life With Luigi, 121, 125–126, 140, 256
Light of the World, 171–173, 256
Lindbergh, Charles, 44–48, 59, 74, 109, 257
Linkletter, Art, 205
Locke, Ralph, 119; photograph, 118. *See also* Papa David (character)
Loeb, Philip, 35, 36, 40n47
Log Cabin Jamboree, 116
Lord, Phillips H., 225, 235
Lou Holtz Laugh Club, 129
Lukas, Paul, 217, 242
Lum and Abner, 108
Lux Radio Theatre, 194–196, 206, 238, 244, 256

M

MacGregor, Kenneth, 181
Mad Russian (character). *See* Gordon, Bert
Malapropisms, 24, 31, 96, 139
Mama Bloom's Brood, 94–97, 103, 256
Mann, Paul, 213
Mann, Rabbi Louis, 163
Mann, Thomas, 220
March, Fredric, 208, 217
March of Time, 198–199, 256
Margolis, Dr. Elias, 162
McCambridge, Mercedes, 140; photograph, 146
McCormick, Myron, 213

McGraw, Walter, 181
McGuire, Dorothy, 238
"Me and Molly" (play), 35, 36
Meet Millie, 127-128, 256
Mercury Theater, 219
Merrill, Robert, 24
Mertz, Ted, 149, 152
Message of Israel, 158, 160, 164–170, 174, 185n38, 189, 229, 256
Message To Israel, 170
Meyer the Buyer, 88–90, 91, 135, 140, 256
Michelson, Albert, 80
Milland, Ray, 238
Miller, Mitch, 108
Millie Bronson (character), 127-128
Mindel, Joseph, 181
Minute of Prayer, 160
Mitchum, Robert, 238
"Molly" movie), 36
"Molly," (play), 36
"Molly," (television), 36
Molly Goldberg (character), 24, 28, 32-33, 148
Moskowitz, Jenny, 193, 194, 244n8
Mount Neboh Temple, 164
"Mr. Cohen Takes a Walk," 211–212, 254
Mr. Cohen/Papale (character), 139, 143-145, 151, 262, 264
Mr. District Attorney, 206, 225, 234, 244, 249n76, 256
"Mr. Ginsberg," 217–218, 254.
Mr. Horowitz (character), 125–126
Mr. Kitzel (character), 106, 116-117, 255
"Mr. Lincoln and the Rabbi," 178
"Mr. Young Disraeli," 242, 255. *See also* "Disraeli"
Mrs. Cohen (Mamale), 139, 143-145, 149-151, 261, 262, 264. *See also* Appel, Anna
"Mrs. G. Goes to College," 36

Mrs. Nussbaum (character), 103, 106, 112–113, 117, 255
Multiculturalism. *See Americans All, Immigrants All*
Muni, Paul, 194, 195
"Murder for Americans," 235, 253
Murrow, Edward R., 203, 228, 257
Mutual network: programs, 30, 121, 123, 160, 170, 171, 211, 223, 228
Myers, Johnny, 141

N

Nagel, Conrad, 120
Nash, J. Carrol, 126
National Association of Broadcasters, 61, 63, 71n54-55
National Jewish Music Council, 163
NBC, 87, 106, 158, 201, 215, 223, programs, 21, 30, 35, 39n32, 75, 83, 92, 99, 101, 111, 112, 120, 123, 139, 160, 161, 164, 171, 174, 191, 208, 209, 214, 217, 220, 223, 226, 232, 235 *See also* Sarnoff, David
NBC University of the Air, 226, 256
Necco Surprise Party, 111
Negroes. *See* African-Americans
Newman, Rabbi Louis, 163
News broadcasts, 197, 203, 228, 246n29. *See also March of Time*
Nichols, Anne. *See Abie's Irish Rose*
Niemoller, Pastor Martin, 133n37, 252n95
No Brass Bands, 240, 256
"No Time For Heartaches," 243, 254
Nolan, Lloyd, 220

O

Oboler, Arch, 217–219, 220
Ochs, Adolph, 242, 254
Ocko, Dan, 179
Office of Education, 75, 76, 81
Office of War Information, 202, 220

Old Testament, 171-173, 212-213
"Operation Nightmare," 236–237, 258
Orson Welles Theater, 219, 256
Ortega, Santos, 181

P
Paley, William S., 15–17, 35, 51; photograph, 14
Papa David (character), 34, 103, 104, 117–120, 207, 212. *See also* Locke, Ralph
Papp, Frank, 181
Parkyakarkas (character). *See* Einstein, Harry
Passover, 24, 31
Passport for Adams, 213, 254
Pearl, Jack, 108
Peary, Harold, 122
Peck, Gregory, 238
Peerce, Jan, 24
Penman, Lea, 100
People Are Funny, 205
Perl, Arnold, 181
Peters, Ken, 126
Petrie, Howard, 141
Phelps, Eleanor, 172
Philco Hour, 111, 192
Picon, Molly, 244n6
Pious, Minerva: photograph, 118. *See* Mrs. Nussbaum (character)
Poet Prince, *See* Feinberg. Rabbi Abraham
Polonsky, Abraham, 38n14
Pool, Rabbi David deSola, 162, 163
Potash and Perlmutter, 92–94, 96, 100, 102n8, 135, 256
Procter & Gamble, 26, 29,119, 121, 147, 152
Programs: appeal to Jews, 28-29, 82, 125, 145-147, 182, 208; appeal to non-Jews, 24, 26, 27, 28, 33-34, 82, 86n18, 145-147, 169, 176, 181-182, 208; closings, 140; complaints about, 125, 205. *See also Abie's Irish Rose;* openings, 95, 98, 119, 139, 141, 172, 177; ratings, 26, 35, 40, 145, 180, 210, 232
"Protocols of the Elders of Zion," 42, 54, 224
Prussing, Louise, 194
Public opinion polls, 202
Pulitzer, Joseph, 80
Putterman, David, 187n68

R
Radio in US homes, 4-5
Radio Chapel of the Air. See Sunday Radio Chapel
Radio Hall Of Fame, 129
Radio Reader's Digest, 242, 256
Raeburn, Bryna, 181
Randolph, Amanda, 141
Ratings. *See* Programs: ratings
Raveth, Irving D., 221
"Red Death," 241, 254
Reed, Alan, 89, 90, 102n4, 109, 112, 126, 140, 237; photograph, 146
Refugees, 78, 178, 207, 211, 218–219, 235,236–237
Religious programs (Judaism), 157–182; conservative, 158, 160, mixed branches, 160, 163, 170, 171, orthodox, 160, 161; reform, 158–159, 160, 164, 183n8. *See also* specific religious programs
Repp, Guy, 181
"Rhode Island Regue," 177. *See also* Touro Synagogue
Rice, Elmer, 194, 245n9
Rich, Doris, 121
Richards, George (Dick), 51, 52, 67n16. *See also* WJR
Richardson, Alexander, 168
"Right To Live," 235, 258
Rinehart, Mary Roberts, 212
Rines, Joe, 14

280 Radio and the Jews

Rise of the Goldbergs, 21-30, 94, 95, 99, 100, 103, 161, 192, 255. *See also Goldbergs*
Rodgers, Richard, 241
Romberg, Sigmund, 241
"Romeo and Juliet" (skit), 111, 192, 254
Ronson, Adele, 89
Roosevelt, President Franklin D., 109, 198, 200
Rose, Norman, 179, 181
Rose, William, 121
Rosenwald, Julius, 79
Rosh Hashanah, 239
Rosten, Norman, 181
Rothschild, Richard C., 147, 148–149, 150, 155n16, 205. *See also* American Jewish Committee and *Abie's Irish Rose*
Rubin, Benny, 217
"Rumor, The," 32, 257
Ryan, Robert, 238
Ryder, Alfred, 25, 31, 38n13

S

Sam Lapidus (character), *See* Holtz, Lou
"Sammy Goldberg's Wedding," 192, 254
"Samson," 212–213, 254
"Samson and Delilah," (skit), 111
Sangster, Margaret, 186n54
Sarnoff, David, 11–15, 83, 174, 215, 216, 223; photograph, 14
"Scapegoats in History: History of Bigotry in the United States," 224, 257
Schwartz, Arthur, 241
Scourby, Alexander, 181
"Second Battle of the Warsaw Ghetto," 221-222, 255
"Second Exodus," 178
Secunda, Sholom, 191, 251n85
Seelye, Dorothea, 83–84, 243

Segal, Cantor Robert, 173, 179, 187n68
Seldes, Gilbert, 76, 78
Seligson, Rabbi David J., 165, 170
"Sensitive Mr. Ginsberg," 217, 253. *See* "Mr. Ginsberg"
Service Bureau for Intercultural Education, 76, 77, 81, 82. *See also Americans All, Immigrants All*
Seymour, Adele and Katherine, 186n54
Shaw, Irwin, 236
Shell Château, 108
Shepherd, Coulson, 170
Sherrill, Henry Knox, 166
Shirer, William L., 203, 245n21
Shlepperman (character), 114–116, 117, 132n30, 255
Shockley, Marion, 140
Sholom Aleichem, 188n72
Siegel, Marc, 181
Silber, Roslyn, 25, 26, 100; photograph, 32
Silver, Monroe, 107
Silver, Rabbi Abba Hillel, 163
Silver Shirts, 63, 74
Skulnik, Menasha, 25, 119, 140, 151, 212; photograph, 146. *See also Abie's Irish Rose*, Mr. Cohen (Papele) and Uncle David
Sloane, Everett, 25, 30, 38n13
Smith and Dale, 108, 130n15
Smith, Gerald L. K.,5, 62–65, 72n62, 74, 109, 257
Smith, Sydney, 140
Smith, Virginia, 149, 152
Soap operas 33-34. *See also Goldbergs, Houseboat Hannah, Life Can Be Beautiful, Light of the World* and *Rise of the Goldbergs*
"Social Justice." *See* Coughlin, Father Charles E.
Sockman, Ralph, 166

Solomon, Haym, 79, 80, 210
Sorin, Lou, 140
Sound effects, 26, 223
Sponsors: censorship, 42, 65n2, 109, 198. *See also* Censorship, Procter & Gamble and Woollcott, Alexander
Stang, Arnold, 30
Stark, Richard, 141
Stereotypes (Jewish). See Jewish: stereotypes
Stevens, Julie, 140
Stewart, Paul, 100
Stone, Sidney, 101
Stopak, Joe, 141
Straus, Nathan, 79, 242, 254
Studebaker, John, 75–76, 84n7
Studio One, 236, 256
"Suffer Little Children," 218–219, 253
Sunday Radio Chapel, 160, 170, 171, 257
Superman. *See Adventures of Superman*
Suspense, 237–238, 244, 257
Sutter, Dan, 181
Swenson, Karl, 181
Swing, Raymond Gram, 211
Synagogue Council of America, 160, 170, 171
Synagogue of Rome. *See* "Jewish Religious Service From Rome"
Syndicated programs, 94–95, 97, 99

T
Take It Or Leave It, 206
Tarshish, Rabbi Jacob. *See Lamplighter*
Taylor, Kathrine Kressmann, 217
Tedro, Henrietta Tedro, 121
"Tel Aviv," 213, 254
Television, 35-36, 40n46, 129
Temple Israel (Boston), 157, 167
"Temple of K'ai-Feng-Fu," 178

Theatre Guild on the Air, 194, 227, 257
They Call Me Joe, 202, 226, 256
Thirty Minutes in Hollywood, 107, 108
Thomas, Ann, 100, 141
Thomas, Lowell, 197, 245n21
Thompson, Dorothy, 200–201
Time Out For Laughs, 129
Today in Europe, 203
Toigo, Avinere, 74, 75-76
Totalitarian Tennis, 206
Totter, Audrey, 127
Touro Synagogue, 177. *See also* Jewish: during Revolutionary War
Town Crier. See Woollcott, Alexander
Trager, Frank N., 215-216
Treasury Agent, 235, 257
Treasury Star Parade, 32, 217, 219, 257
Trommers Troupers Show, 129
Tucker, Sophie, 243, 254
Tunick, Irv, 181
Twenty-six by Corwin, 212

U
U.S.S. Dorchester, 224
Uncle David (character), 25, 31, 32-33, 119, 140, 151, 212
Union of American Hebrew Congregations, 158-159, 163, 165
United Jewish Appeal, 203, 235, 236
United Jewish Laymen's Committee, 163, 164, 165, 185n38
United States Steel Hour. *See Theatre Guild on the Air*
United Synagogues of America, 158
University of Chicago Round Table, 214–216, 257
Usher, May, 192, 193, 254

V
Vallee, Rudy, 153, 191–192, 241. *See also Fleischmann's Yeast Hour*

Van Ronkel, Alfred, 139
Van Rooten, Louis, 181
"Vanishing Jew," 130n11, 229
Vaudeville, 106-108, 110, 112, 128, 132n22, 147, 192
Verdugo, Elena, 127
Victory Front, 120, 219, 255
Vitaphone Jubilee Hour, 110
Voutsas, George, 181

W

WABC, 89, 111, 158
Waksman, Selman A., 242
Wald, Lillian, 79
Walden, Bertha, 100
"Wall," 223, 258
War This Week, 203
Warburg, Felix M., 162, 170
Warsaw Ghetto. See "Battle of the Warsaw Ghetto," "Second Battle of the Warsaw Ghetto," and "Wall,"
Washington, George, 79, 178
Waters, James R., 25, 37n12, 100; photograph, 32
WCCO, 89
WCNW, 162
WCSH, 161
WEAF, 158, 161, 174, 208
Weiner, Lazar, 168
Weist, Dwight, 141, 153
Welles, Orson, 194, 219
Welsh, Lou, 94
Werfel, Franz. See "Jacobowsky and the Colonel"
WGBS, 91
WGN, 160
WGY, 161
WHAS, 89
Whipple, Clark "Doc," 172
White, Alfred, 140
WHO, 161
WHN, 174
Williams, Florence, 141

Wincelberg, Shimon, 181
Winchell, Walter, 106, 130n11, 197, 244n6
Winkler, Betty, 140, 153
"Winner Takes Life," 242, 254
WINS, 170
Wise, David, 165, 166, 167, 169, 170, 185n29
Wise, Rabbi Jonah B., 162, 163, 164–165, 168, 169, 170, 184n26, 186n40; photograph, 179. *See also Message of Israel*
Wise, Rabbi Stephen Wise, 162, 163, 183n8, 190. *See also* American Jewish Congress and American Jewish Congress Rally
"Wise Men of Chelm," 180
Wishengrad, Morton, 174–175, 181, 182, 222, 227
WHBI, 58
WIND, 58
WISN, 89
WJAS, 89
WJAX, 161
WJJD, 58
WJR, 49, 50, 51, 52, 61, 62, 67n16
WJZ, 21, 92, 157, 162, 164
WLS, 161
WLTH, 190
WLW, 49
WMAL, 89
WMAQ, 49, 122
WMCA, 20, 58-59, 60, 70n41, 190
WNAC, 157
Wolf, Johnny: photograph, 118. *See* Izzy Finkelstein (character)
Woollcott, Alexander (*The Town Crier*) 65n2, 197, 245n16
Woolley, Dr. Mary, 167
WOR, 69n28, 101, 160, 211, 228
Words at War, 223–224, 257
World War II: Jews and entry into, 46–47; programs during, 120, 202-203; 208, 212-213, 216-227,

228 references to 31-32, 39n37, 122
WOW, 161
"Would-be Pauper," 180
WRNY, 158
WTAG, 161
WTAQ, 89
WWJ, 161
WXYZ, 72n69, 160
Wyler, Marjorie, 175. *See also Eternal Light*
Wynn, Ed, 107

Y

Yiddish dialect,23, 31, 88, 103–106, 107, 108, 110, 129n1, 192, 193, 229, 244n6, 250n81; characters using 24, 31, 89, 91, 94, 96, 98, 101, 110-111, 112-113, 114-115, 116-117, 119, 121, 122, 123-125, 126, 127, 128, 139, 193, 211-212, 217; opposition to using, 105-106, 112-113, 125,147, 149-150, 261-263. *See also* Malapropisms
Yom Kippur, 29, 79, 80, 240, 251n9
Youmans, Vincent, 241
Young, Robert, 238
"Young Man in a Hurry," 242, 254
Youth Aliyah Movement, 198

Z

Ziegfeld Follies of the Air, 108
Zolli, Rabbi Anton, 209, 254

www.ingramcontent.com/pod-product-compliance
Lightning Source LLC
Chambersburg PA
CBHW060555230426
43670CB00011B/1838